THE SITUATIONISTS AND THE CITY

THE SITUATIONISTS AND THE CITY

EDITED BY TOM McDONOUGH

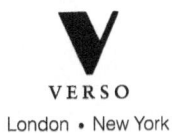

VERSO
London • New York

First published by Verso 2009
In the collection © Verso 2009
Translation and introduction © Tom McDonough

All rights reserved

The moral rights of the author have been asserted

1 3 5 7 9 10 8 6 4 2

Verso
UK: 6 Meard Street, London W1F 0EG
US: 388 Atlantic Ave, Brooklyn, NY 11217
www.versobooks.com

Verso is the imprint of New Left Books

ISBN-13: 978-1-84467-332-2 (hbk)
ISBN-13: 978-1-84467-364-3 (pbk)

British Library Cataloguing in Publication Data
A catalogue record for this book is available from the British Library

Library of Congress Cataloging-in-Publication Data
A catalog record for this book is available from the Library of Congress

Typeset by Hewer Text UK Ltd, Edinburgh
Printed in the United States

For Tim Clark and Anne Wagner

Contents

1 Introduction by Tom McDonough — 1
2 Critique of Functionalism and Modernization — 32
3 Paris, Modern Myth — 68
4 Consolidation — 88
5 The Architectural Interlude — 105
6 The Critique of Urban Planning — 139
7 Festival and Urban Revolution — 168
8 Toward a Synoptic Theory — 198

Acknowledgements — 223
Bibliography — 225
Index — 233

Introduction

TOM McDONOUGH

We think we know, after more than two decades of scholarship and a burgeoning bibliography of publications, what place the Situationist International (hereafter, S.I.) has in the history of architecture and urban planning. The group, whose existence was marked by the publication between 1958 and 1969 of twelve numbers of a collectively edited review of the same name, consisted of a small number of individuals around the influential figure of Guy Debord whose common purpose may be said to have been the revitalization of Arthur Rimbaud's famous injunction, "*Il faut changer la vie.*" "We must change life," the poet had written, and so the Situationists set out to transform everyday life in the modern world through a comprehensive program that included above all else the construction of "situations"—defined in 1958 as moments of life "concretely and deliberately constructed by the collective organization of a unitary ambiance and a play of events"[1]—but that also necessarily entailed the supersession of philosophy, the realization of art, the abolition of politics, and the fall of the "spectacle-commodity economy." If at first these tasks would be undertaken by Debord in collaboration with figures from the world of contemporary art, most notably the Danish painter Asger Jorn and his Dutch colleague Constant, political practice soon took the upper hand, culminating in the prominent role played by the S.I. in the events leading up to May '68. Such, in its most schematic form, is the trajectory within which the more specialized histories of the group's concern with architecture and the city have been written.

Those histories have tended to see the S.I. as occupying something of a crux, as a movement that effected the transition from the "loyal opposition" to modernist planning precepts of Team 10 to the visionary designs of a

---

1 See "Definitions" (1958), in *Situationist International Anthology*, ed. and trans. Ken Knabb (Berkeley, Calif.: Bureau of Public Secrets, 1981), 45 (trans. modified).

generation of architects that came of age in the 1960s, like the members of Archigram. In this formulation, the seeds of the Situationist critique of modernism were germinated over the course of the 1950s, amid the triumph of functionalist architecture and planning and of the anti-urban biases of Le Corbusier's Athens Charter, with its calls for razing traditional cities and their replacement by broadly spaced towers surrounded by parkland. Those seeds would come to flower in a brief period stretching from the group's founding in 1957 to around 1962, particularly with the seductive designs for a future city—the so-called "New Babylon" project—produced by Constant. With his resignation in 1960, this high point of Situationist engagement in the redefinition of architecture and urbanism is generally seen to come to a close, followed by a period of ever more abstract and rigid theorizing, even as the writings and models of the earlier moment grew in influence over an architectural world in ferment. As even the most cursory glance at the writings on Situationist critiques of architecture reveals, the vast majority of research in recent years has devoted itself to the rediscovery of that rather brief moment of 1957–62, what we might call the group's "architectural interlude."

Such a bias is of course entirely understandable on the part of scholars working within a disciplinary subspecialty like architectural history, and their work has been undeniably fruitful in restoring to us a fuller picture of the range of the activity conducted under the aegis of the S.I. But it has just as undeniably resulted in a fundamental misrecognition of the group's history and of its true originality in this field. For the most interesting aspects of the Situationists' engagement with the contemporary city reside precisely in what *resists* incorporation into the mainstream history of twentieth-century architecture and urbanism, what *cannot* be assimilated to the trajectory of postwar neo-avant-gardes in these fields. This brief essay, and the anthology it introduces, aim to trace an alternate history, one that does not privilege the architectural interlude that has been at the center of earlier scholarship. Its essential premise is that the S.I., at its most innovative, was not so much concerned with changing modern architecture, as with leaving it behind—the group's aim here, as in so many other fields of cultural and social endeavor, was to challenge its very premises and accepted ways of thinking. (And it did so, we should note, in dialogue with a variety of thinkers and activists on the French left, most notably with Henri Lefebvre and those in his circle in the late 1960s.) Unlike their contemporaries working within the architectural field, the Situationists were not involved in a restorative attempt to return to the putative roots of modernism, or in a regressive withdrawal to premodern forms; their ideas cannot honestly be mobilized to justify any of the subsequent maneuvers within this professional domain. Their significance lies elsewhere.

At its core, what we find in the twenty-odd year articulation of Situationist writings on the city is the outline of what we might call a Hegelian urbanism. For the S.I. the city was less a physical container—an assemblage of structures and routes, of functions and their interrelations—than the space constituted by and constitutive of the drama of self-consciousness and mutual recognition that lay at the heart of Hegel's *Phenomenology*. We have long recognized the crucial role played by that text in the formulation of much of what is most original in twentieth-century French philosophy, but its centrality to the Situationists has often been overlooked, or relegated to discussions of their political theory alone;[2] the dialectic of lordship and bondage however was also played out in their writing on urban space, as we will see, with the city figuring as a space of possible recognition—of the self, of the other, and at its limit of the collectivity in its revolutionary becoming. From being the site of alienated labor and passive consumption, the city was reformulated as the locus of a potential reciprocity and community, the crucial spatial stake of any project of radical social transformation. The history and development of this Hegelian urbanism, of the contribution of the S.I. to our understanding of the modern city and its future, is the subject of this introduction, and of the writings collected herein; they will be traced through seven loosely chronological thematic categories, each represented by an emblematic image, commencing with the pre-Situationist investigations of the early 1950s and concluding with their most elaborated theoretical statements of the late 1960s and early 1970s.

Critique of functionalism and modernization

The first image is a photograph taken in May 1955 (fig.1.1), two years prior to the founding of the S.I. In it we see Jacques Fillon, a rather obscure member of the pre-Situationist formation known as the Lettrist International (hereafter, L.I.), standing on a parapet atop the so-called Palais Idéal, a fantastic structure built over a thirty-odd year period between 1879 and 1912 by the postman Ferdinand Cheval (1836–1924) near his home at Hauterives in the Drôme in southeastern France. Fillon had traveled there in the company of Debord and his partner Michèle Bernstein, in one of two trips made at that time to particularly charged architectural monuments outside Paris, and in fact we also have a photograph of Debord himself from this visit, standing in one of the Palais' grottoes beneath an

---

2 On Hegel's place in twentieth-century French philosophy, see Judith P. Butler, *Subjects of Desire* (New York: Columbia University Press, 1987).

4 THE SITUATIONISTS AND THE CITY

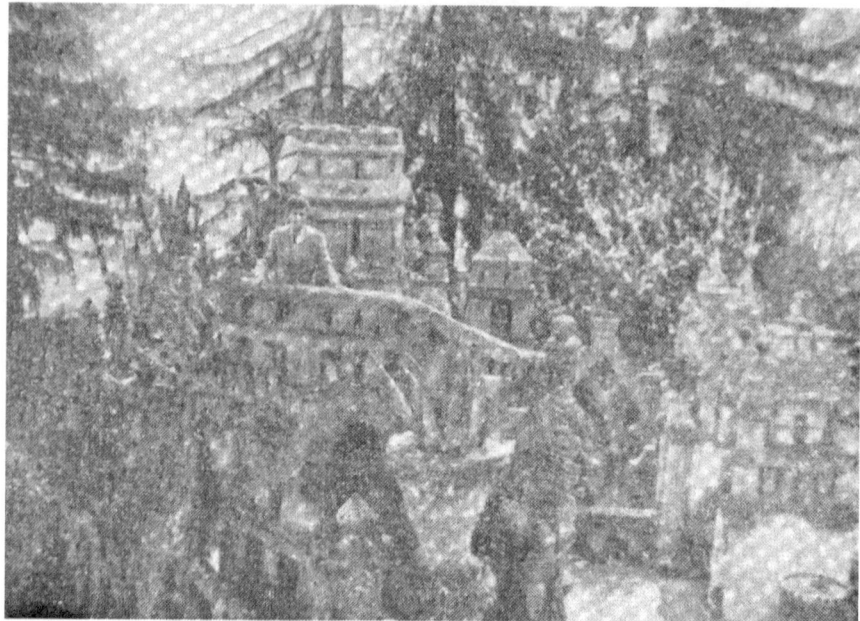

Fig.1.1   Jacques Fillon at the Palais Idéal, May 1955. From *Potlatch* no. 20 (May 30, 1955).

inscription reading "Where dreams become reality." (fig.1.2)[3] The postman Cheval had begun this structure at the age of forty-three, when one day during his deliveries he came across a stone of fascinating shape; upon finding others like it, he decided to collect them in a wheelbarrow each day after his rounds and work into the night on his ideal palace, whose forms echoed both the local landscape and the illustrations found in geography textbooks—it is in fact a kind of fanciful concatenation of French imperial topography, mixing forms derived from Roman monuments (the Maison Carrée in Nîmes), medieval castles, and Swiss chalets, with those from overseas colonies (the temples of Angkor, the Kasbah of Algiers), with of course a strong dose of pure fantasy that seems to share some of the spirit of contemporary phenomena like the art of Antoni Gaudí, art nouveau sculpture, or the sets of Georges Méliès's films.

The Situationists' early interest in the postman Cheval's construction in fact extended back to the previous summer, when his name first began appearing in the L.I.'s newsletter. In particular it was discussed in a short

---

3   Both photographs are preserved in the Situationist archive at the Silkeborg Kunstmuseum in Silkeborg, Denmark. This visit was conducted under the rubric "Construct a little situation without a future for yourself" and announced in a leaflet of the same name. The posting of this tract around Paris, "chiefly in psychogeographically favorable places," was announced in "Rédaction de nuit," *Potlatch* no. 20 (May 30, 1955). Its title derives from a collage made by Ivan Chtcheglov two years earlier, in 1953, and now apparently lost.

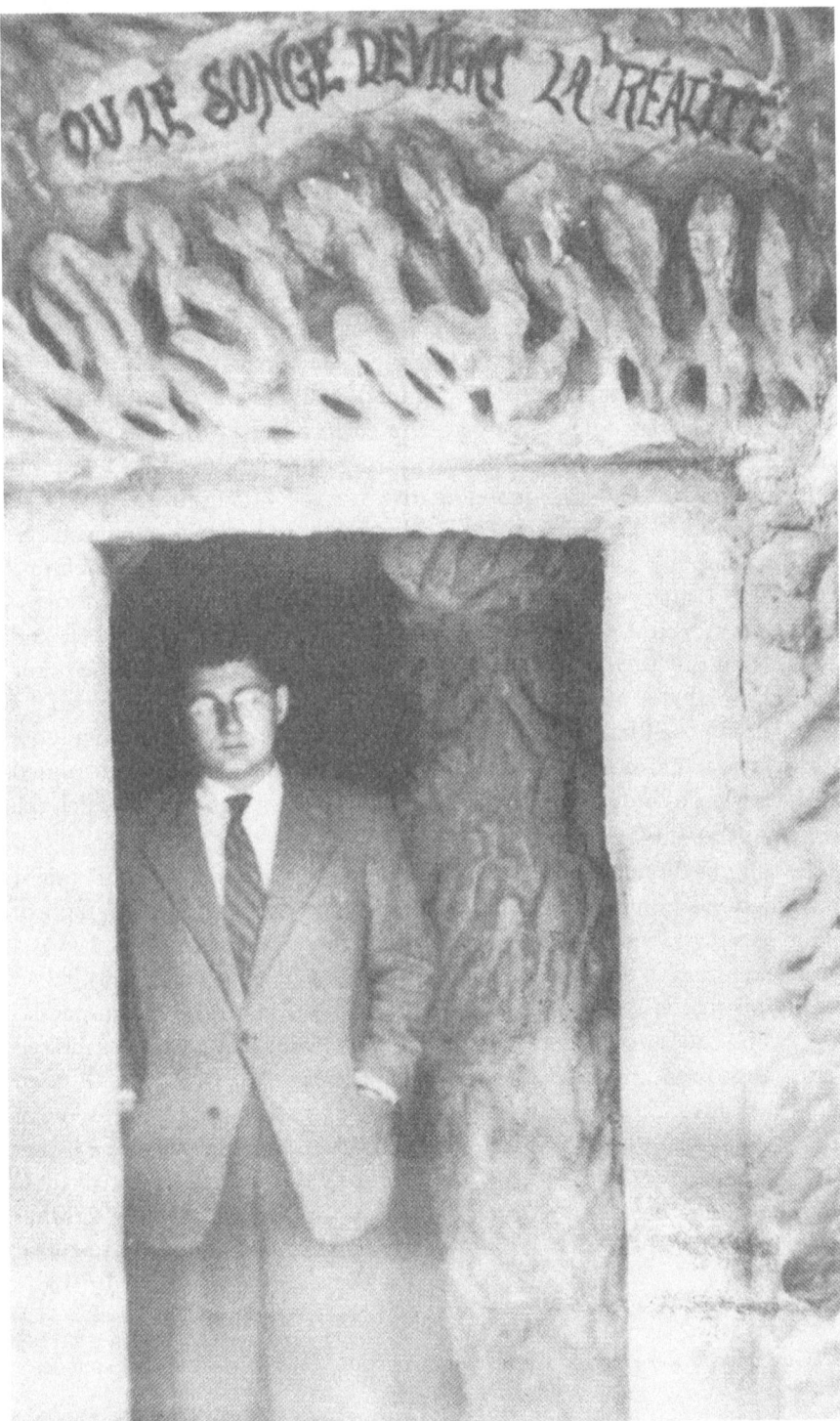

Fig.1.2 Guy Debord at the Palais Idéal, May 1955.

article titled "Next Planet," where it was called "the first expression of an architecture of disorientation," a building "of use only for losing oneself."[4] What the Situationists valued most in the Palais Idéal was not the single-mindedness of its designer, who worked on undeterred by the mockery of his neighbors, but rather the way that his labor resulted in the revelation of "a strange passion that remains unarticulated." Indeed passion—and its notable absence—was the dominating term in their early discussions of architecture: "Architecture must become *thrilling*," Debord and Fillon wrote programmatically around that time, insisting that "we could not take into consideration more restrained construction ventures."[5] Extravagance, gratuitousness, and disorientation became their watchwords, posed against the increasing hegemony of postwar functionalist architecture, which had triumphed as France desperately attempted to address the crisis posed by the four million families displaced during the Second World War. If that architecture had one representative for the Situationists, it was Le Corbusier, whose massive Unité d'Habitation, a 340-unit apartment block outside Marseilles, was completed in 1952, just as the L.I. was defining itself. The Unité's cellular arrangement (inspired by traditional monasteries), its substitution of the internal corridor for the public street, and its focus on the nuclear family and the domestic everyday life of the home were all anathema to the young Situationists. (Although, to be fair, Le Corbusier himself had hoped his design might work to re-establish a sense of the cosmic harmony of humanity with nature that had been disrupted by the advent of industrialization and urbanization—a goal with which the Situationists could only have sympathized.)

But all this discussion of Cheval's Palace and Le Corbusier's Unité might have sounded rather familiar in the mid-1950s. Even the photograph of Fillon visiting Hauterives would have seemed easily recognizable. It was a clear reiteration of a picture of the Surrealist André Breton (fig.1.3), taken during his first visit in September 1931, a trip made on the recommendation of his colleague Jacques-Bernard Brunius, who had already embraced this strange monument. The photograph of Breton had only recently been published in 1955, the same year as the L.I.'s excursion, appearing as one of the illustrations inserted into the new edition of his book *Communicating Vessels* (originally published in 1932).[6] From 1931 forward, the Palais Idéal would become the site of repeated Surrealist pilgrimages, along with other structures of the past such as the eighteenth-century folly of the so-called

---

4   "Next Planet" (1954), trans. in this volume, 42–44.
5   Guy Debord and Jacques Fillon, "Summary 1954" (1954), trans. in this volume, 46.
6   See André Breton, *Communicating Vessels* (1932), trans. Mary Ann Caws and Geoffrey T. Harris (Lincoln and London: University of Nebraska Press, 1990), 143.

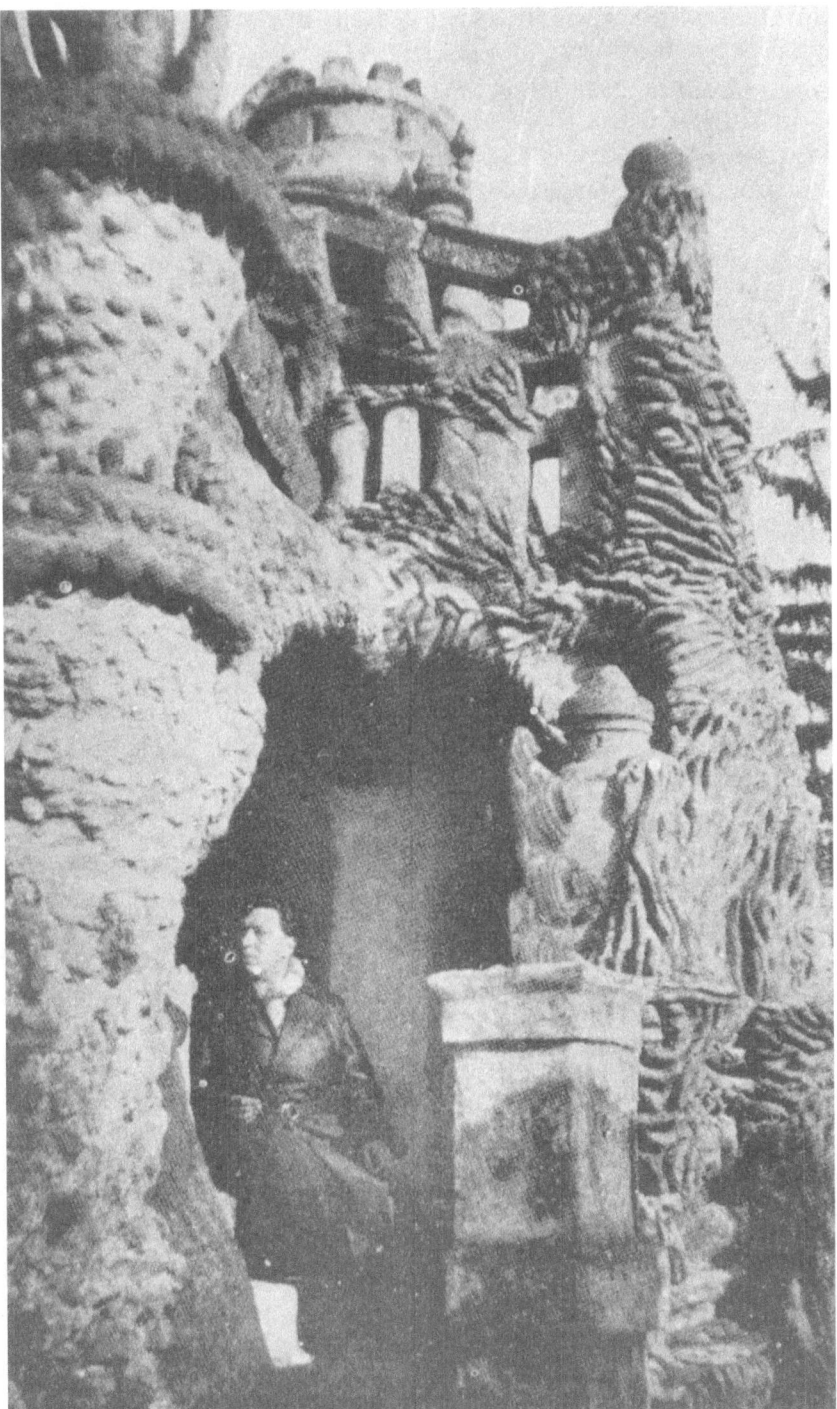

Fig.1.3 André Breton at the Palais Idéal, September 1931. From Breton, *Communicating Vessels*, 1955 edition.

Désert de Retz (which was also visited by Debord in May 1955). For Breton, the Palace represented a "concrete irrationality" that had "tried to burst all limits," and a clear challenge to the dominant "rationality and coldness" of functionalist architecture, once again figured by Le Corbusier.[7] The interest of the Situationists, then, was prefigured by that of the Surrealists, and indeed much of the former's critique of modernist architecture was quite consciously developed as a continuation of the latter's own positions.

That debt is signaled clearly in the itinerary of the three friends Bernstein, Debord, and Fillon in the late spring of 1955, a journey undertaken in the footsteps of their elders, but it is no less clearly evident in the body of writing published by the L.I. over the three or four years preceding the foundation of the Situationist International, from Ivan Chtcheglov's foundational "Formulary for a New Urbanism" through Debord's "Introduction to a Critique of Urban Geography." That early history was in many ways one of rearticulating the insights of interwar Surrealism, rediscovering its key texts, while simultaneously insisting on the concrete realization of its homage to desire. Debord explained that attitude in 1955, quoting Breton's statement "The imaginary is what tends to become real," and insisting that "such an assertion, in its involuntary restrictiveness, could serve as a touchstone and do justice to a few parodic literary revolutions: what tends to remain unreal is empty chatter."[8] The value of Cheval's Palace lay not its builder's imagination, but in its physical realization of his fantasy as a space "where dreams had become reality."

Paris, modern myth

As alluring as were eccentric structures such as the Palais Idéal or the Désert de Retz, the ultimate stake of the realization of desire lay in the city, the only place in which what Chtcheglov called a "symbolic urbanism" could assume a truly collective scale. For the members of what would become the S.I., this meant Paris, and the physical setting and history of that city played an absolutely central role in their definition of a revolutionary architecture. Our second image is a novel sort of map, or perhaps we might better say a work that stands halfway between the realms of art and cartography: Debord's *Axis of Exploration and Failure in the Search for a Situationist "Great Passage,"* made in 1957 (fig.1.4). This was one

---

7   Breton, "Surrealist Situation of the Object" (1935), in *Manifestoes of Surrealism*, trans. Richard Seaver and Helen R. Lane (Ann Arbor: University of Michigan Press, 1972), 261.
8   Debord, "Introduction to a Critique of Urban Geography" (1955), trans. in this volume, 63.

INTRODUCTION 9

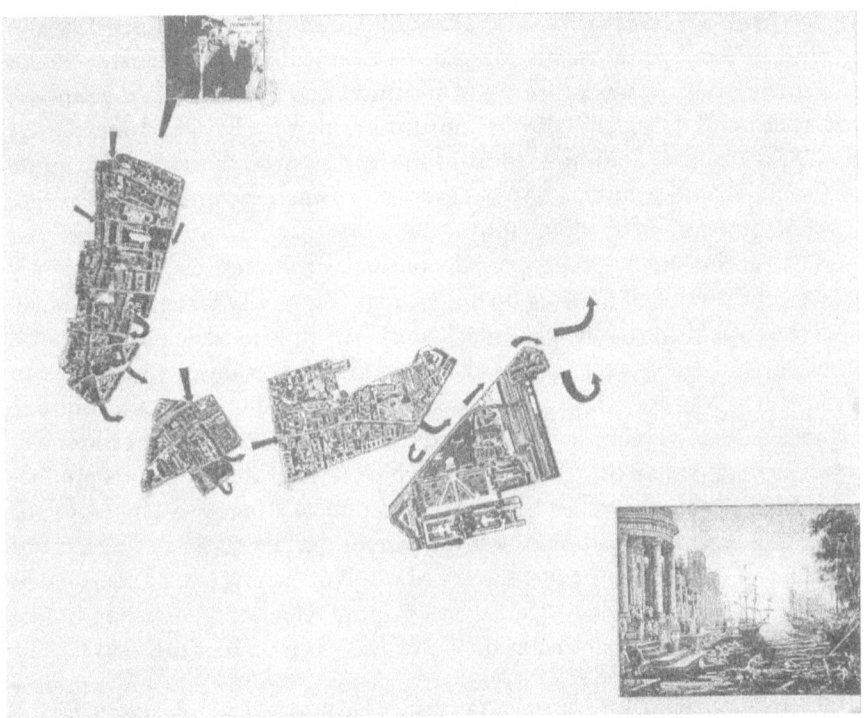

Fig. 1.4 Guy Debord, *Axis of Exploration and Failure in the Search for a Situationist "Great Passage,"* 1957.

of a series of so-called "psychogeographic" maps he made of Paris at that moment, maps that intended to chart "the specific effects of the geographic milieu, consciously planned or not, acting on the affective comportment of individuals."[9] It in fact records one particular expedition—what the Situationists called *dérive*, or urban drifting—undertaken three years earlier by Debord and Chtcheglov (seen in the photograph at the top left), across their favored neighborhoods on the Left Bank, pictured in four collaged aerial photographs linked by arrows signaling various possible routes of entry and egress from one "ambiance" to another. At the bottom right we find a poetic emblem of this voyage, a reproduction of Claude Lorrain's *Seaport with the Embarkation of Saint Ursula* of 1641 (National Gallery, London). The three elements together—along with the work's title, which characteristically unites a rather dry, technical description with the fanciful reference to the "great" (that is, northwest) passage sought by explorers from Christopher Columbus forward in their quest for a more direct route to the East—produce an idiosyncratic plan of the city, one that privileges psychology as much as topography.

Once again, the Surrealist precedents are clear. Breton had only recently written of the value of drawing up unique maps of the city for each individual, ones that would show "the places he haunts [...] in white, the ones he avoids in black, and the rest in various shades of gray according to the degree of attraction or repulsion."[10] Debord would quickly take up this call, and urge his colleagues to develop "a transformed cartography" through "the forging of psychogeographic maps," the results of which were evidenced by his productions of 1957.[11] Even earlier, Chtcheglov had made a suggestive map of Paris by pasting bits of a world map over the plan of the city's Métro. The cut-out segments of the map—the northwest coast of North America, Hudson's Bay, Greenland, China, Afghanistan, Africa, Central America—correspond quite closely to those foregrounded in the Surrealists' own map of the world, overlaying their valorization of non-Western cultures onto the postwar *métropole* of the decaying French empire. (Indochina, about to be lost in the wake of the defeat at Dien Bien Phu, features prominently in one fragment.) One needn't have recourse to imperial exotica, this modest collage suggests, for otherness is to be found right around the corner, or at most a subway ride away.

Dérive was, at some essential level, the search for an encounter with otherness, spurred on in equal parts by the exploration of pockets of class, ethnic

---

9   See "Definitions" (1958), in *Situationist International Anthology*, 45 (trans. modified).
10 Breton, *Free Rein* (1953), trans. Michel Parmentier and Jacqueline d'Amboise (Lincoln and London: University of Nebraska Press, 1995), 222.
11 Debord, "Introduction to a Critique of Urban Geography" (1955), trans. in this volume, 62.

and racial difference in the postwar city, and by frequent intoxication. The fledgling Situationists frequented North African bars in the Fifth arrondissement and Spanish ones north of the city in Saint-Denis, all the while projecting their own desires for alterity onto the sometimes recalcitrant subjects conscripted into their adventures—a resistance apparent in many of the accounts of *dérive* written by participants. This technique of urban wandering has often been compared to its nineteenth-century forebear, the poetic *flânerie* practiced by Charles Baudelaire and other inhabitants of the metropolis, and indeed something of the privilege of the *flâneur*—the paradigmatically male stroller who, equipped with his encyclopedic knowledge of the city and its denizens, travels incognito through the most varied milieus—remained a component of the S.I.'s approach to Paris. What we might call the ambivalence of the *flâneur* paradigm, its unstable mix of desire for and condescension toward the other, is detectable in some of the Situationist writing on *dérive* and would only dissipate in early 1960s as the final holdovers of romantic thought were purged from the group.

However, for the Situationists these plans cannot be reduced to a purely individual response to the urban terrain; cities were for them profoundly historical landscapes, whose current appearances were shaped—as geological strata underlay physical landscapes—by the successive events that time has buried, though never completely effaced. Throughout the years prior to the founding of the S.I., an important strain in their writings reflected a desire to rediscover and reconnect with that history, and specifically with the revolutionary legacy of the city in its most radical guises. Recollections of the Terror of 1848 and of the Commune appeared again and again as antidotes to the closed perspectives of their own day. The city assumes the guise of a vast storehouse of slumbering memories awaiting potential awakening.[12]

Nowhere was this more true than in Paris, which for over a century prior to the foundation of the S.I. had fostered a particular relation between itself and its inhabitants, a certain representation of the city that had held sway from the time of Balzac and that was composed in equal parts of a "poeticization of urban civilization" and "a truly emotional attachment to the modern city." This was what Roger Caillois had called the "modern myth" of Paris, and in many ways what we find in the early work of the Situationists is its final, post-Surrealist articulation.[13] It would be

---

12 On this particular vision of the historical city, and its basis in Surrealist writing, see Margaret Cohen, *Profane Illumination* (Berkeley: University of California Press, 1993).
13 Roger Caillois, "Paris, a Modern Myth" (1938), trans. Claudine Frank and Camille Naish, in *The Edge of Surrealism*, ed. Claudine Frank (Durham, N.C.: Duke University Press, 2003), 181–182.

difficult to stress how profoundly this city shaped Situationist thought, from Chtcheglov's foundational "Formulary" of 1953 through Debord's late autobiographical writings. But what should equally be recognized is their profound ambivalence toward modern Paris: to the extent that it was composed of the "ruins of the bourgeoisie" (to echo Walter Benjamin), it would have to be remade through the most radical plan of "rational improvement." The secrets held within the urban landscape, which *dérive* attempted to unlock, were the secrets to this city's own supersession—the "Great Passage" out of the capitalist urban grid toward a new city form where, for the first time, individual desire and architectural morphology might coincide. (Hence Debord's fascination with Claude's harbor scenes that, as he wrote in 1955, present in particularly moving form "a *sum of possibilities*" and a Baudelairean invitation to the voyage.)[14] The mythical Paris of the modernist imagination receives its greatest homage and most penetrating critique in these works and the writings that accompany them.

Consolidation

The Situationist International was formally founded in July 1957 through the unification of the Paris-based Lettrist International of Debord and the International Movement for an Imaginist Bauhaus (hereafter, I.M.I.B.), an anti-functionalist regrouping of artists headed by Danish painter Asger Jorn. This moment of the close of the 1950s represents not only, or perhaps not even primarily, a new start, but rather a period of consolidation of the advances of the previous five years, and of the sometimes uncomfortable conjoining of the L.I.'s intransigency with more open currents stemming from the artistic milieu of the I.M.I.B. One of the first tasks the newly founded S.I. set itself was the propagation of key texts from the preceding years, and early issues of its journal were marked by the republication of essays written during the Lettrist phase: Chtcheglov's "Formulary" of 1953 appeared, in a slightly modified version, in the first number of *Internationale situationniste* (1958), establishing the continued significance of psychogeography; while Debord's "Theory of the *Dérive*" came out in the next issue (also 1958), ensuring that this technique of urban exploration also would remain central. But the key term emerging from the moment of the founding of the S.I. was another neologism: "unitary urbanism."

Its place in the structure of Situationist thought was made clear in a tract published in 1958, titled "New Theater of Operations in Culture." (fig.1.5) Underneath that heading appeared an aerial photograph of

---

14 Debord, "Introduction to a Critique of Urban Geography" (1955), trans. in this volume, 62.

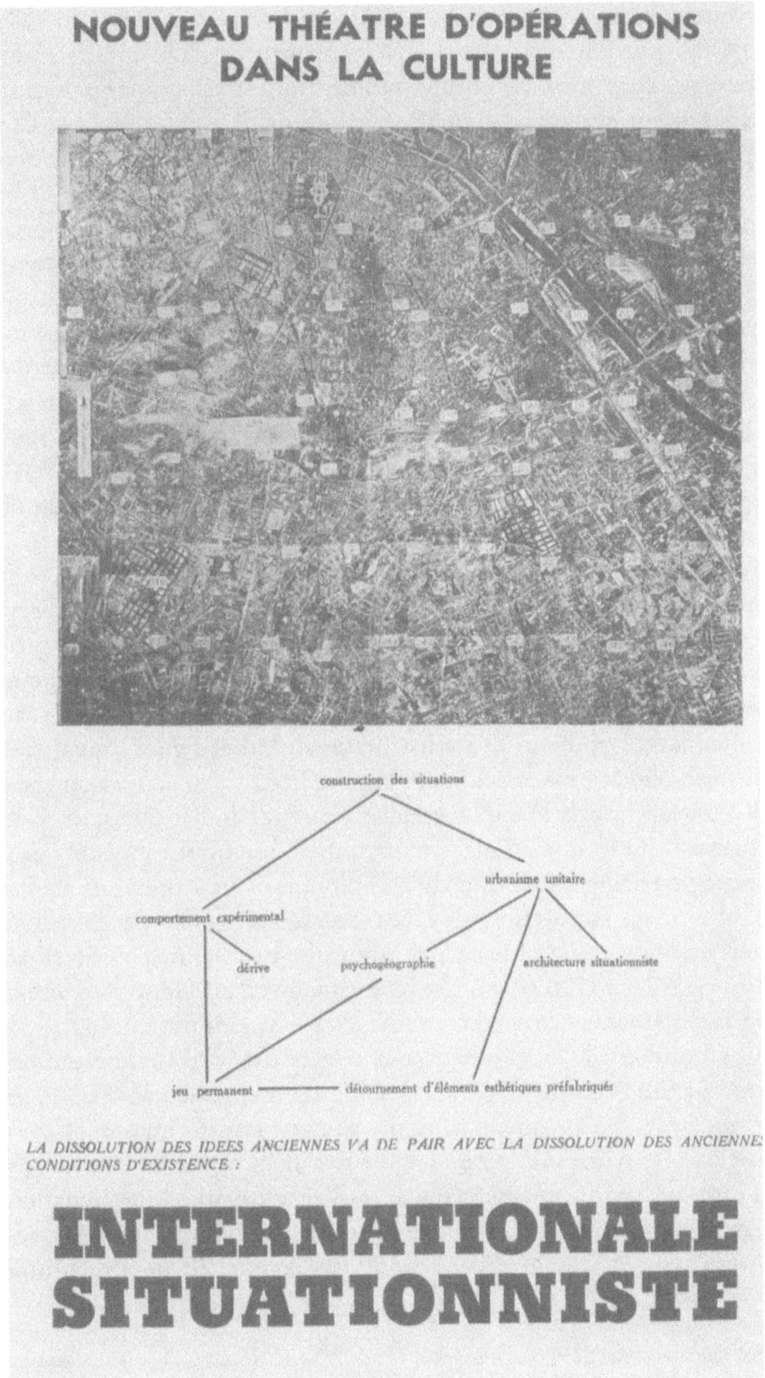

INTRODUCTION 13

NOUVEAU THÉATRE D'OPÉRATIONS DANS LA CULTURE

```
                    construction des situations

    comportement expérimental        urbanisme unitaire

         dérive    psychogéographie     architecture situationniste

    jeu permanent ———— détournement d'éléments esthétiques préfabriqués
```

LA DISSOLUTION DES IDEES ANCIENNES VA DE PAIR AVEC LA DISSOLUTION DES ANCIENNES CONDITIONS D'EXISTENCE :

INTERNATIONALE SITUATIONNISTE

Fig.1.5   "New Theater of Operations in Culture," 1958.

southeastern Paris—the same neighborhoods featured in Debord's collaged plan of the previous year—and a diagram showing the interrelations of the concepts central to the group's radical cultural experimentation. If the construction of situations remained its ultimate aim, unitary urbanism (along with "experimental comportment") was the privileged path toward this end. In this chart, it would appear to have been based on the interaction of three dependent elements: psychogeography, the appropriation (*détournement*, in Situationist parlance) of prefabricated aesthetic elements, and Situationist architecture. The S.I. also provided a definition in the first issue of its journal: unitary urbanism was the "theory of the use of the whole of arts and techniques combined in the integral construction of an environment in dynamic connection with behavioral experiments."[15] Throughout the documents that prefigured and announced the foundation of the group, we find this term employed not only as a concrete aim to be worked toward, but also as the very ground for the unification of the disparate alliances from which the S.I. was formed.

"New Theater of Operations" also signaled a fundamental shift in Situationist approaches toward the city. Until now, the role of Surrealist precedent had been predominant, at times even overwhelming, in the group's writings on architecture and urbanism; it is only a slight exaggeration to say that the L.I. had continuously been engaged in an oedipal struggle to at once honor and annihilate its Bretonian father-figure. But there had always been another current underlying the Lettrists' polemics on the city: for all their appropriation of Surrealist concepts and techniques, Debord and his colleagues had studiously refused the often mystical quality of their forebears, preferring to ground their explorations in a pseudo-sociological prose. Indeed, an important reference—one might almost say guidebook—for their understanding of urban form was the two-volume study *Paris and the Parisian Region* (1952), written by sociologist Paul-Henry Chombart de Lauwe and his team of researchers at the Musée de l'Homme.[16] In this publication, Chombart de Lauwe had been concerned with understanding the situation of the Parisian working class and with elucidating the large-scale structures and processes involved in the postwar transformation of the city; his insights into what he described as the two alien worlds of Paris—a proletarian east confronting a bourgeois west—clearly marked the Situationists' own maps of the city, as did his analyses of the bourgeois reconquest of its eastern part. Much of this research was conducted on the ground in

---

15 See "Definitions" (1958), in *Situationist International Anthology*, 45 (trans. modified).
16 For an account of the remarkable interdisciplinary research involved in the writing of this book, see Paul-Henry Chombart de Lauwe, *La fin des villes: mythe ou réalité?* (Paris: Calmann-Lévy, 1982), 205–209.

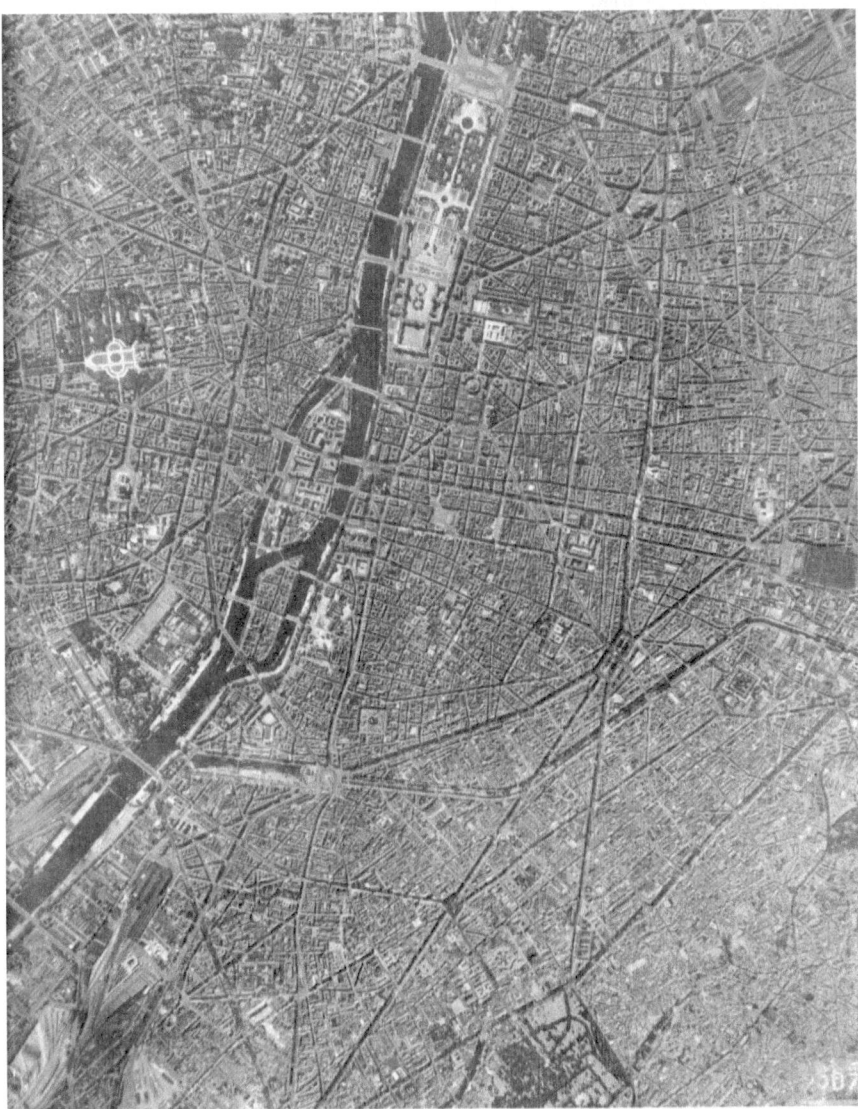

Fig.1.6 "Paris (vertical view). The high altitude overview of central Paris and the surrounding area provides a better understanding of certain structures and the opposition between different kinds of urban fabric." From Paul-Henry Chombart de Lauwe's *Paris and the Parisian Region*, 1952.

working-class residential neighborhoods, but Chombart de Lauwe was also an early champion of the role of aerial photography in the study of human geography, and the Situationists' interest in such photographs of Paris also owes much to his work.[17]

The tract announced this shift away from Surrealist vocabulary toward more "objective," although certainly no less committed, modes of analysis. The stakes of culture would no longer be found within the artist's studio or architect's atelier, nor inside the rarified institutions of official (i.e., State-sponsored) representation, but out in the city's streets themselves. This was where an "integral" synthesis of the arts—that much-desired unification of painting, sculpture, and architecture seen as so decisive to a rejuvenation of culture in the later 1950s—would occur: at the level of everyday life itself. The fledgling Situationists were breaking out of the small world of Left Bank bohemia that had defined their existence, both physically and intellectually, over the previous decade (the subject of Debord's 1959 retrospective film *On the passage of a few people through a rather brief moment in time*, and of his collage-autobiography *Memoirs* of the same year), and discovering a larger urban context and a more coherent articulation of their approaches toward it.

However unitary urbanism at this moment also revealed an essential instability. The official definition, for all its specialized vocabulary ("integral construction of an environment," "behavioral experiments"), seems in the end rather imprecise; as one historian of the movement has noted, "it was never made clear [...] whether unitary urbanism was a project for the here-and-now or for post-revolutionary society," and a certain utopian irresolution clung to it.[18] That irresolution was not coincidental, and did not result simply from a lack of clarity in the Situationists' analysis of the city. It was rather the result of a necessary compromise between the Parisian Lettrists, who had already through their apprenticeship in post-Surrealism begun to outline an anti-architectural critique of the contemporary city, and their newfound colleagues coming from more mainstream artistic backgrounds, for whom some grounding in studio-based creation retained its urgency. Unitary urbanism was comfortably expansive enough at this stage to accommodate both wings, although the next five years of the S.I. would be devoted in large measure to the struggle over which vision would prevail.

---

17   See Chombart de Lauwe, "La vision aérienne du monde," in *La découverte aérienne du monde*, ed. Paul-Henry Chombart de Lauwe (Paris: Horizons de France, 1948), 19–52; and Anthony Vidler, "*Terres Inconnues*: Cartographies of a Landscape to be Invented," *October* no. 115 (Winter 2006): 13–30.

18   Simon Sadler, *The Situationist City* (Cambridge, Mass. and London: The MIT Press, 1998), 157.

The architectural interlude

If the conflicted project of unitary urbanism may be associated with any single name, it is that of Constant, the Dutch artist turned visionary architect, and founding member of the S.I. alongside Debord. Constant recently has been the subject of much scholarly interest within the realm of contemporary art and architecture (see the bibliography under his name at the end of this volume), and looking at the photograph of his model for *Orange Construction* of 1958 (Gemeentemuseum, The Hague), it is not hard to understand why. The spidery construction, with its abstract forms built of wire and Plexiglas, appeals both to our revived attention to twentieth-century utopian design (with its echoes of Soviet Constructivist experimentation of the early 1920s) and to our fascination with mid-century modernism (of whose aesthetic it wholly partakes). As photographed here (fig.1.7) by Jan Versnel (1924–2007)—one of the greatest Dutch photographers of architecture and interiors in the last century—the modestly scaled maquette assumes monumental proportions, becoming a light megastructure that hovers over the cars below.

This was perhaps the most reproduced image of Constant's New Babylon project within Situationist circles; it had an almost emblematic quality for the group in the years following its making. It first appeared in *Potlatch* in 1959, captioned as a "pre-Situationist model, with contemporary automobile traffic," illustrating an article by Constant that announced the program of this project that would occupy him for almost two decades. Premised upon a futuristic mechanization, in which human labor will have become obsolete, New Babylon envisaged a space where people were free to engage in creative work, shaping the world in accordance with their desires. Suspended above the earth's surface, its flexible structure would provide a suitable environment for these new types of inhabitant who might collectively elaborate the mobile elements of its interior.[19] It appeared again later that same year as an uncaptioned illustration to Constant's essay, "A Different City for a Different Life," published in *Internationale situationniste*.[20] Finally, it was also included in a monograph devoted to the artist that was published in 1960, now titled *Ambiance of a Future City*, with the adjoining text, appropriated from Chombart de Lauwe's book on Paris:

---

19 Constant, "The Great Game to Come" (1959), trans. Gerardo Denís, in *Theory of the Dérive and Other Situationist Writings on the City*, eds. Libero Andreotti and Xavier Costa (Barcelona: ACTAR and Museu d'art contemporani, 1996), 62–63.
20 Constant, "A Different City for a Different Life" (1959), trans. John Shepley, in *Guy Debord and the Situationist International: Texts and Documents*, ed. Tom McDonough (Cambridge, Mass. and London: The MIT Press, Coll. "OCTOBER Books," 2002), 95–101.

18 THE SITUATIONISTS AND THE CITY

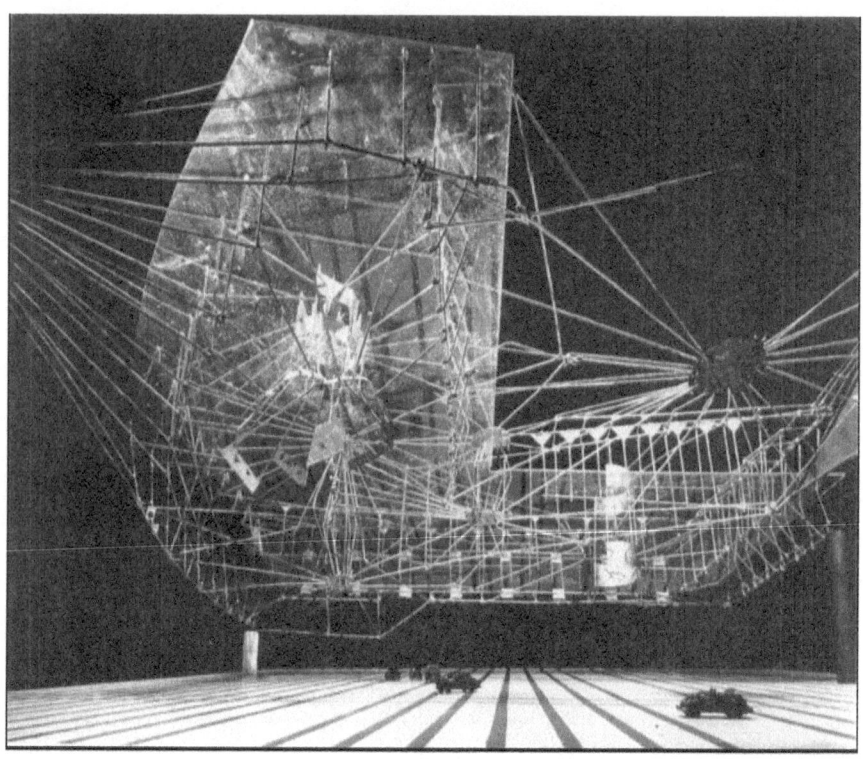

Fig.1.7 Constant, *Orange Construction*, 1958. Gemeentemuseum, The Hague. © 2009 PICTORIGHT.

Humanity comes profoundly under the influence of the milieu and humanity can, with the help of means currently at its disposal, alter this milieu just about however it wishes. The current drama stems from the fact that it is rarely the same people who most strongly come under these influences of the milieu that dispose of the means to change it.[21]

Undoubtedly chosen by Debord, this caption represented an exemplary attempt to reconcile the two contradictory components of S.I. at this stage, conjoining visionary model making with more grounded analysis of the present-day urban milieu.

The terms for that reconciliation were perhaps best expressed in a short essay of 1961, published by the sociologist and philosopher Lefebvre, who was at that time rather close to Situationist circles. In it, he defended the concept of what he called "experimental utopia," which he defined as "*imaginary variations* on themes and exigencies defined by the real as understood in the broadest sense: by the problems posed by reality and by the virtualities held within it." It was "the exploration of human possibilities, with the help of the image and the imagination, accompanied by a ceaseless criticism and a ceaseless reference to the given problematic in the 'real.'"[22] What he posed here was a radical alternative to the dominant models of invention in contemporary architecture and planning, which we could say were bifurcated between, on one hand, the reigning empiricism within contemporary modernism, and on the other hand the a priori assumptions characteristic of so-called visionary or utopian design. With this concept of experimental utopia, Lefebvre laid out a crucial set of terms for understanding Constant's New Babylon project and, more broadly, what we might call the architectural interlude of the S.I.—its period of active investigation of future architectural and urban forms—that extended from the group's founding in 1957 into the early 1960s.

New Babylon has come down to us above all as its creator's vision of a world in which people could invest all their energy in a playful experience of freedom. It was, as Lefebvre might have written, "a virtual object" constructed "from information about reality and a definite problematic." Here was the precocious realization of Lefebvre's experimental utopia, an imaginative response to a concrete problematic. (Indeed, the latter's concept likely owed much to his knowledge of Constant's work at this time.) It is not sufficient, then, to call New Babylon a "utopian" architecture—at its best it was not, in Lefebvre's words, an "abstract utopia," attending to "the ideal city without connection to definite situations," but rather an attempt to test hypotheses regarding

---

21 Chombart de Lauwe, *Paris and the Parisian Region* (1952), trans. in this volume, 74–75.
22 Henri Lefebvre, "Experimental Utopia: Toward a New Urbanism" (1961), trans. in this volume, 105–106.

particular conditions of life in the postwar world. These included, not least, the reality of cross-border migrations: the initial spur for New Babylon lay in Constant's never-realized design for a Gypsy camp (fig.1.8), begun in 1956 at the behest of Italian artist and fellow Situationist Pinot Gallizio, who had welcomed onto his lands in the Piedmont Romany people driven off the surrounding countryside. The question was whether those hypotheses proved correct or not, and as Constant became increasingly concerned with the formal problems of his designs—at the expense of the conceptions of nomadism and social space that had been at their origin—the flaws in their premises became clearer. New Babylon regressed, we might say, from an experimental utopia to an abstract one, without even the virtues of concrete realization that saved the Palais Idéal from mere folklorism. Constant's project failed to the precise degree that it could be captured for the professional realm of architecture and turned into just one of many neo-avant-garde proposals marking the 1960s (as his numerous exhibitions, lectures, and publications of that decade attest).

But there was another aspect to the Situationists' architectural interlude, one that has received significantly less attention from subsequent scholarship. In the wake of Constant's resignation from the S.I. in 1960, as the group attempted to reassess the architectural practice of unitary urbanism, it turned—if only briefly—to the work of architect Günther Feuerstein.[23] Feuerstein's rejection of an increasingly antiseptic modernism—of its fetishization of technology and abstraction, of its inhuman scale—appealed to the group just as it echoed other contemporary subjectivist responses to functionalist architecture (most notably Hundertwasser's "Mold Manifesto Against Rationalism in Architecture," of 1958).[24] Introducing Feuerstein's essay, German members of the S.I. wrote:

> Contrary to the urbanistic hyper-planning called for by Constant, Feuerstein's unpremeditated architecture is revealed as absolutely subversive, based as it is on micro-regions, chance, process, emotion, human conduct, the intimate sphere, new units of measure, new conceptions of material, etc.[25]

---

23 Feuerstein's essay "Theses on Unpremeditated Architecture" (a version of which is translated in this volume, 125–133) was published in the German Situationist journal *Spur* no. 5 (June 1961), in a special number devoted to unitary urbanism. This essay was then mentioned, in a predominantly critical light, in "Critique of Urbanism" (1961), trans. in this volume, 152.
24 See Hundertwasser, "Mould Manifesto against rationalism in architecture" (1958), trans. Michael Bullock, in *Programmes and Manifestoes on 20th-Century Architecture*, ed. Ulrich Conrads (London: Lund Humphries, 1970), 157–60. This collection, originally published in Germany in 1964, also contains four texts by the S.I., representing an early appearance by the group in mainstream architectural circles.
25 This introduction may be found, in French translation, in *Archives situationnistes*, vol. 1 (Paris: Contre-Moule and Parallèles, 1997), 53.

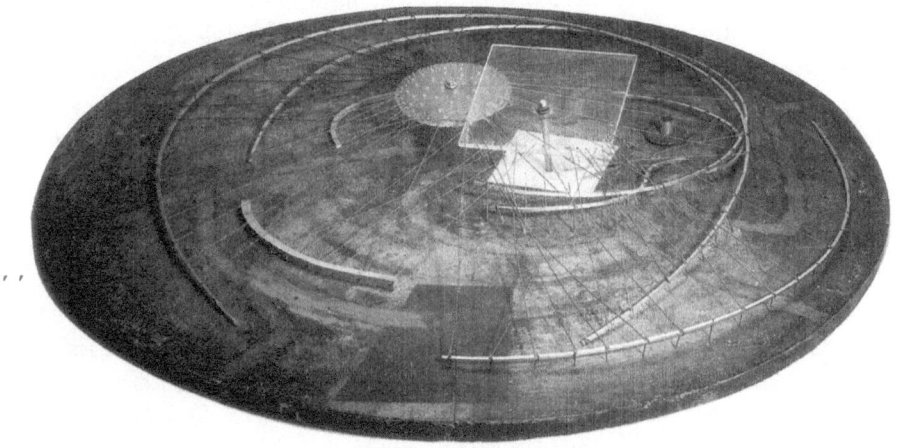

Fig 1.8 Constant, *Project for a Gypsy Camp*, 1956–58. Gemeentemuseum, The Hague.
© 2009 PICTORIGHT

Here was another, albeit short-lived, vision of a potential Situationist architecture, and one that was notably more in line with emerging valorizations of the small-scale within the New Left.

The critique of urban planning

Ultimately neither Constant nor Feuerstein's vision of a Situationist architecture would prevail, and in fact a consensus was already developing by the time of the former's resignation that all prospective models for a future city were doomed in advance to cooptation by the outer reaches of capitalist research and development. That prognosis was quickly borne out: by 1962 Constant's New Babylon was being featured in *Architecture d'aujourd'hui*, the professional journal of record in France, alongside other technocratic plans by collectives such as G.E.A.M. (Study Group for Mobile Architecture) or G.I.A.P. (International Group for Prospective Architecture), with whose work Constant's designs showed striking parallels.[26] Characteristically, the S.I. assumed its distance from these trends, and at the very moment when the architecture and planning professions began to allow for at least a modicum of dissent from modernist doxa, it chose an even more profound obscurity—or, to be more exact, it chose to exile itself further from the realms of professional specialization. Taking seriously the Marxist refusal of utopian model-building, the S.I. would devote itself increasingly to the task of critique, developing over the first half of the 1960s one of the most compelling analyses of contemporary planning available on the Left.

Perhaps the most powerful explication of that analysis is to be found in a 1961 article in the group's journal, titled "Critique of Urbanism." Among the illustrative material for this text, which summarized the failure of the architectural interlude and began laying out the groundwork for a more comprehensive appraisal of the built environment, was an entirely banal photograph of Mourenx, a city in the far southwest of France near the border with Spain (fig.1.9). Mourenx had been built in the 1950s to house employees of natural gas and oil concerns, which were exploiting nearby deposits in Lacq. The photograph depicts a familiar landscape of the era—a geometric arrangement of regularized towers and slabs, interspersed with vegetation—that, if not for the Pyrénées rising in the distance, could be the Alton Estate at Roehampton (itself built in 1959) or any number of other new towns springing up in England and Scandinavia at this time. The anonymous authors of "Critique of Urbanism" caption it as follows:

---

26 See "Constant: Néo-Babylone," *L'Architecture d'aujourd'hui* no. 102 (June–July 1962): 77. This was a special issue devoted to "Fantastic Architecture." On the visionary technocratic tendency in French architecture of this moment, see Larry Busbea, *Topologies* (Cambridge, Mass. and London: The MIT Press, 2007).

INTRODUCTION 23

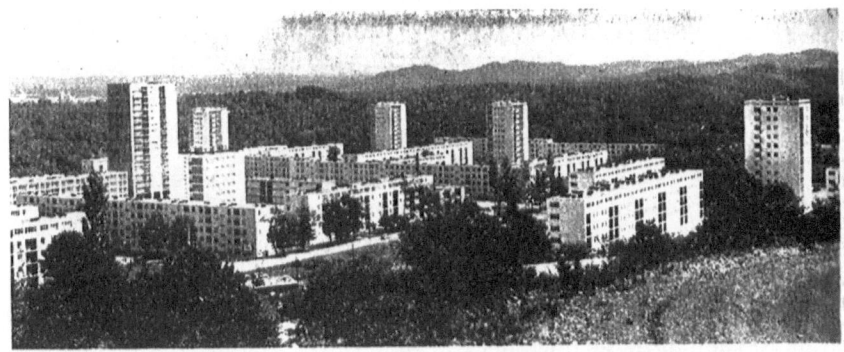

La ville de Mourenx. Les 12.000 habitants logent dans les blocs horizontaux s'ils sont mariés, dans les tours s'ils sont célibataires. A droite de l'image s'étend le petit quartier des cadres moyens, composé de villas identiques, symétriquement partagées entre deux familles. Au-delà, dans le quartier des cadres à plus haut salaire, se reproduit un autre type de villa entièrement dévolue à son occupant. Les cadres plus réellement dirigeants du travail effectué à Lacq sont implantés à Pau, Toulouse et Paris.

Fig.1.9 "Critique of Urbanism," photograph reproduced in *Internationale situationniste* no. 6 (August 1961).

The city of Mourenx. 12,000 residents live in the horizontal slabs if they are married, in the towers if they are unmarried. To the right of the picture lies the small neighborhood of mid-level personnel, composed of identical villas symmetrically divided between two families. Beyond, in the neighborhood for higher-paid personnel, we find repeated a different type of villa assigned entirely to its occupant. The personnel who most truly manage the labor carried out at Lacq are lodged in Pau, Toulouse, and Paris.[27]

What the Situationists perceived in this planning, then, went beyond the criticisms that reformers were commonly making of such monotonous towers and slabs, which had by the early 1960s come to dominate official French architectural production in the so-called *grands ensembles*. Minister of Construction Pierre Sudreau had launched a policy developing such self-sufficient suburbs in the mid-1950s, each to be provided with its own shopping-centers, lycées, theaters, and other communal facilities; they very quickly had been subject to attack, both within and outside of the architectural community, for aesthetic deficiencies; for the lack of social and cultural equipment, of transportation, and of local industries; and lastly for the unhappy and empty lives of their inhabitants. The Situationists, however, were uninterested in proposing discrete features that might ameliorate the designs; for them Mourenx and other new towns were nothing less than physical embodiments of the hierarchical organization of advanced capitalism, a concrete expression of the graduated set of rewards that awaited the new cadres of an ever-modernizing France. This impoverished urban form was for them as distant from the traditional city—the space of heterogeneity, of encounter, of freedom, in a word—as it was from the rural landscape of the past.

In choosing a photograph of Mourenx rather than the more famous Sarcelles, for example (a new town outside Paris that gave rise to the term "Sarcellitis," to describe the particular ennui suffered by its residents), the S.I. was also signaling its debt to Lefebvre, who had grown up not far from the site of the future city, and who would write about the contrast between it and his home of Navarrenx around this time. For Lefebvre, the dominant issue in the new town was its lack of history. In the stones of Navarrenx, he wrote, "I can read the centuries, rather as botanists can tell the age of a tree by the number of rings in its trunk."[28] But Mourenx was without history. If the traditional city may be compared with a natural organism—tree or seashell—that grows over time, the new town is defined by its having been planned once and for all. The question then becomes whether its inhabitants

---

27 See *Internationale situationniste* no. 6 (August 1961), 149–155 8; "Critique of Urbanism" is translated in this volume, 149–155.
28 Lefebvre, *Introduction to Modernity* (1962), trans. John Moore (London and New York: Verso, 1995), 116.

will "do what the plan expects them to do, shopping in the shopping center, asking for advice at the advice bureau, doing everything the civic center offices demand of them like good, reliable citizens?" The entire city functioned for Lefebvre like a binary code, telling its residents "do this, don't do that"—a purely legible text laid out in the form of abstract Corbusian "machines for living in" shorn of location in place and time.[29] The S.I. would wholly concur with this assessment, and in their writings of this time we find a diagnosis of modern planning that—in a colder, more analytic style—echoed that of their erstwhile ally.

Festival and urban revolution

In their critique of urban planning, the Situationists were responding to the particular conditions they faced in a France undergoing a period of active urbanization; in a veritable rural exodus, more than one million people arrived in Paris from the provinces between 1945 and 1960. By that date, 46% of those living in the Parisian region had been born elsewhere; moreover, one in ten were not French, but came from the working classes of North Africa, Spain, or Portugal. This was nothing less than a vast reordering of the social structure of the country, and was accompanied —as we have seen—by a determined spatial strategy of class segregation, with the last working-class quarters ("slums") being cleared out of the old urban centers in a process of "rehabilitation," while the suburbs were sown with *grands ensembles*, characterized by their repetitive, banal architecture and their total rupture from the existing city. The period stretching from the early 1950s to the mid-1970s has rightly been termed one of a "new Haussmannization," a reprise of the mid-nineteenth century renovation of Paris that sought to displace the city's restive working class and create a more sympathetic environment for the bourgeoisie. The rapid urbanization of the postwar years was nothing less than a new push in this long-term process of capitalist modernization.

If Baron Georges Haussmann's depredations of a century earlier had been justified as providing Paris with a healthier environment, with new parks and open-air spaces, and with an easier traffic flow, by the mid-twentieth century even mainstream voices could recognize that his true motives were rather more political—that is to say, they lay in the maintenance of order: "He tore down unhealthy quarters in so far as they were the haunts of rebels. He created roads that were straight and wide, so that the cavalry could more easily charge down them and the regular troops could make

---

29 Lefebvre, *Introduction to Modernity* (1962), 118–119. See the discussion in Andy Merrifield, *Metromarxism* (New York and London: Routledge, 2002), 80–84.

use of their long-range weapons."³⁰ Yet however much Haussmann and his master, Napoléon III, believed in the preeminently strategic nature of their plan, the events of the Commune in the spring of 1871 put paid to their hope that urbanism could render insurrection obsolete. For several weeks the proletariat of Paris, under the conditions of the most extreme duress, reconquered the city from which it had been excluded and established what has often been described as a carnivalesque interval of participatory democracy before being brutally crushed by troops loyal to the conservative Versailles government. It should hardly be surprising that, at the same moment that the S.I. was studying the neo-Haussmannization affecting Paris and its suburbs, it would also undertake a close examination of the legacy of the Commune.

For both the Situationists and Lefebvre—mutually pursuing the study of the Commune in the early 1960s—a key term would prove to be that of festival: Paris in the spring of 1871 represented liberation from the miseries and humiliations of everyday life and rebirth of the *fête*. Revolution and festival were thereby conjoined, in an insistence that the tasks of social transformation were not to be "restricted to the spheres of economy, politics, and ideology," but had necessarily to aim at the destruction of everyday life itself, as the primary site of alienation in modern society. Inspired by the example of the Commune, Lefebvre wrote, "the revolution of the future will put an end to the everyday, it will usher in prodigality and lavishness and break our fetters, violently or peaceably as the case may be."³¹ If modern urbanism was premised on the physical implantation of separation and segregation, the revolutionary urbanism embodied in festival founded itself on the collapse of boundaries, the removal of obstacles, and the possibility of mutual recognition of subjects in the social space created therein.

But however important the Commune was for the Situationists—providing as it did *"the one realization of a revolutionary urbanism"*³²—its example remained primarily historical, and it took contemporary events happening a continent away to actualize its lessons. In August 1965 the predominantly African-American neighborhood of Watts, in Los Angeles, exploded in several days of rioting that saw pitched battles with the forces of order, the looting of stores, and a state of generalized insurrection that the S.I. understood as the herald of a new extremism in the resistance to capitalist

---

30 Pierre Lavedan, *Histoire de l'urbanisme: Époque contemporaine* (Paris: Henri Laurens, 1952), 107–108.
31 Lefebvre, *Everyday Life in the Modern World* (1968), trans. Sacha Rabinovitch (New York: Harper & Row, Coll. "Harper Torchbooks," 1971), 36 (trans. modified).
32 Guy Debord, Attila Kotányi, and Raoul Vaneigem, "On the Commune" (1962), translated in this volume, 170.

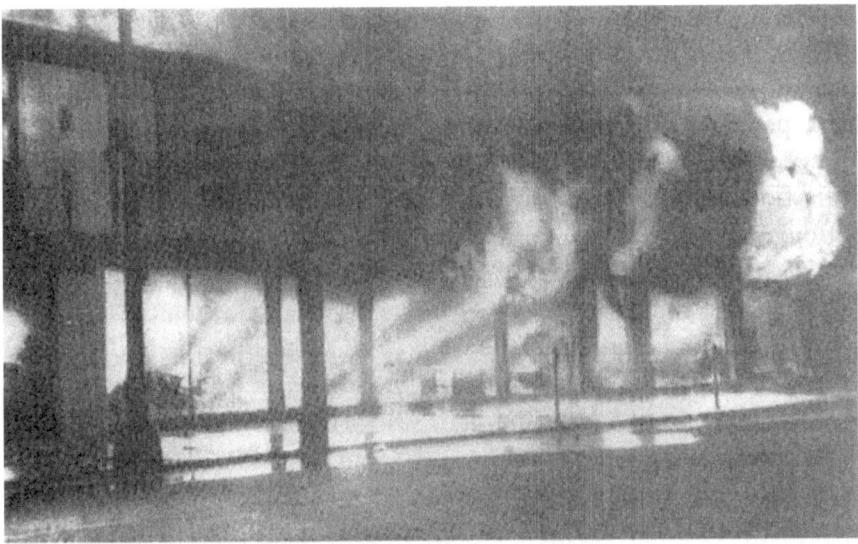

Fig.1.10 "Critique of Urbanism (Los Angeles Supermarket, August 1965)," from *Internationale Situationniste* no. 10 (March 1966).

America immediately has stooped over to examine this new wound. For several months, sociologists, politicians, psychologists, economists, and experts of all sorts have sounded its depths. ... It is not a 'neighborhood' in the true sense of the word, but a hopelessly stretched-out and monotonous plain ... 'one-story America' in all its breadth, everything most dismal in an American landscape, with its flat-roofed houses, its shops that all sell the same thing, its hamburger joints, its service-stations, all of them weathered by poverty and meanness. ... Traffic is less thick there than elsewhere, but pedestrian traffic is hardly thicker, so scattered is the housing and so discouraging are the distances. ... White passersby attract stares, stares in which if not hate, at least sarcasm can be read (you often hear 'more researchers and other sociologists looking for explanations instead of giving us jobs'). ... As for housing, no doubt it could be improved physically, but one scarcely sees how it would be possible to prevent whites fleeing en masse any neighborhood into which blacks begin to move. The latter will continue to feel abandoned to themselves, particularly in this city beyond measure that is Los Angeles, lacking a center, without even a crowd into which to blend, where whites only catch a glimpse of their fellows through the windshields of their cars. ... The reverend Martin Luther King [spoke] in Watts a few days later and [called] for his brothers of color "to extend a hand," someone shouted in the crowd: 'and burn, baby, burn!' ... It is a tonic sight to see, some distance from Watts, so-called 'middle-class' neighborhoods where blacks of the new bourgeoisie mow their lawns in front of comfortable houses." Michel Tatu, *Le Monde*, November 3, 1965.

modernization. In 1966 a photograph taken during the riots appeared in the pages of the group's journal; it had been appropriated from *Time* magazine, where it had first appeared the previous summer in an account of the uprising (fig.1.10). Characteristically, the American magazine had expressed outrage and puzzlement over what it called this "orgy of rapine," and the photo's original caption read "Pillaged furniture store blazing out of control." When it reappeared in the *Internationale situationniste* seven months later, it bore a new caption: "Critique of urbanism." That transformation was crucial, expressing as it did the Situationists' belief in the eminent rationality of the Watts rioters; the festival of the Commune had taught them to see in the methodical looting and burning of stores during the nights of unrest in Los Angeles a form of constructive appropriation of capitalist space.

When the S.I. changed captions on this press photograph, it was not however simply coopting the spontaneity of the Watts riots for its own pre-established critique of modernist city-planning; there was more to this act than a kind of theoretical imperialism, whereby Continental intellectuals would provide the unthinking acts of African-American insurgents with ex post facto justification. If anything, the polarity of influence was the opposite: through Watts, the S.I. learned to recognize the currency of the Commune and its own antagonism toward the realm of the everyday. Even as an explicit concern with architecture began to fade in the group's writings, the joined notions of urban revolution and festival assumed greater and greater importance, providing a crucial impulse for the Parisian uprising of May–June 1968. Here too, as in the Commune almost a century earlier, the struggle was articulated around the hope that "the antithesis between the everyday and the Festival—whether of labor or of leisure—will no longer be a basis of society."[33]

Toward a synoptic theory of capitalist urbanization

By the late 1960s the S.I. had traveled far from its origins within a post-Surrealist discourse, and had equally marked itself off from the growing chorus of internal critiques of postwar urbanism's foundational Athens Charter (such as Team 10) as well as critiques stemming from a neo-avant-garde position (such as Yona Friedman, Paul Maymont, or Nicolas Schöffer). The Situationist analysis of urbanism, and its elaboration of a theory of festival and urban revolution, was cut off from these more mainstream debates, ignoring those discussions taking place within the professional realm of architecture and being ignored in turn. (Tellingly, when critic Françoise Choay published her epochal anthology on modern city-planning

---

33 Lefebvre, *Everyday Life in the Modern World* (1968), 36–37.

in 1965, the S.I. went unmentioned.)[34] Having categorically refused all architectural experimentation—having made the position of architects within the S.I. utterly impossible (like artists, if they deigned to engage their profession, they would be excluded)—by this point the Situationists had become all but invisible within the arguments that were shaking up architecture and urbanism at this time. In its place, the S.I. was developing a disabused theory of the place of building and city-planning in advanced capitalism, and sketching the outlines of its negation. Above all in Debord's *The Society of the Spectacle*, published in 1967 and made by him into a film six years later, we find the articulation of a Hegelian urbanism.

"Hegelian," of course, because the theory Debord expounded was based upon his close reading of early Marx and of Hegel's *Phenomenology*, but more profoundly because at its heart we find the expression of a dynamic —conveyed within and through our built environment—of alienation, not only internal to the self, but of self from other. Contemporary architecture and urbanism were nothing less than the logic of alienation and reification writ in stone, the capitalist refashioning of space "into its own décor," as Debord wrote in *The Society of the Spectacle*.[35] The aim of revolution would then lie not only in the abolition of class society (the social basis of this alienation) but in the construction of a world in which the reciprocal recognition of subjects would replace their mutual misrecognition; the end of commodity relations would also be the end of the other apprehended as an object, as a thing in a world of things. The Commune in the nineteenth century, and Watts in the recent past, pointed to what such a society might look like: festival-spaces where individuals and social classes could become conscious of themselves for the first time as subjects, or rather, as fully human.

Debord spoke of revolution as *"that critique of human geography* whereby individuals and communities must construct places and events commensurate with the appropriation no longer just of their labor, but of their total history."[36] Here, with a nod back to his own earlier insistence in a 1955 essay that "the sole thrilling direction" in the theater of the everyday was "the fragmentary search for a new way of life," he recast the terms of a revolutionary practice of architecture and urbanism.[37] The discovery of that new way of living would not take place through the disciplines of the

---

34 See Françoise Choay, *L'urbanisme: utopies et réalités, une anthologie* (Paris: Éditions du Seuil, 1965).
35 Debord, *The Society of the Spectacle* (1967), trans. Donald Nicholson-Smith (New York: Zone Books, 1994), 121.
36 Debord, *The Society of the Spectacle* (1967), 126.
37 Debord, "Introduction to a Critique of Urban Geography" (1955), trans. in this volume, 59.

built environment, but only through their thoroughgoing transformation into a collective practice whereby people can come to recognize themselves and each other. When in 1973 Debord sought an image of that future, he found it in Pieter Brueghel the Elder's *Tower of Babel* of c. 1563 (Museum Boymans-van Beuningen, Rotterdam) (fig.1.11); in this context, the Biblical story of overweening human pride was appropriated and re-signified to convey the triumphant effort of humanity united in constructive effort, and the end to all separations and alienations (Babylon being that great cosmopolitan city that united humanity under a common tongue).

But in taking Brueghel's *Tower* as an image of post-revolutionary place making, Debord was also reinventing an origin story for the city. After all, American urban historian Lewis Mumford had located the origin of monumental architecture and organized urban life in the river valley civilizations of Mesopotamia, such as Babylon. Their great ziggurats had been the earliest examples of "megamachines"—the products of hierarchical organizations of human beings unified into machine-like units. Mumford's magisterial *City in History* (1961, translated into French in 1964) had been of great influence in Situationist circles, and particularly marked Debord's thought, but here we see him turning Mumford's story of human devolution upon its head. If Mumford had written a history in which the city —from deepest antiquity through the present—more often than not had functioned as the site where human powers were alienated from those who exercised them, Debord would insist that human freedom would also take an urban form. Considered dialectically, what the megamachine figured negatively was nothing less than the infinite possibilities of human creation when freed from its class-based bonds.

We began with a piece of fantastic architecture, the postman Cheval's Palais Idéal, which had—within the objective limits of a single individual's means—expressed the imperious human need to shape one's environment, to create surroundings that somehow speak of and to oneself; we end with a piece of imaginary architecture, a Biblical tower made over into a premonitory sign of the future collective construction of our world. Whatever the profound changes that "consumer society" or the "society of the spectacle" have undergone in the meantime, and however much their territories have also been altered, the Situationists' critical study of modernity and of its supersession contained between these two images has hardly been exhausted. We continue to await the construction of those more concrete collective spaces announced in the pages that follow.

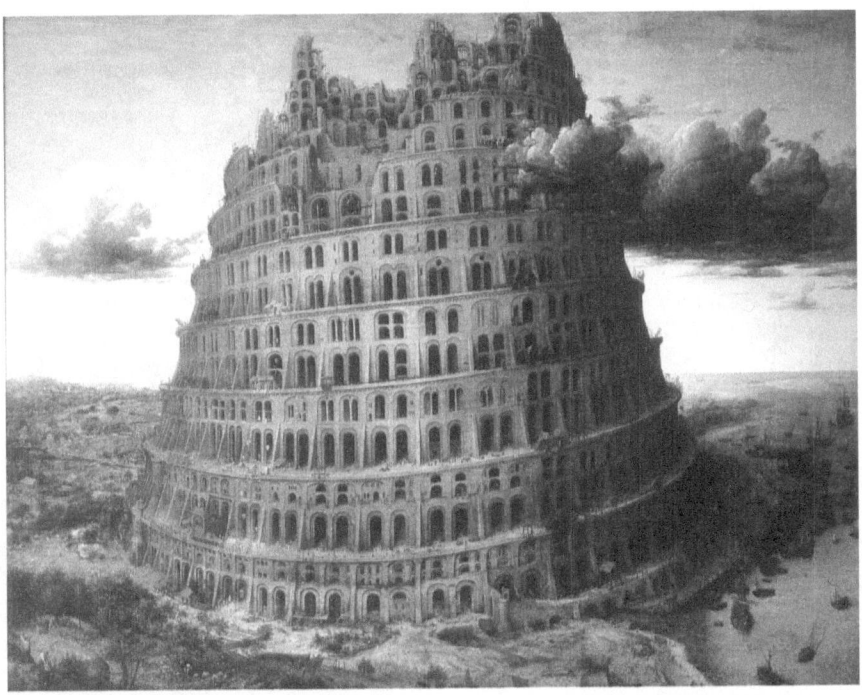

Fig.1.11 Pieter Brueghel the Elder, *Tower of Babel*, c. 1563. Museum Boymans-van Beuningen, Rotterdam.

2.

Critique of Functionalism and Modernization

FORMULARY FOR A NEW URBANISM[1]

GILLES IVAIN (PSEUDO. IVAN CHTCHEGLOV)

In 1958 the Situationist International would define "psychogeography" as the "study of the precise effects of the geographical environment, consciously organized or not, acting directly on the affective comportment of individuals."[2] *However Gilles Ivain (pseudonym of Ivan Chtcheglov) had already undertaken studies in this field five years earlier, in his "Formulary for a New Urbanism" of September 1953. Ivain opens on a poetic note, remarking on the predominant experience of boredom in the contemporary city and concluding the first section of his essay with the famous statement: "You will never see the hacienda. It does not exist. The hacienda must be built." (The reference to haciendas, those vast Spanish estates of the New World, probably derives from popular fictions like Johnston McCulley's* Zorro *and its filmic adaptations.) This is, then, an architectural problem at least in part, and Ivain goes on to comment on the role of architecture as a means of expressing and effecting spatio-temporal experience, and to call for a modifiable built environment that might change with the desires of its inhabitants. Those desires demand a program of propaganda and action that might counter the ever-expanding banality of contemporary life. The realization of desire, he concludes, requires its own architectural and urban setting: most notably, a city whose quarters*

---

1 First published in *Internationale situationniste* no. 1 (June 1958): 15–20, in a version edited by Guy Debord from the original manuscript drafted in September 1953. The following translation is based on the full text as found in Ivan Chtcheglov, *Écrits retrouvés*, ed. Jean-Marie Apostolidès and Boris Donné (Paris: Editions Allia, 2006), 7–16. [Ed.]

2 "Definitions" (1958), in *Situationist International Anthology*, 45 (trans. modified). [Ed.]

CRITIQUE OF FUNCTIONALISM AND MODERNIZATION

might correspond to differing emotional states and whose inhabitants devoted themselves to a continual wandering among them.

Sire, I am from the other country.

We are bored in the city, there is no longer any temple of the sun. Between the legs of women walking by the Dadaists would have liked to find an adjustable wrench, and the Surrealists a crystal goblet—that's lost. We know how to read all the promises on faces, latest state of morphology. The poetry of posters lasted twenty years. We are bored in the city, to still discover mysteries on the signs along the street, latest state of humor and poetry, requires getting damned tired:

> BAIN-DOUCHES DES PATRIARCHES
> MACHINES À TRANCHER LES VIANDES
> ZOO NOTRE-DAME
> PHARMACIE DES SPORTS
> ALIMENTATION DES MARTYRS
> BÉTON TRANSLUCIDE
> SCIERIE MAIN-D'OR
> CENTRE DE RÉCUPÉRATION FONCTIONELLE
> AMBULANCE SAINTE-ANNE
> CINQUIÈME AVENUE CAFÉ
> RUE DES VOLONTAIRES PROLONGÉE
> PENSION DE FAMILLE DANS LE JARDIN
> HÔTEL DES ÉTRANGERS
> RUE SAUVAGE

And the swimming pool of the rue des Fillettes. And the police station of the rue du Rendez-vous. The medico-surgical clinic and the free employment agency of the quai des Orfèvres. The artificial flowers of the rue du Soleil. The hôtel des Caves du Château, the bar de l'Océan and the café du Va et Vient. The hôtel de l'Epoque.

And the strange statue of Doctor Philippe Pinel, benefactor of the insane, disappearing in the last evenings of summer. Exploring Paris.

And you, forgotten, your memories ravaged by all the sorrows of the map of the world, stranded in the Red Caves of Pali-Kao, without music and without geography, no longer setting out for the hacienda *where the roots call up the child and the wine is drunk down to fables from an old almanac*. Now that game is lost. You will never see the hacienda. It does not exist.

The hacienda must be built.

All cities are geological and three steps cannot be taken without encountering ghosts, bearing all the prestige of their legends. We maneuver within a *closed* landscape whose landmarks constantly draw us toward the past. Certain

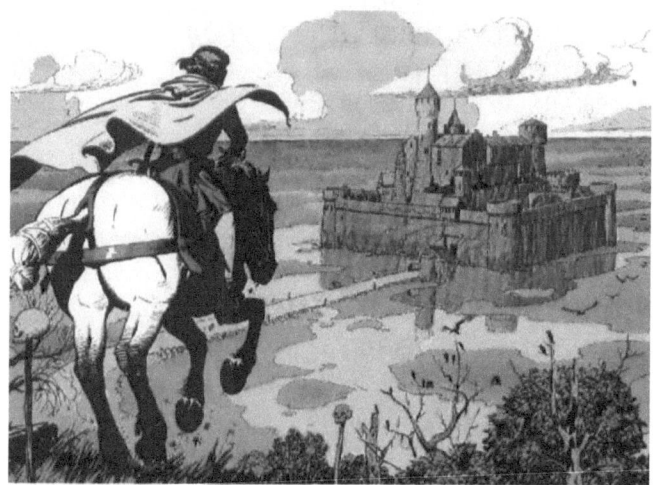

Fig.2.1.1   Harold Foster, "Prince Valiant," created 1937. Prince Valiant ©
1937 DISTRIBUTED BY KING FEATURES SYNDICATE

shifting angles, certain *receding* perspectives allow us to glimpse original conceptions of space, but this vision remains fragmentary. It must be sought in the magical locales of folkloric tales and surrealist writings: castles, endless walls, little forgotten bars, Mammoth Cave, mirrors of Casinos.

These dated images retain a small catalyzing power, but it is almost impossible to use them in a *symbolic urbanism* without rejuvenating them by giving them a new meaning. There was good in seahorses, in yellow dwarfs of destiny, but they are in no way adapted to the requirements of modern life. This is the twentieth century, after all, although few people suspect it. Our intellect, haunted by old-fashioned key images, has remained far behind our perfected machines. The various attempts to fuse modern science into new myths remain inadequate. Since then, the Abstract has invaded all the arts, contemporary architecture most of all. Pure plasticity, without anecdote but lifeless, relaxes the eye and chills it. Elsewhere other fragmentary beauties can be found, while the land of promised syntheses is further and further away. Everyone wavers between the emotionally still-alive past and the already dead future.

We will not prolong mechanical civilizations and the *architecture froide* that ultimately lead to boring forms of leisure.

We propose to invent new, changeable decors.

We leave to monsieur Le Corbusier his style that suits factories as well as it does hospitals. And the prisons of the future: is he not already building churches? I do not know what this individual—ugly of countenance and hideous in his conceptions of the world—is repressing to make him want thus to crush humanity under ignoble heaps of reinforced concrete, a noble material that ought to permit an aerial articulation of space superior to Flamboyant Gothic. His power of cretinization is vast. A model by Corbusier is the only image that brings to my mind the idea of immediate suicide. With him moreover any remaining joy will fade. And love—passion—liberty.

Darkness draws back from lighting and the seasons from air conditioning: night and summer are losing their charms, and dawn is disappearing. The human being of the cities thinks he or she is escaping from cosmic reality and does not dream any the more for it. The reason for it is clear: dream has its point of departure in reality and is realized in it.

The latest state of technology allows unbroken contact between the individual and cosmic reality, while eliminating its disagreeable aspects. The glass ceiling lets the stars and the rain be seen. The mobile house turns with the sun. Its sliding walls enable vegetation to invade life. Mounted on tracks, it can go down to the sea in the morning, and return to the forest in the evening.

Architecture is the simplest means to *articulate* time and space, to *modulate* reality, to engender dreams. It is not only a matter of plastic articulation and modulation—expression of an ephemeral beauty—but of a modulation producing influences, in accordance with the eternal spectrum of human desires and of progress in the realization of these desires.

The architecture of tomorrow will thus be a means of modifying present conceptions of time and space.

The architectural complex will be modifiable. Its aspect will change partially or totally in accordance with the will of its inhabitants.

A new architecture can only be spoken of if it expresses a new civilization (it is clear that there has been neither civilization nor architecture for several centuries, but only experiments, the majority of which have failed: one can speak of Gothic architecture, but Marxist or capitalist architecture does not exist, although these two systems show similar tendencies and common aims).

Hence everyone has the right to ask us upon what outlines of a civilization we want to found an architecture. I will quickly recall the bases of a civilization:

- a new conception of space (whether based on a religious cosmogony or not).
- a new conception of time (numeration starting from zero, various *ways* for time to unfold).
- a new conception of comportment (in moral nature, sociology, politics, law. The economy is only one part of the laws of comportment to which a civilization agrees).

Past collectivities offered the masses an absolute truth and incontestable mythic examples. The appearance of the idea of *relativity* in the modern mind allows one to glimpse the EXPERIMENTAL aspect of the next civilization, although that word doesn't please me. Let's say more fluid, more "entertaining." (For a long time it was believed that the Marxist countries were on this path. Now we know that this attempt has followed the old standard evolution, in order to arrive in record time at the hardening of its doctrines and at forms frozen in their decadence. A renewal is perhaps possible, but the question cannot be dealt with here.)

On the bases of this mobile civilization, architecture will be, at least in the beginning, a means of testing a thousand ways of modifying life, with a view toward a synthesis that could only be commemorated in legend.

A mental disease has swept the planet: banalization. Everyone is hypnotized by production and comfort—sewage system, elevator, bathroom, washing machine.

This state of affairs, which arose out of a struggle against poverty, overshoots its ultimate goal—the liberation of humanity from material cares—and becomes an obsessive image hanging over the present. Between love and a garbage disposal, young people of all countries have made their choice and prefer the garbage disposal. A complete and sudden change of the spirit has become essential, by bringing to light forgotten desires and creating entirely new ones. And by an *intensive propaganda* in favor of these desires.

Guy Debord already has pointed out the necessity of constructing situations as one of the basic desires upon which the next civilization will be founded. This necessity of *absolute* creation has always been closely linked to the necessity of *playing* with architecture, time, and space. As evidence I need only point to the sheet that the Palais de Paris distributes along the streets. (Manifestations of the collective unconscious always correspond with the assertions of creators.)

VANISHED NEIGHBORHOODS
Great events
PERIOD MUSIC
ILLUMINATIONS

PARIS BY NIGHT

COMPLETELY BROUGHT TO LIFE

The Cour des Miracles: impressive three hundred square meter reconstruction of an old medieval neighborhood with leprous houses peopled with vagrants, beggars, prostitutes, all subjects of the frightful KING OF THUNE, who dispenses justice from atop his cask.
The Tour de Nesle: The ominous Tower silhouettes its impressive bulk against the dark sky, where black clouds race. The waters of the Seine lap gently. A barge comes in. Two swordsmen lie in wait for their victim.
etc.

Other examples of this desire to construct situations have reached us from the past. Thus Edgar Poe and his story of the man who devotes his fortune to constructing landscape gardens.[3] Or the painting of Claude Lorrain. Many of his admirers have no idea to what to attribute the charm of his canvases. They speak of their light. Its effects are indeed strange, but not

---

3 Edgar Allan Poe, "The Landscape Garden" [The Domain of Arnheim]" (1847), in *The Unabridged Edgar Allan Poe* (Birmingham, Ala.: Sweetwater Press, 1997), 1097–1110. [Ed.]

sufficient to explain their ambiance of *perpetual* invitation to the voyage.⁴ This ambiance is caused by an *unusual architectural space*. The palaces give directly onto the sea, they have "useless" hanging gardens whose vegetation appears in the most unexpected places. Incitation to *dérive* is caused by the lack of distance between the portals of the palaces and the ships.

One of the most remarkable precursors in architecture remains de Chirico. He was grappling with the problem of absences and presences through time and space.

We know that an object, not consciously noticed at the time of a first *visit*, provokes by its absence during subsequent visits an indefinable impression: as a result of a retrieval in time, *the absence of the object becomes a perceptible presence*. More precisely: although remaining generally indefinite, the quality of the impression nevertheless varies with the nature of the removed object and the importance accorded it by the visitor, ranging from serene joy to terror (little does it matter to us that in this specific case the vehicle of these feelings is memory. I only selected this example for its convenience).

In de Chirico's painting (Arcades period) an *empty space* creates a *well-filled time*. It is easy to imagine the future that we will reserve for such architects, and what will be their influences on crowds. Today we can have nothing but contempt for a century that relegates such *models* to so-called museums. Without going so far as to offer de Chirico the opportunity to freely arrange the place de la Concorde and its Obelisk, businesses could entrust him with the drawing up of those gardens that "decorate" several entrances to the capital.

This new vision of time and space that will be the theoretical basis of future constructions, is not in the right state and will never wholly be so before testing comportments in cities set aside for this effect, cities in which will be systematically assembled—in addition to the organizations necessary for a minimum of comfort and security—buildings charged with a great power of evocation and influence, symbolic edifices representing desires, forces, events past, present, and to come. A rational expansion of the old religious systems, of old tales, and above all of psychoanalysis to the profit of architecture becomes more urgent each day, as all the reasons for becoming impassioned disappear.

In a way everyone will live in his own personal "cathedral." There will be rooms more conducive to dreams than drugs, and houses where one cannot help but love. Others will be irresistibly alluring to travelers ...

This project could be compared with Chinese and Japanese *trompe-l'oeil* gardens—with the difference that those gardens are not designed to be lived in

---

4 A reference to the poem of Charles Baudelaire, "Invitation to the Voyage," in *Les Fleurs du mal*, trans. Richard Howard (Boston: David R. Godine, 1982), 58–59.[Ed.]

CRITIQUE OF FUNCTIONALISM AND MODERNIZATION 39

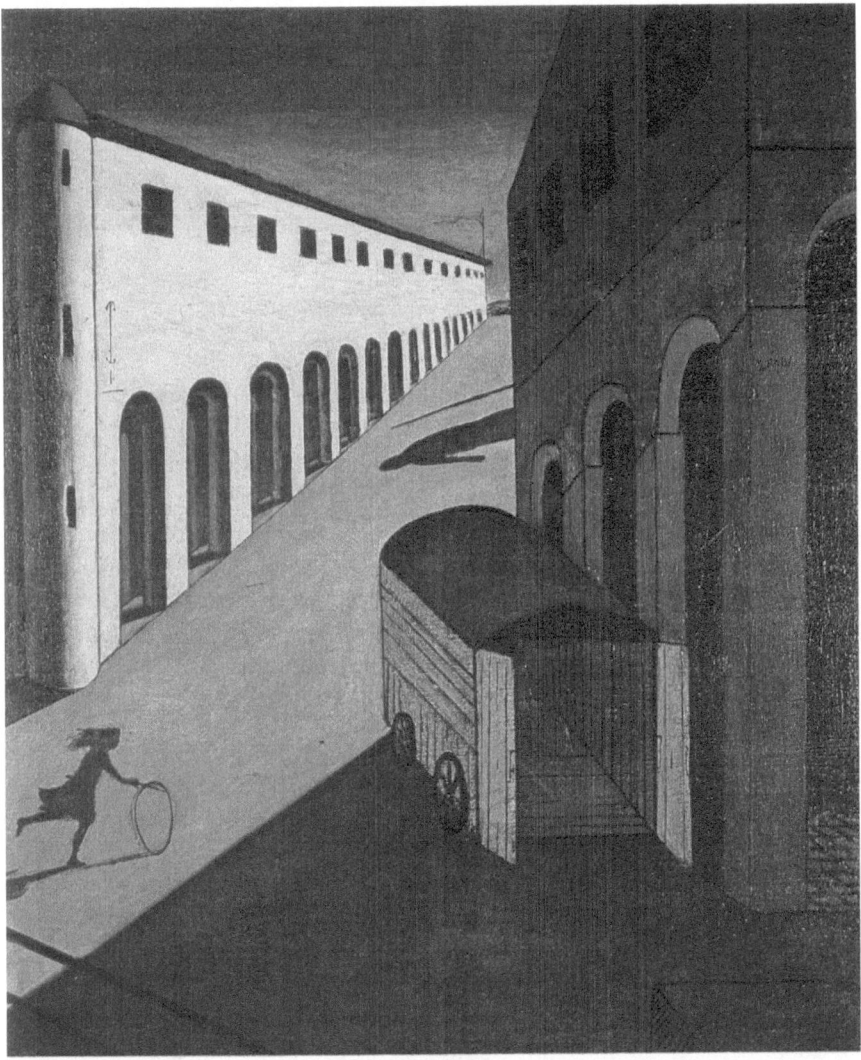

Fig.2.1.4 Giorgio de Chirico, *Melancholy and Mystery of a Street*, 1914. Private collection. © 2009 SIAE

all the time—or with the ridiculous Labyrinth in the Jardin des Plantes, at the entry to which can be read, height of protective stupidity, Ariadne unemployed:

GAMES ARE FORBIDDEN IN THE LABYRINTH

This city could be envisaged in the form of an arbitrary assemblage of castles, grottoes, lakes, etc. It would be the baroque stage of urbanism considered as a means of knowledge. But this theoretical phase is already outdated. We know that a modern building could be constructed that would have no resemblance to a medieval castle but that preserved and enhanced the poetic power of the *Castle* (by the conservation of a strict minimum of lines, the transposition of certain others, the positioning of openings, the topographical location, etc.).

The quarters of this city could correspond to the catalog of diverse feelings that are encountered *by chance* in daily life.

Bizarre Quarter—Happy Quarter, specially reserved for habitation—Noble and Tragic Quarter (for good children)—Historic Quarter (museums, schools)—Useful Quarter (hospital, tool shops)—Sinister Quarter, etc. And an *Astrolaire* that will group plant species in accordance with the relations they manifest with the stellar rhythm, a Planetary Garden comparable to that which the astronomer Thomas intends to establish in Vienna at the Laaer Berg. Indispensable for giving the inhabitants a consciousness of the cosmic. Perhaps also a Death Quarter, not for dying in but in which to *live in peace*, and here I think of Mexico and of a principle of innocent cruelty that becomes dearer to me each day.

The Sinister Quarter, for example, will favorably replace those holes, those mouths of hell, that many peoples once possessed in their capital: they symbolized the evil forces of life. The Sinister Quarter would have no need to harbor real dangers, such as traps, dungeons, or mines. It would be difficult of access, hideously decorated (piercing whistles, alarm bells, sirens of irregular cadence, grotesque sculptures, motor-driven mechanical mobiles) and as poorly lit at night as it is blindingly lit during the day by an excessive use of the phenomenon of reflection. At the center, the "Square of the Appalling Mobile." Saturation of the market with a product causes the product's price to fall: the child would learn in exploring the Sinister Quarter not to fear the anguishing occasions of life, but to be amused by them.

The principal activity of the inhabitants will be CONTINUOUS *DÉRIVE*. The changing of landscape from one hour to the next will result in complete disorientation.

Couples will no longer spend their nights in their houses dedicated to habitation and reception, the customary *social* reason for banalization. The chamber of love will be more remote from the center of the city: it will completely naturally re-create for the partners the notion of *ex-centricity*, in a place less open to the light, more hidden, in order to return to the atmosphere of the secret. The contrary move, the search for a center of thought, will proceed by the same technique.

Later, at the time of the inevitable wearing down of these gestures, this *dérive* will partially leave the realm of the lived for that of representation.

Note: A certain Saint-Germain-des-Prés, on which no one has yet written a word, was the first unit working at the scale of history on this ethics of dérive. *This egregore,[5] secret until now, is the lone explanation for the enormous influence that* three blocks of houses *have exerted over the world, and that people have tried to rationalize through the insufficient fields of clothing and song, and more stupidly through questionable aptitudes for prostitution (what then of Pigalle?).*

In future books we will define what in Saint-Germain would make for the coincidence of days and their occurrences *(*The New Nomadism *by Henry de Béarn,* Beautiful Youth *by Guy Debord, etc.). From them will appear not only an "aesthetic of comportment" but practical means for founding new units, and above all a complete* phenomenology *of couples, encounters, and duration toward which mathematicians and poets will be profitably predisposed.*

Finally, to those who will object that a people cannot live on *dérive* alone, it is useful to recall that in each group individuals (whether priests or heroes) are entrusted as specialists with representing its tendencies, in agreement with the double mechanism of projection and identification. Experience demonstrates that a *dérive* favorably replaces a mass: it is better fitted to introduce the whole of our energies into communication, to collect them for the benefit of the collectivity.

The economic objection does not hold up to closer scrutiny. It is known that the more a place is *set aside for the freedom of play*, the more it influences comportment and the greater is its force of attraction. The immense prestige of Monaco, of Las Vegas, is proof of it. And Reno, caricature of free love. Yet it is only a question of mere gambling. This first experimental city would live largely off a tolerated and controlled tourism. Future avant-garde activities and productions would gravitate there of their own accord. In a few years it would become the intellectual capital of the world, and would be universally recognized as such.

---

5   "Egregore" is an occult concept closely associated with Rosicrucianism describing an autonomous psychic entity made up of, and influencing, the thoughts of a group of people. [Ed.]

SLUM CONSTRUCTION[6]

ANDRÉ-FRANCK CONORD

The viewpoints developed by Ivain in his "Formulary" also arose as a reaction to the architecture of the 1950s, a decade that saw the generalization of modernist planning principles and the triumph of reinforced concrete. The protagonists of the Lettrist International saw the resulting "machines for living in" as products of an irrational rationality that was destroying a sense of the human scale and generating a style of housing that lay halfway between the factory and the barrack. The architect Le Corbusier was of course the most famous representative of this development, and so he suffered the L.I.'s first salvoes against functionalist architecture—a target of heated critique at the same moment by Asger Jorn and the CoBrA movement.

Within the framework of the social policy programs of the past few years, the construction of slums as a means to avert the housing crisis is continuing feverishly. The ingenuity of our ministers and our architect-urbanists can only be admired. To avoid any disruption of harmony, they have developed a few standard slum types whose plans can be used anywhere in France. Reinforced concrete is their preferred building material.—This material lends itself to the most flexible of forms, but is employed only to make square houses. The greatest success of the genre seems to be the "Cité Radieuse" by general Corbusier, although the productions of the brilliant Perret run a close second.[7]

In their works, a style is developed which sets the standards of Western thought and civilization for the mid-twentieth century.—It is the "barracks" style and the 1950s house is a box.

Setting determines gestures: we will build passionate houses.

NEXT PLANET[8]

Their builders are lost, but uncanny pyramids resist the banalizations of travel agencies.

By working every night of his life, the postman Cheval built in his Hauterives garden his indefensible "Ideal Palace," which is the first expression of an architecture of disorientation:

---

6 *Potlatch* no. 3 (July 6, 1954): n.p. [Ed.]
7 A reference to Auguste Perret (1874–1954), a French architect specializing in reinforced concrete construction; his reconstruction of Le Havre after the Second World War, begun in 1947, was characterized by a rather dry, modern classicism. [Ed.]
8 *Potlatch* no. 4 (July 13, 1954): n.p. [Ed.]

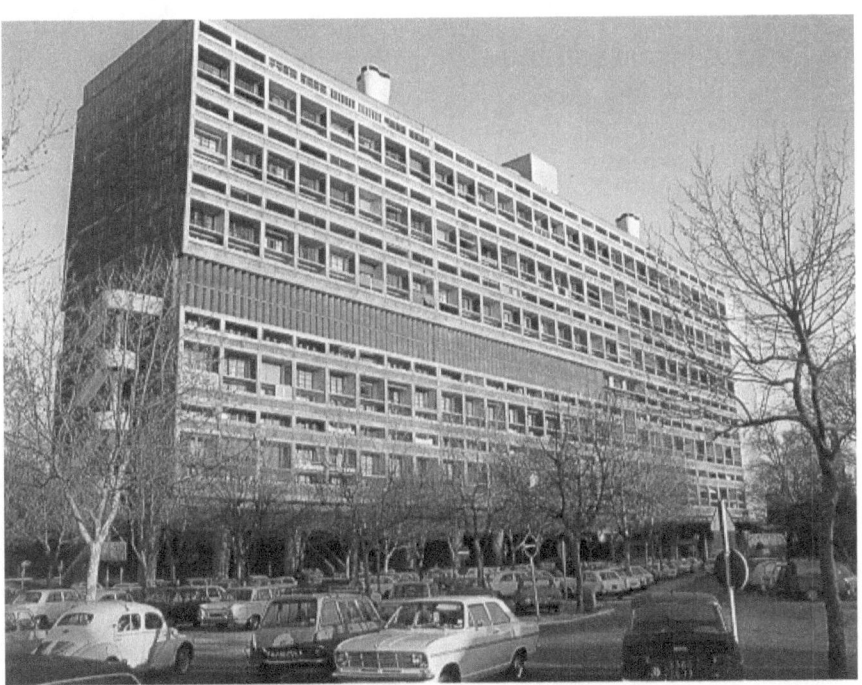

Fig.2.2.1 Le Corbusier, Unité d'Habitation, Marseilles, France. Completed 1952.

This baroque Palace, which *appropriates* [*détourne*] the forms of various exotic monuments (and which is made of stone vegetation), is of use only for losing oneself. Its influence will soon be immense. The sum of the labor supplied by a single man with an incredible obstinacy is not, of course, appreciable in itself, as customary visitors think, but revealing of a strange passion that remains unarticulated.

Struck by the same desire, Ludwig II of Bavaria erected at great expense a few delirious artificial castles in the forested mountains of his kingdom—before disappearing in shallow waters.

The underground river that was his theater or the plaster statues in his gardens draws attention to this *absolutist* enterprise, and its drama.

Here are certainly to be found all the grounds of an intervention for psychiatric scum; and yet more slavering pages for paternalistic intellectuals who from time to time pursue a "naïf."

But the naivety is theirs. Ferdinand Cheval and Ludwig of Bavaria built the castles that they wanted, to the dimensions of a new human condition.

SKYSCRAPERS BY THE ROOTS[9]

LETTRIST INTERNATIONAL

In this epoch more and more placed, in all domains, under the sign of repression, there is one particularly repugnant man, clearly more of a cop than the average. He is building cellular *unités d'habitations*, he is building a capital for the Nepalese, he is building vertical ghettoes, morgues for an age that has good use for them, *he is building churches*.

The modulor Protestant, Le Corbusier-Sing-Sing, the dauber of neo-Cubist smears, is making the *"machine for living in"* work for the greater glory of God, who created carrion and crows [*corbusiers*] in his own image.

It should not be forgotten that if modern Urbanism has not yet been an art—and even less a setting for life—it has on the other hand always been inspired by Police directives; and after all Haussmann only gave us these boulevards to more conveniently bring in the cannon.

But today, when we are informed that Le Corbusier longs to *abolish the street*, the prison becomes the model for housing and Christian morality triumphs without rejoinder. He even brags about it. Here's the program: life definitively divided up into closed blocks, into communities under observation; the end of opportunities for insurrections and encounters; automatic resignation. (Let us note in passing that the existence of the automobile is useful to all—save, of course, for a few of the "underprivileged"—: likewise the recently deceased Chief of Police, the unforgettable Baylot, declared

---

9   *Potlatch* no. 5 (July 20, 1954): n.p. [Ed.]

after the last post-graduation student parade that street demonstrations were henceforth incompatible with traffic requirements. And, every 14 July, it's proven to us.)[10]

With Le Corbusier, the games and forms of knowledge that we have a right to expect from a truly surprising architecture—daily disorientation—have been sacrificed to the garbage disposal that will never be used for the prescribed Bible, already in place in hotels across the U.S.A.

You would have to be a real fool to see a modern architecture here. It is nothing but a wholesale return to the old, not properly buried Christian world. At the turn of the last century, the mystic from Lyon Pierre-Simon Ballanche, in his *Ville des expiations* ["City of Expiations"][11]—whose descriptions prefigure the "cités radieuses"—had already voiced this ideal of existence:

> The City of Expiations must be a living image of the monotonous and sad law of human vicissitudes, of the unbending law of social necessities: all customs, even the most innocent, must be attacked head-on; everything must be a constant reminder that nothing is stable, and that man's life is a journey through a land of exile.

In our eyes, however, earthly voyages are neither monotonous nor sad; social laws are not unbending; customs that must be attacked head-on should give way to an ceaseless renewal of marvels; and the first comfort that we wish for will be the elimination of ideas such as these, and of the police spies that spread them.

What does Monsieur Le Corbusier presume to know of human *needs*? The cathedrals are no longer white. And you'll notice that we're delighted about it. A "ration of daylight" and a place in the sun, you know the routine —cue the M.R.P. organs and drums[12]—and heavenly pastures where late architects graze. "Enlevez le boeuf, c'est de la vache."[13]

---

10   Jean Baylot (1897–1976), Prefect of Paris Police 1951–1954, notorious for his anticommunism. At the 1953 Bastille Day parade, seven Communist Party militants were killed by his police in street fighting. Baylot was also the author of *La circulation à Paris et dans le Département de la Seine* (Paris: Pref. Police, 1953). He resigned from his post in mid-July 1954, having fallen out with the Mendès-France government. [Ed.]
11   Pierre-Simon Ballanche (1776–1847) was a French counterrevolutionary religious and social philosopher; his unfinished *Ville des expiations* was the projected third and final volume of his lifework, entitled *Essais de palingénésie sociale* ("Essays on Social Palingenesis"), in which he sought to outline the regeneration of society through Christianity. [Ed.]
12   A reference to the Mouvement Républicain Populaire, a French Christian-democratic party founded in 1944 and a mainstay of the Fourth Republic. [Ed.]
13   Slang term, a concluding phrase. [Ed.]

SUMMARY 1954[14]

GUY DEBORD AND JACQUES FILLON

Big cities favor the pastime we call *dérive*. *Dérive* is a technique for locomotion without a goal. It depends on the influence exerted by the setting.

All houses are beautiful. Architecture must become *thrilling*. We could not take into consideration more restrained construction ventures.

The new urbanism is inseparable from (happily inevitable) economic and social upheavals. We may assume that the revolutionary demands of an epoch are a function of the idea that this epoch has of happiness. The valorization of forms of *leisure*, then, is no joke.

We remind you that it is a question of inventing new games.

ARCHITECTURE AND PLAY[15]

GUY DEBORD

In this article, Debord insists that the only motive behind the Lettrists' interest in architecture and urbanism was their "passion for play." Architectural ideals mirroring life ideals, the author betrays his taste for those "desolate zones" of Paris' popular quarters where members of the L.I. undertook their dérives. *He also turns Le Corbusier's words against him, so that the architect's own residential schemas (most famously, his* Unité d'Habitation, *Marseilles, 1947–52) are conceived as sites of underdevelopment produced by the postwar period's increasing prosperity.*

In his *Homo Ludens: A Study of the Play-Element in Culture*, Johan Huizinga shows that "in its earliest phases culture has the play-character, that it proceeds in the shape and the mood of play."[16] The author's latent idealism and his narrowly sociological appreciation for the higher forms of play do not lessen the great contribution made by his work. It is futile, moreover, to search in our theories on architecture or *dérive* for any other motive than the passion for play.

To the extent that the spectacle of almost everything that happens in this world provokes our anger and our disgust, so we nevertheless increasingly know how to make fun of it. Those who understand by this that we are given to irony are being too simple-minded. Life around us is made to obey absurd necessities, and tends unconsciously to satisfy its true needs.

---

14 *Potlatch* no. 14 (November 30, 1954): n.p. [Ed.]
15 *Potlatch* no. 20 (May 30, 1955): n.p. [Ed.]
16 Johan Huizinga, *Homo Ludens: A Study of the Play-Element in Culture*, trans. R. F. C. Hull (London: Routledge & Kegan Paul, 1949), 46. [Ed.]

These needs and their partial fulfillments, their partial understandings, everywhere confirm our hypotheses. For example, a bar called AU BOUT DU MONDE (The End of the World), at the frontier of one of Paris' strongest units of ambiance (the quarter around the rues Mouffetard-Tournefort-Lhomond), is not there by chance. Events depend upon chance only so long as the general laws governing their category are unknown. We must strive toward the highest degree of consciousness of the elements that determine a situation, beyond utilitarian imperatives whose sway will anyhow diminish.

What one wants to make of an architecture is a verdict fairly close to what one would like to make of one's life. Beautiful adventures, it is said, can only have beautiful quarters as settings and origin. The notion of what constitutes beautiful quarters will change.

At present already, it is possible to savor the ambiance of a few desolate zones, as suitable for *dérive* as they are scandalously unsuitable for habitation, where the system nevertheless shuts in the laboring masses. Le Corbusier himself acknowledges, in *Urbanism is a Key*, that if the miserly and anarchic individualism of construction in highly industrialized countries is taken into account, "underdevelopment may be as much the consequence of a *surplus* as of a *scarcity*."[17] This remark can naturally be turned on the neo-medieval promoter of the "vertical commune."

Widely disparate individuals have sketched, through seemingly identical moves, some intentionally baffling architectures, which range from the famous castles of King Ludwig of Bavaria to that house in Hanover that the Dadaist Kurt Schwitters had—it seems—tunneled through and confused with a forest of columns made of collected objects. All these constructions arise from the baroque character, which is always found clearly marked in attempts at an integral art, and which would be completely determinant. In this connection, it is significant to note the connections between Ludwig of Bavaria and Wagner, who himself must have been seeking an aesthetic synthesis in the most painful and, on the whole, the most useless manner.

It clearly has to be said that if the architectural manifestations to which we are inclined to grant particular value fall in some way under the rubric of naïve art, we value them for another reason altogether, namely for their concretization of the unexploited future powers of a discipline economically inaccessible to the "avant-gardes." In the exploitation of commercial values strangely attached to most means of expressing naivety, it is impossible not to recognize the display of a categorically reactionary mentality, closely related to the social attitude of paternalism. More than ever, we believe that the men who are deserving of some esteem must have been able to answer all questions.

---

17 See Le Corbusier, *Architecte du bonheur, l'urbanisme est une clef* (Paris: Presses d'Ile de France, Coll. "Cahiers Forces Vives, nos. 5-6-7," 1955). [Ed.]

We will not cease to hold as our goal the greatest possible participation in the real elaboration of the risks and powers of urbanism, which we are presently happy to use.

We are well aware that the provisional, the free realm of ludic activity —which Huizinga believes to be opposed, as such, to "ordinary life" characterized by a sense of duty—is the lone field of true life, though it be constrained fraudulently by taboos claiming to be eternal. The compartments we love tend to establish all the conditions favorable to their full development. Now it is a question of getting rid of arbitrary and conventional rules of the game in favor of ones with a moral basis.

LIMEHOUSE NIGHTS IN THE 1930s AND LETTRIST INTERVENTION[18]

London's Chinatown is threatened with extinction. That labyrinth of squalid streets, mysterious passages, and shuttered hovels a mile or two east of Aldgate Pump is doomed. The planners have been told to go ahead. By the end of the year much of Pennyfields will have been demolished to make room for blocks of flats. After that, it is only a question of time before the rest of it will vanish like an opium smoker's dream.

Tenacious as the type of Oriental who jumps ship and settles within the purlieus of London's Docklands is, he is helpless under the New Order. Whatever he and his compatriots may feel, they cannot hope to frustrate the designs of the modern builder. The series of rabbit warrens, from which a Chinese head was once wont to pop out with disconcerting suddenness, must give place to neat and tidy dwellings fitted with "h. and c." and a sanitation calculated to make the old time denizen of London's Chinatown shudder.

For it has never been the dwelling place of the Mandarin, much less the hiding place of the Communist plotter. But it has been, and still is, the home-from-home of the Chinese Common Man, who, sick of the sea, has found the precarious existence to be derived from gambling, catering for his fellows, or pandering to curious visitors much to his liking.

A Safe Guide

In the 1930s, for reasons that would take too long to explain, I spent many nights in London's Chinatown. Indeed, there were long periods when I was almost a nightly visitor. An old friend of mine in the Aliens Immigration

---

18   Anonymous, "Limehouse Nights in the 1930s: Chinatown of Romance and Fable Receives Its Death Blow from the Planners," *London Times*, August 31, 1955: 10; and *Potlatch* no. 23 (October 13, 1955): n.p. [Ed.]

CRITIQUE OF FUNCTIONALISM AND MODERNIZATION

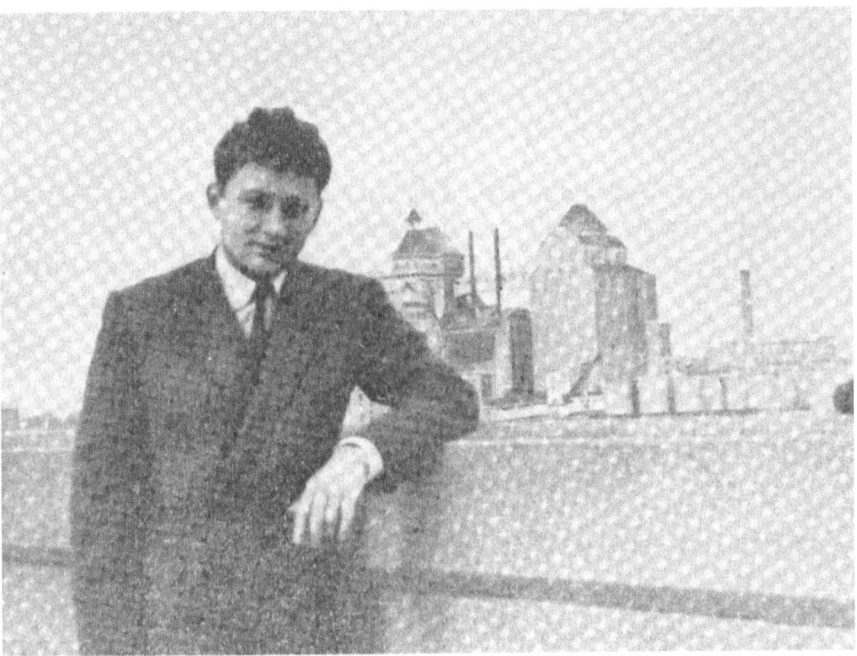

Fig.2.6.2 Guy Debord in Aubervilliers. From *Potlatch* no. 20 (May 30, 1955).

Department held the power almost of life or death over the Orientals who sneaked into Limehouse knowing that to identify them was practically impossible. If they got into trouble through opium smuggling or kindred offenses, he sometimes had them deported. But he knew they would soon be back, and they invariably were.

Thomas Burke and other writers wove romances, in which luxurious opium dens that were pure figments of their imagination loomed large. The role I played on many occasions was akin to that of The Man from Cooks. I gained a reputation as a safe guide (unpaid), who was always ready to conduct one, or at most two, persons through the mysterious precincts of Limehouse Causeway and Pennyfields.

At one time or another I conducted an American bishop, an Egyptian prince, a Harley Street specialist, a Covent Garden opera singer, and many others on a tour of Chinatown.

My friends numbered dope traffickers, cocaine addicts, and, of course, detectives, who were ever on the alert to prevent possible tragedy not to mention unhappiness that might result through the intermingling of a few Orientals on the prowl for impressionable white girls.

In spite of such vigilance it was not uncommon to find a girl listed at Scotland Yard as missing consorting with some Chinese loafer, and apparently unconcerned at the grief of relatives or the anomaly of that situation.

Ceremonial Libations

Occasionally I was admitted to the tiny Confucian Temple to which few were allowed to penetrate, and where libations in the "wine of the country" —interpreted by the Chinese as whisky—were ceremoniously poured out.

My entry to the hallowed place, whose locale was unknown excepting to the faithful followers of the Great Philosopher, I owed to my Immigration Officer friend who took our welcome for granted.

Invariably my itinerary was much the same. First, as the evening shadows fell, a call at the back room, reached by a dark alleyway, where three inscrutable Chinese sat at tables ready to accept six-pences—or larger coins—for the next "race," as the lottery was dubbed by white devotees.

It was generally understood that a small investment on *Pa ko pï o*—or as freely translated by the man in the street *Pukapoo*—might yield £1,000, and those in charge of the bank were credited with having almost unlimited funds. But neither I nor any of the personages I introduced to the gamble ever won anything.

The Ritual of the Game

Yet, like them, I was fascinated by the ritual of the game. To all who proffered a coin a card, bearing Chinese characters, was given for marking, usually done by the punter with a pen. The card was then handed back, and the Chinese recipient would use a small brush to make the marking more effective to the point of obliterating the characters already partly expunged. After that there was nothing to be done but wait for the result. This I never did, being satisfied that, so far as I was concerned, the game was up.

But at times the craze for *Pukapoo* became so rife that the police forbade it. It still went on, however, and for years its promoters played hide-and-seek with the police. By selecting a different den every night, and paying the occupier well, they were able to snap their fingers at the law and its guardians.

From the gambling dens to a little Chinese restaurant in Limehouse Causeway was but a step, and there my party would look at a menu they could not decipher, and then order ham and eggs, which they were always asked if they would like "flied blown." Some were daring enough to order noodles of one kind or another, but never dried seaweed, dried fish, soya bean sauce, bamboo shoots, or other of the delicacies favored by Chinese customers.

After the meal chopsticks of sandalwood were unostentatiously offered for sale for a mere trifle, and just as unobtrusively bought.

Then to Charlie Brown's, a pub packed with ivory relics, supposed to come from Chinese palaces, though cynics said that Charlie had collected them in Tottenham Court Road.

From that time anything might happen. By influence I could take my protégés into a real, though not ornate, opium den well above street level so that the sickening odor was unlikely to be detected by the police.

I was shocked now and again by some of those I shepherded up rickety staircases, for they were not merely willing but eager to try the pipe that brings oblivion. But I drew the line at that, and told them that they must come there alone to indulge in opium orgies.

"No Smokee, No Workee"

Devotees of the fruit of the poppy were numerous among the Chinese. But, as one explained while he drew deeply and contentedly on his pipe, the habit to him was no more baneful than tobacco smoking to the white man. "Me on board ship work hard if can have pipe, all the same as English sailor want tobacco. But no smokee, no workee," he said laconically.

One English addict in Limehouse told me more about the effects of opium smoking than any other person I have ever met. "It makes your dreams come true," he said. "If you love one woman in your conscious moments, she is the woman of your dreams. These are not just voluptuous or sensual, but in accord with your highest ideals."

In any event, it matters little now, for though the community that was once Chinatown may be scattered, but try to re-form, modern building will prevent a revival of the old customs, vices, and crimes that were formerly a menace. Drug smuggling by Chinese ne'er-do-wells into Limehouse is now rare, the traffic that once flourished in shady West London night clubs is virtually ended.

As for the Chinese folk, and the half castes inevitable from the mixed marriages of the past, they too are a dwindling quantity. Limehouse, at any rate, will never be the same again. For the romance that once hung over it like a halo is dead. Few who knew it in reality will mourn its passing.

MICHÈLE BERNSTEIN, GUY DEBORD, and GIL J. WOLMAN

Sir,

The Times has just announced the projected demolition of the Chinese quarter in London.

We protest against such moral ideas in town-planning, ideas which must obviously make England more boring than it has in recent years already become.

The only pageants you have left are a coronation from time to time, an occasional royal marriage which seldom bears fruit; nothing else. The disappearance of pretty girls, of good family especially, will become rarer and rarer after the razing of Limehouse. Do you honestly believe that a gentleman can amuse himself in Soho?

We hold that the so-called modern town-planning which you recommend is fatuously idealistic and reactionary. The sole end of architecture is to serve the passions of men.

Anyway, it is inconvenient that this Chinese quarter of London should be destroyed before we have the opportunity to visit it and carry out certain psychogeographical experiments we are at present undertaking.

Finally, if modernization appears to you, as it does to us, to be historically necessary, we would counsel you to carry your enthusiasm into areas more urgently in need of it, that is to say, to your political and moral institutions.

EXCERPTS FROM *IMAGE AND FORM*[19]

ASGER JORN

Although the CoBrA group was short-lived, its brief existence had been marked by a struggle against the geometric abstract painting and the influence of Piet Mondrian and De Stijl that still dominated contemporary exhibitions, as well as by opposition to functionalism in architecture and design. These two currents had led to the privileging of elemental expression and the complete freedom of spontaneous, abstract forms. The same critique would be focused against the New Bauhaus at Ulm, a design school conceived in 1950 and directed by the Swiss artist Max Bill; this program attempted to take up once again the theories of the original Bauhaus of Walter Gropius at Weimar, for whom architecture needed to be unified with the other "major" arts of painting and sculpture through a close collaboration of artist and craftsman. By emphasizing the machine as a tool worthy of the artist, the curriculum had worked to abolish the separation between art and industry, and to conjoin mass production with aesthetic invention. In this way the New Bauhaus integrated the aims of the old, which was to experiment and produce prototypes of common objects for standardization. But for Bill, the production of industrial design had in the meantime become the sole function of the artist in society. The functionalists were succeeding in creating a world that was more and more controlled, ordered, rationalized, and boring, and it was against this trend that Asger Jorn, a founding member of CoBrA, would rebel in his book Image and Form.

Regarding the current value of the concept of functionalism

The past few years have seen an ever-growing discontent with the rationalist ideas of functionalism. More and more, people speak of a revolution against its unbearable constraints and this revolution plainly appears to be inevitable. But before throwing it all out as so much rubbish, we really should think about what a true revolution might be, because the latter cannot take place by destroying just anything.

We should keep what seems alive in the heritage of functionalism. At the

---

19 From Asger Jorn, "Image et forme" (1954), in *Pour la forme* (Paris: L'Internationale situationniste, 1958), 9–16. First published as *Immagine e forma*, trans. Sergio Dangelo (Milan: EPI, 1954); excerpts published in *Potlatch* no. 15 (December 22, 1954): n.p., with the following prefatory note: "Today we publish some excerpts from *Image and Form*, Asger Jorn's book on architecture and its future, a problem that we have continually raised here. (See in particular 'Next Planet' in *Potlatch* no. 4 and 'Skyscrapers by the Roots' in no. 5.)" The text appears here courtesy of Donation Jorn, Silkeborg. [Ed.]

moment the latter rose up against an outmoded classicism, it declared that "the house is a machine for living in," "the kitchen is a machine for nourishment," etc. These arguments triumphed because of their undeniable truth.

The functionalists created a rational analysis of structure and functions, they reduced form to the aspect most economical for the satisfaction of our needs, and to this end they created an entirely new way of understanding the object and the tool. Beyond this objective functionalism, they lay claim to a humanist analysis of the social and ethical functions of our surrounding milieu, issuing from belief in democracy and supported by an "urbanistic concept" that stipulated humanity's right to housing that ensured a healthy and peaceable existence.

In formulating an irrational architecture, leaving out these capital facts would be unthinkable. It is easy and undoubtedly amusing to come up with new ideas opposed to the previous ones, but culture consists in just the opposite: it is the continual elaboration and transformation of pre-existing phenomena. The functionalist slogan can always be useful for us. Utility and function will always remain the point of departure of any formal critique; it's merely a question of transforming the functional program. The most effective result is always best sought through the most economical means. But if we are in agreement on this point, why say we're dissatisfied with functionalism? Because of its aesthetic, which was never willing to see aesthetic qualities as an autonomous function of human activity. Aesthetics is the "science of the beautiful and the ugly." Starting from platonic ideas, the functionalists ended up denying beauty's autonomous existence by saying that "what is true and good is always beautiful": that is, that beauty is contained within logic and ethics themselves.

Because of this false idea, they devised an aesthetic belief in making the exterior of an object a reflection of the practical functions of the interior and of the constructive idea. Yet these analyses of utility and necessity that, according to their beliefs, should be the basis for the construction of any object created by humanity become immediately absurd once we analyze all the objects being manufactured today. A fork or a bed cannot come to be considered necessary for humanity's life and health, and yet retain a relative value.

They are "learned necessities." Modern human beings are suffocating under necessities like televisions, refrigerators, etc. And in the process making it impossible to live their real lives. Obviously we are not against modern technology, **but we are against any notion of the absolute necessity of objects**, to the point even of doubting their real utility.

Functionalists moreover are unaware of the psychological function of our surroundings. Just as coffee has no benefit for humanity's health, but only a psychological and sensory importance, the exterior appearance of the structures and objects that surround us and that we use has a function independent of its practical utility. The exterior of a house should not reflect the interior, but should be a source of poetic feeling for the viewer. [...]

Some elementary laws of the evolution of human technology

Because of their ideas of standardization, the functionalist rationalists thought that it was possible to attain ideal, definitive forms of the different objects relating to humanity.

Contemporary development shows that this static conception is wrong. We must arrive at a dynamic conception of form, we must face the truth that any human form is in a continual state of transformation. We must not, like the rationalists, shun this transformation; the bankruptcy of the rationalists lay in their failure to understand that the only way of avoiding the anarchy of change is to become aware of the laws governing transformation and to make use of them. Since the rationalists consequently denied style's very reason for being, we are obliged to go back to the old classical conceptions of stylistic evolution. That rather simplistic conception of stylistic decadence was modeled on the evolution of ancient Greek art, and distinguishes four stages in the rhythm of style. It begins with an uncertain and primitive experimental style; followed by the high style characterized by a lofty power; followed by the noble style characterized by a complete refinement; this last declines to a (decadent) style characterized by formal excesses and disequilibrium. This is a position that cannot hold up against a confrontation with reality, and the facts of history only fit into its mold if they are forced. Formal evolution is much more complex than all this and is a problem that has to be studied with close attention. In archaeology the study of style has had to be investigated thoroughly, since not a single hint has been communicated to us from prehistory and only the objects themselves can speak; this study has been able to freely take shape because no one today is very interested in archaeology. We can gather some laws from that study, laws that are applicable to human creations not only in the evolution of architectural style, but also in mental, social, political, etc. evolution, as they apply wherever it is a question of style.

1. **Formal evolution advances through sharp breaks.** In order for a form to have a collective importance, it must be transformed from a unique phenomenon into a typical phenomenon. The formation of a "type" happens by leaps. For each functional "type" there is a limit point at which the type reaches its greatest active potential, at which all its possibilities are exhausted. This represents its ideal form, which cannot be improved upon. Moreover, such a form cannot be surpassed without its functional value being diminished until the moment we pass to another material, another "type" for the same function.
2. **Use produces ideal form.** Every human creation is invented in the mind. We can dream of new types of functions, then realize them through experiments. But we can never imagine the ideal, definitive form of new

types, nor arrive at it through laboratory experiment. Only through adaptation, and the attentive analysis of this "use," can the definitive form be found.

3. **Conservatism of forms.** When a new "type" is invented to satisfy a function, its form is influenced by the "type" it is replacing or by the form of other known, familiar types. Unfamiliar objects are always given familiar forms: for example, the first clay vases were modeled on woven baskets or gourds or leather sacks, whose forms up to that point were suitable for these functions. Hence the first bicycles were equipped with a horse-head, a residue of the preceding form. It is important to understand that such conservatism of forms is thoroughly illogical because it is not the result of not knowing the object's ideal, definitive form, but rather of the fact that humanity becomes worried when it does not find some element of "déjà vu" in the unfamiliar phenomenon: for example, the first boats with diesel engines were made without smokestacks, but no passenger wanted to get onboard until false smokestacks were added, so that they looked like steamships.

4. **Radicalism of forms.** If a new model once created meets with much success on account of its greater efficiency than its predecessor, it lends certain neighboring forms a formal radicalism, which attempts to borrow from the appearance of the new form: for example, bronze tools that had reached the furthest development of their utility had a disastrous influence on stone tools, warping them toward an elegance that could only be attained in bronze. Today aviation has imposed its aerodynamic forms even on baby strollers and irons. This radicalism of forms is a result of the fact that people become bored when they do not find some unexpected element in the familiar. This radicalism might seem illogical, as the advocates of standardization believe, but we must not forget that discovery is only made possible by this need of humanity.

EXCERPT FROM "THE COMMANDER'S GAIT"[20]

MARCEL MARIËN

We could already try to lend a hand, to intervene if only by simply moving objects around. This would be better, on the whole, that waiting for the thick wall encircling life to brutally make the first move. (As happens during wartime.)

But this reminds me of another story. It happened just before 1940,

---

20 Marcel Mariën, "Le Pas du Commandeur," *Les Lèvres Nues* no. 5 (June 1955): 15–17. [Ed.]

when the Belgian army was being mobilized. I was a soldier, and chance had taken us to a small village where we halted before resuming our march along I don't know what road for our camp. We had stopped near a church around which spread a cemetery. At loose ends, I strolled between the tombs when suddenly an idea hit me, an idea for an act that seemed apt to favorably stimulate the minds of those who visited this spot—the living who had buried some dead person there. In all truth, I would have preferred tombs of the rich, but my scheme being rather singular and my physical means limited, I had little choice but to fall back on tombs of the modest.

My project was uncomplicated. Simply switch around the crosses so that visitors, if they had become accustomed to appearances, would now have some trouble finding them. Here was, I have always thought, a very moral act. Undoubtedly only a slight disorder in the visitor's mind, but all things considered just enough to cause a certain deep pleasure. Already his very presence, the trust he feels toward these hallowed places, the bewitching silence, those hands that join effortlessly in reverence: everything tempts him to believe in miracles. If he only would be consistent, he would not fail to find the thing decent and altogether natural. So I did what I said and I uprooted a few light crosses, planting Paul's on the tomb of Marie, that of Marie on Jean's sepulcher, Jean's with Paul, and so on. I have no idea what the outcome of my undertaking was, having had to quickly get back on the road, but I cannot believe it was indifferent, so long as Marie, Paul, and Jean had left behind conscientious survivors.

You can see only too well what I wanted to get at. If it is true that a statue, once erected, vanishes into the ether, why not move it elsewhere, give it the opportunity to garner other glances and win other hearts! Our tourists, no longer having to move, would experience a perpetual fairyland right at home. Opening the window in the morning or at their jobs, their city would perpetually transform itself. Those who, despite everything, have retained a taste for travel would never know ahead of time what they might see on their voyages. Organizations of international exchange, less inane that our present day so-called cultural services—whose only job is to cultivate boredom—would be founded to this end. No one would quibble over the cost or the scope of the operation; whole war budgets would be spent to display Bartholdi's Liberty to the residents of Leningrad, in exchange for which those of New York would welcome for a few days the equestrian statue of Peter the Great. And we have the technological means to carry out such an enterprise. Including aviation, which would allow us to secretly drop by parachute, or to carefully guide by radio-control toward the right spot, Michelangelo's *David* or some Eastern Buddha. But if one of these sculpted personages should be damaged on the way, I don't think we need shed any tears. Think of the success of the Venus de Milo or the Victory of Samothrace, who are admired no less for their lack of arms or head—damage that is to us like a joyful sorrow, a misfortune illuminated by delight.

Yes, an entire world of happy possibilities is revealed to us, and the spice of adventure is restored to us at the same time. In order to mitigate the untold trash soiling the people in the form of statues we will try to mislay as many as we can, since in the end it is a matter of getting rid of these stone nuisances that for centuries we have dragged along with us. Certain will be painted in bright colors to stand out against the gray facades. Others, ingeniously made buoyant, will be thrown into the sea like the proverbial bottle: they will seem to walk on the water. In this manner we could rescue from the Northern mists, where she shivers on her rock, the little mermaid of the Sund, who will be pushed by favorable winds into the hands of those who dwell along the banks of the Nile or those of the Tuamotu islanders. Others finally will fill up an entire train that will slowly cross the continents, stopping at each station, a famous head at each window—an eternal sleeping car. Each one will be considered, no one will be forgotten. Including having the Kaaba wander all over, so that Muslims will have to continually change the direction of their prayers.

Yet other means are given us that, as opposed to certain all too necessary removals, make use of a different method: multiplication. So it cannot be denied that the statue of Joséphine de Beauharnais, in Martinique, is quite beautiful. But it is no less evident that much of this is due to its setting, to the brilliant sun that strikes her marble throat, a marble that is no longer allegorical, and lastly to the nine coconut palms encircling her—a majestic halo. Nevertheless if I frequented these places, I suspect that I would soon fail to see its charm. So, provisionally, perhaps there would be some interest in inverting the roles, that is, in encircling a single giant palm, planted right in the center, with nine marble Joséphines. Already the ethical idea appears. After all, Joséphine isn't worth it, she hardly deserves it. This lady was rather insignificant; it's high time to put her in her place.

The swarms of emperors, kings, and princes can be dealt with the same way. Best would be to gather all of them in some desert, and as they are generally mounted on horseback, this would compose a rather amusing cavalry of ghosts. In passing, we won't fail to baffle the pitiful spirit of responsibility that plagues our times. To hell with history and dates, with their useless lessons! No need, then, to arrange them chronologically or even in alphabetical order, as in dictionaries. Helter-skelter, any which way, would be all the better—like on the battlefield—and let the wolves finally devour each other.

For truly great men, we will prove to be more flexible, more delicate, more patient; although it also matters, in the long run, that we get rid of them. They can be scattered as we wish, but here too multiplication may be put to good use. So for example, one will happily see all around Moscow a gigantic white garland woven of the Stalins from all over Russia, placed side by side after having been stolen from every square—the final gathering before the great departure.

INTRODUCTION TO A CRITIQUE OF URBAN GEOGRAPHY[21]

GUY DEBORD

Of the many sagas in which we take part, with or without interest, the sole thrilling direction remains the fragmentary search for a new way of life. The greatest detachment toward a few disciplines—aesthetic or otherwise—whose inadequacy in this regard is readily evident, goes without saying. Some provisional terrains of observation should therefore be delineated, among them the observation of certain processes of chance and predictability in the streets.

The word *psychogeography*, suggested by an illiterate Kabyle to designate the general phenomena with which a few of us were preoccupied around the summer of 1953, is relatively defensible. It does not stray from the materialist perspective of the conditioning of life and thought by objective nature. Geography, for example, recognizes the determinant action of general natural forces, such as soil composition or climatic conditions, on the economic structures of a society, and, through them, on the conception that it might have of the world. *Psychogeography* will aim to study the precise laws and specific effects of the geographic milieu, consciously planned or not, acting directly on the affective comportment of individuals. The adjective *psychogeographic*, preserving a rather amusing vagueness, can thus be applied to the data ascertained through this type of investigation, to the effects of their influence on human feelings, and even more generally to any situation or any conduct that seems to arise from the same spirit of discovery.

It has already been a long time that one has been able to say the desert is monotheistic. Would it seem illogical, or devoid of interest, to declare that the quarter running in Paris between the place de la Contrescarpe and the rue de l'Arbalète inclines rather to atheism, to oblivion, and to the disorientation of customary routines?

It is right to possess a historically relative idea of the utilitarian. The concern to have at one's disposal open spaces allowing for the rapid circulation of troops and the use of artillery against insurrections was at the origin of the beautification plan adopted by the Second Empire. But from any standpoint other than that of law and order, Haussmann's Paris is a city built by an idiot, full of sound and fury, signifying nothing. Today, the main

---

21 *Les Lèvres nues* no. 6 (September 1955) 11–15. [Ed.]

problem that urbanism must resolve is that of the smooth circulation of a rapidly increasing quantity of motor vehicles. It is not forbidden to think that a future urbanism will apply itself to structures, no less utilitarian, taking into the largest account psychogeographic possibilities.

Moreover the present abundance of private cars is nothing other than the result of the non-stop propaganda through which capitalist production persuades the mob—and this case is one of its most confounding successes—that the possession of a car is specifically one of the privileges our society reserves for its privileged members. (Anarchic progress negating itself, one can furthermore savor the spectacle of a police prefect using a filmed advertisement to invite Parisian automobile owners to use public transportation.)

Since we run into, even with such slight justification, the idea of privilege, and since we know with what blind fury so many people—who are nevertheless so little privileged—are willing to defend their mediocre advantages, we are forced to declare that all these details partake of an idea of happiness, a received idea among the bourgeoisie, maintained by a system of advertising that includes Malraux's aesthetics as well as the imperatives of Coca-Cola, and whose crisis must be provoked on every occasion, by every means.

The first of these means are undoubtedly the spreading, with an aim of systematic provocation, of a host of proposals tending to make of life an integral, thrilling game, and the unceasing depreciation of all customary amusements (to the extent, of course, that they cannot be appropriated [*détournés*] to be of use in constructions of more interesting environments). It is true that the greatest difficulty in such an undertaking is to pass on with these apparently delirious proposals a sufficient quantity of *genuine seduction*. To obtain this result, a clever use of currently prized means of communication can be imagined. But moreover a sort of strident abstention, or manifestations aiming at the thorough disappointment of lovers of these same means of communication, undeniably sustain—at little expense—an uneasy atmosphere extremely favorable for the introduction of a few new notions of pleasure.

This idea—that the realization of a chosen affective situation depends solely on the rigorous comprehension and intentional application of a certain number of concrete mechanisms—inspired this "Psychogeographical Game of the Week" published, despite everything, with some humor in *Potlatch* no. 1:

> Depending on what you are after, choose a region, a more or less densely populated city, a more or less lively street. Build a house. Furnish it. Make the most of its decoration and its surroundings. Choose the season and the time. Gather together the most fitting people, with suitable records and drinks. Lighting and

conversation must, of course, be appropriate, along with the weather or your memories.

If there has been no error in your calculations, you should find the outcome satisfying.[22]

We must occupy ourselves in throwing onto the market (even if for the moment merely the intellectual market) a load of desires whose wealth does not exceed humanity's present means of action on the material world, but only the old social organization. It is thus not without political interest to contrast publicly such desires to the basic desires that we must not be surprised to see endlessly rehashed by the film industry or psychological novels like those of that old corpse Mauriac.[23] ("In a society founded on *poverty* the *poorest* products have the fatal prerogative of being used by the greatest number," Marx explained to poor Proudhon.)[24]

The revolutionary transformation of the world, of all aspects of the world, will prove right all the dreams of abundance.

The abrupt change of environment in a street, within the space of a few meters; the obvious division of a city into zones of distinct psychic atmospheres; the strongly sloping contour (with no relation to the unevenness of the terrain) that aimless walks must follow; the appealing or repellent nature of certain places—all this seems to be neglected. In any case, it is never envisaged as depending on causes that can be revealed by a thorough analysis and turned to account. People are quite aware that there are gloomy quarters and others that are agreeable. But they generally convince themselves that elegant streets trigger a feeling of satisfaction and that poor streets are depressing, with almost no more nuance than that. As a matter of fact, the variety of possible combinations of environments, analogous to the dissolution of pure chemical bodies in an infinite number of mixtures, entails feelings as differentiated and as complex as those provoked by any other form of theater. And the slightest clear-headed search makes evident that no distinction, whether qualitative or quantitative, between the influences of diverse settings built in a city can be inferred from an architectural era or style, much less from housing conditions.[25]

---

22 "Le jeu psychogéographique de la semaine," *Potlatch* no. 1 (June 22, 1954): n.p. [Ed.]
23 François Mauriac (1885-1970), a Roman Catholic French author, who won the Nobel Prize in literature in 1952 "for the deep spiritual insight and artistic intensity with which he [...] penetrated the drama of human life." [Ed.]
24 Karl Marx, "The Poverty of Philosophy" (1847), in Karl Marx and Frederick Engels, *Collected Works*, vol. 6 ("Marx and Engels: 1845–48") (London: Lawrence & Wishart, 1976), 133–134. [Ed.]
25 This paragraph echoes André Breton in his essay "Pont-Neuf" (1950), in which he writes: "The steps that, for no external reason, bring us year after year

The enquiries that we are thus called on to lead into the arrangement of the elements of the urbanistic setting, in close connection with the sensations they provoke, will not progress without making use of bold hypotheses that must constantly be corrected in light of experience, by critique and self-critique.

Certain canvases by de Chirico, which are manifestly provoked by sensations of architectural origin, may exert an effect in return on their objective base, to the point of transforming it: they tend to become themselves models. Disturbing quarters of arcades could one day carry on, and complete, the attraction of this oeuvre.

I see little but those two harbors at nightfall painted by Claude Lorrain —which are at the Louvre, and which show the very frontier of two of the most diverse possible urban environments—that rival in beauty with the metro maps postered around Paris. It will be understood that in speaking here of beauty I don't have in mind plastic beauty—the new beauty can only be a beauty of situation—but solely the particularly moving presentation, in one case and the other, of a *sum of possibilities*.[26]

Among various more difficult means of intervention, a transformed cartography seems fit for immediate exploitation.

The forging of psychogeographic maps, and even various impostures like correlating (with little justification or even completely arbitrarily) two topographical representations, can contribute to illuminating certain displacements of a nature indeed not so much gratuitous but utterly *insubordinate* to usual attractions—attractions of this order being cataloged under the term tourism, that popular drug as repugnant as sports or purchasing on credit.

A friend recently told me that he had just traveled through the Harz region, in Germany, by means of a map of the city of London whose directions he had blindly followed. This sort of game is obviously only a mediocre beginning compared to the complete construction of architecture and urbanism—a construction whose power will someday be

---

to the same spots in a city prove how increasingly sensitive we become to some of its parts, which appear in some obscure fashion to be either favorable or inimical. If one pays attention while walking along a single street that is moderately long and presents sufficient variety along the way [...], one will discover between two spots that could be pinpointed alternating zones of wellbeing and discomfort." See André Breton, *Free Rein* (1953), trans. Michel Parmentier and Jacqueline d'Amboise (Lincoln and London: University of Nebraska Press, 1995), p. 222. [Ed.]

26 This paragraph, and the preceding, owes an obvious debt to the ideas first put forward by Gilles Ivain (pseudo. Ivan Chtcheglov) in "Formulary for a New Urbanism" (1953), translated in this volume, 37–38. [Ed.]

conferred upon everyone. Meanwhile, several levels of partial, less difficult productions can be distinguished, beginning with the mere displacement of elements of embellishment that we are accustomed to finding in positions set in advance.

So Mariën, in the preceding issue of this journal, proposed gathering together in disorder—when global resources have ceased to be squandered on the irrational enterprises that are imposed on us today—all the equestrian statues of every city on a single desert plain.[27] This would offer to passersby—the future belongs to them—the spectacle of a mock cavalry charge, which could even be dedicated to the memory of the greatest slaughterers of history, from Tamerlane to Ridgway.[28] Here we see reappear one of the chief requirements of this generation: educational value.

As a matter of fact, there is nothing to wait for but the coming to consciousness, by the masses in action, of the living conditions imposed on them in all domains, and of the practical means of changing them.

An author, whose name I have since forgotten because of his notorious intellectual misconduct, might have written "the imaginary is what tends to become real."[29] Such an assertion, in its involuntary restrictiveness, could serve as a touchstone and do justice to a few parodic literary revolutions: what tends to remain unreal is empty chatter.

Life, for which we are accountable, encounters, at the same time as great motives for discouragement, an infinity of more or less vulgar diversions and compensations. There isn't a year when people we have loved don't vanish, for want of clearly understanding the possibilities in view, to some conspicuous surrender. But they do not strengthen the enemy camp, which already numbers millions of imbeciles, and in which one is objectively condemned to imbecility.

The first moral deficiency remains indulgence, in all its forms.

---

27 Marcel Mariën, "Le Pas du Commandeur," *Les Lèvres nues* no. 5 (June 1955), pp. 10-21; excerpts translated in this volume, 56–59. [Ed.]
28 Tamerlane (1336–1405), Turkic ruler and conqueror who has been considered one of the greatest military campaigners in history, having led his armies on far-flung expeditions from southern Russia to India, and from Central Asia to Turkey. He is also the subject of an early poem by Edgar Allan Poe, "Tamerlane" (1827). Matthew Bunker Ridgway (1895–1993), an American military officer, had commanded United Nations forced in Korea from 1951 and was later Supreme Allied Commander in Europe, 1952–53. [Ed.]
29 André Breton, "The Pistol With White Hair" (1932), in *Earthlight*, trans. Bill Zavatsky and Zack Rogow (Los Angeles: Sun & Moon Press, 1993), 90. [Ed.]

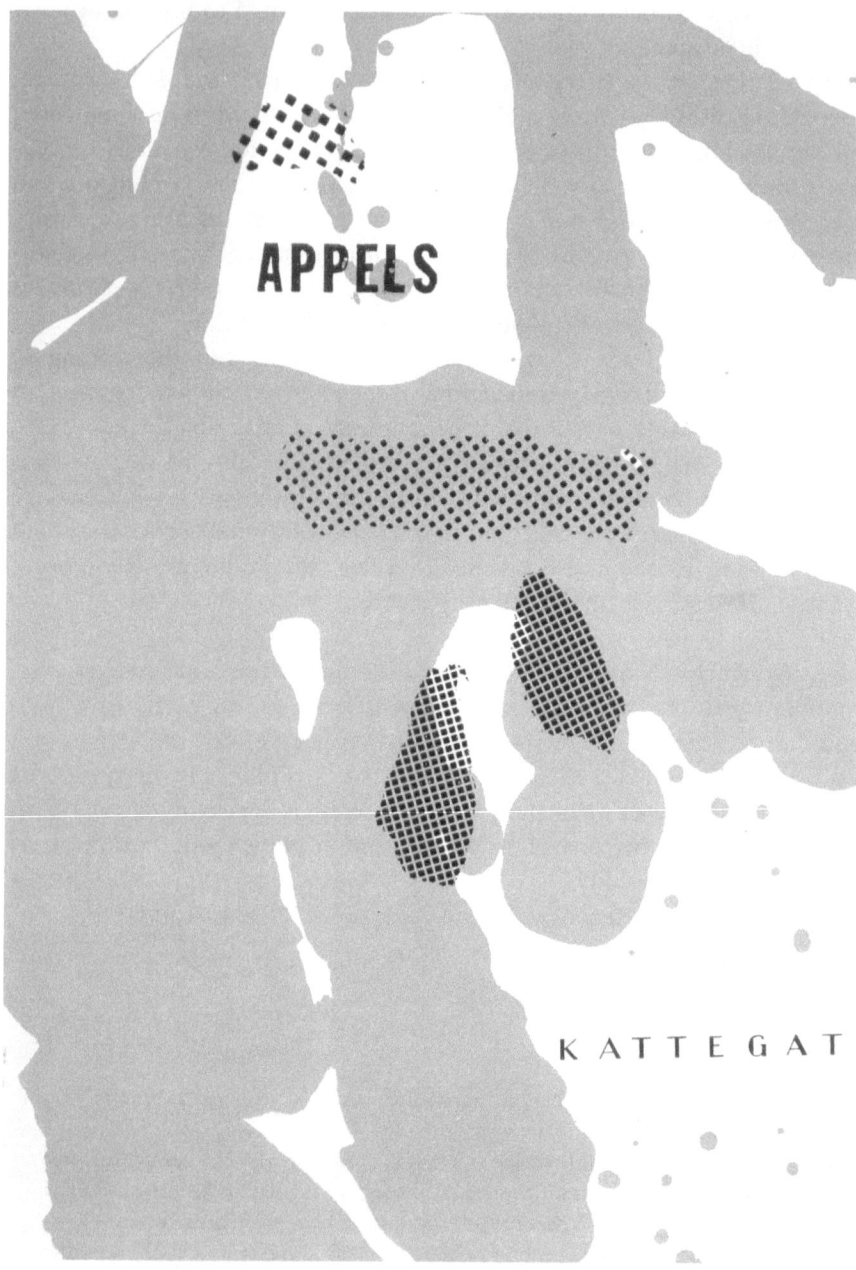

Fig.2.11.1   Page from Asger Jorn and Guy Debord, *Fin de Copenhague*, 1957.

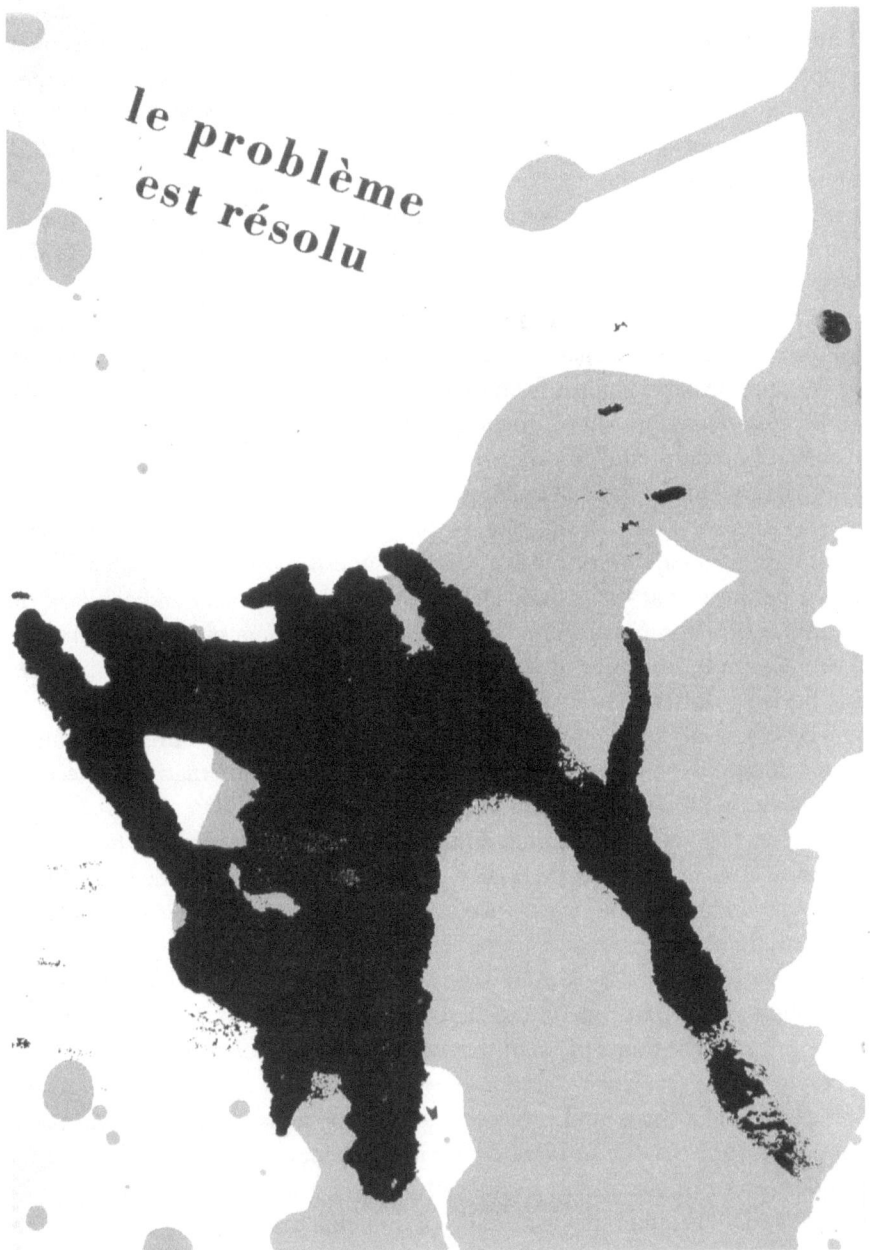

Fig.2.11.2   Page from Asger Jorn and Guy Debord, *Fin de Copenhague*, 1957.

JORN'S COPENHAGEN[30]

The old Futurist and Dadaist techniques of insult, abuse and satire die hard, if only because the Modern Movement that grew out of them has developed almost as many pomposities, inhumanities and hypocrisies as the attitudes it has replaced. Among the most salutary recent eruptions of the grand old method is Asger Jorn's *Fin de Copenhague*, an edition-de-luxe limited to 200 copies and bound in flong, that uses the combined techniques of collage and action-painting to satirize *gemütlich* Europe in general, the author's native Copenhagen in particular, and Le Corbusier in passing. Thus, much of the "text" has been clipped from steamy newspaper serials and confronted with clippings from the ultimate guardian of middle-class morality, the agony column of *Elle*; noisy slogans (APPELS, Votre Vie Transformée, Le Problème est Résolu) have been culled from many sources, but all recall the propaganda for *la Ville Radieuse*; and Copenhagen is satirized not only as the seat of ancestral boredom, and in other standard terms, but also for being a "well-planned city," in the sense of making a pretty pattern of black and green in the planner's report—only in this case the pretty pattern is produced by applying place-names to patches of mechanical tint superimposed on (apparently) an action painting that has "run." The result has the elegance, and the lack of meaning, of a zoning diagram, and the paper-planners pretensions are cut down to size by the accurately backhanded caption "Un splendide paysage que Bernard Buffet a souvent peint."

The whole of this urbanistic cold douche was realized—one understands—in a single afternoon of inspired exasperation, and is a remarkable piece of improvisation among the techniques of graphic reproduction. All the collage material for the text and pictorial illustrations was the product of a lunchtime excursion to a single news-stand and—when pasted-up—provided the plates for the second, black and white, printing on the pages. The first run through the press, for the color-work, however, resulted in what are virtually monotypes, the color being applied by Jorn himself, and somewhat different on every sheet. The whole cavalier attitude to the sacred rituals of printing may be taken as a fair example of the frame of mind that prompts Jorn to refer to himself and his colleagues as the *Bauhaus Imaginiste* or even the *Bauhaus Imaginaire*. The scope of the original Bauhaus ran from typography to town planning as well, and one hopes that Jorn may be inspired or exasperated enough in the near future to demolish some of the middle sections of this spectrum—the home and furniture magazines should provide a wealth of over-ripe material.

---

30 *Architectural Review* (October 1957). [Ed.]

CRITIQUE OF FUNCTIONALISM AND MODERNIZATION 67

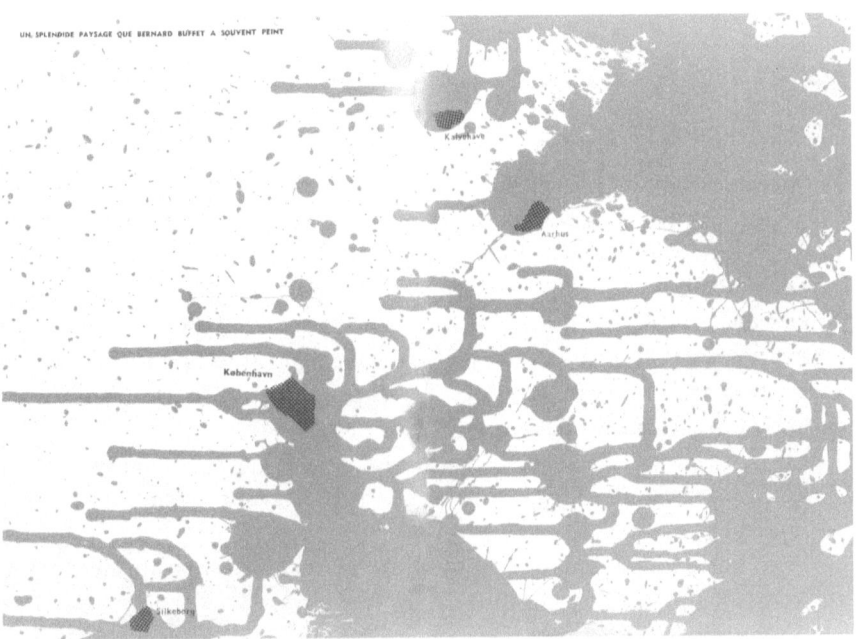

Fig.2.11.3   Spread from Asger Jorn and Guy Debord, *Fin de Copenhague*, 1957.

3.

Paris, Modern Myth

WHILE AWAITING THE BOARDING UP OF CHURCHES[1]

Despite that calendar of 1793 that attempted to impose a different usage, the unpleasant word "saint" continues to sully the walls of a great many Parisian streets whose appellation it commands.[2]

For a few months now, we have enjoyed campaigning for the suppression of this word, in correspondence as well as in our conversations.

Street names are ephemeral. What will the future retain of them, except perhaps, for the record, the Impasse de l'Enfant Jésus (15th Arrondissement, metro Pasteur)?

From now on, the administration of the P.T.T.[3] will bow to the wishes of its clientele: letters will arrive at boulevard Germain and rue Honoré.

We invite the sound part of opinion to support this public health effort.

---

1 *Potlatch* nos. 9-10-11 (August 17–31, 1954): n.p. [Ed.]
2 It was actually only in 1794 that the Convention would require that the word "saint" be removed from street names as part of the program of dechristianization undertaken during the Terror; the Public Works Commission of the Commune de Paris ordered the work begun in late December that year, which continued to mid-July 1795. [Ed.]
3 Postes, Télégraphes, Téléphones, the French General Post Office. [Ed.]

PLAN FOR RATIONAL IMPROVEMENTS TO THE CITY OF PARIS[4]

This article is an interesting, concrete application of the critique of functionalism and modernization being developed in the same years by the Lettrist International. It opens by specifying: "no constructive viewpoint has been envisaged," since the most urgent task appears to be "clearing the ground." This is followed by a number of propositions, ranging from alterations of the city's public spaces (allowing individuals to wander through the metro's tunnels late at night, when the trains had ceased running; opening up the rooftops of Paris, etc.) to a debate over the possible use of certain monumental structures. Churches present perhaps the greatest dilemma to the group, with Debord recommending their demolition and Jacques Fillon suggesting that they be transformed into haunted houses; in any event, unanimity is found in the shared rejection of their preservation on account of aesthetic beauty. Train stations, cemeteries, museums, and prisons are also addressed, and the article ends with proposals for public statuary and "cretinizing" street names.

Lettrists present September 26 have jointly put forward the solutions reported here to various problems of urbanism raised at random during discussion. They call attention to the fact that no constructive viewpoint has been envisaged, clearing the ground appearing to all to be the most urgent task.

Open the metro at night after the trains stop running. Keep the corridors and tunnels poorly lit by means of weak, intermittently functioning lights.

With a careful rearrangement of fire escapes, and the creation of walkways where needed, open the roofs of Paris for strolling.

Leave the public gardens open at night. Keep them dark. (In some cases, a weak lighting may be justified by psychogeographic considerations.)

Put switches on every street lamp; lighting should be at the disposal of the public.

With regard to churches, four different solutions were put forward and acknowledged as defensible until trial by *experimentation*, in which the best will promptly win:

G.-E. Debord declared himself an advocate of the total destruction of religious buildings of all denominations. (No trace should remain of them, and the resulting space should be made use of.)

Gil J. Wolman proposed to preserve churches by draining them of all religious belief. Treat them as ordinary buildings. Let children play in them.

---

4   *Potlatch* no. 23 (October 13, 1955): n.p. The title and subject of this essay are obvious echoes of the Surrealist article on the "irrational embellishment of a city": "Recherches expérimentales sur certaines possibilités d'embellissement irrationnel d'une ville," *Le Surréalisme au service de la Révolution* no. 6 (1933). [Ed.]

Michèle Bernstein wanted churches to be partially demolished, so that the remaining ruins would no longer betray their former purpose (the Tour Jacques, boulevard de Sébastopol, would be an unintentional example). The perfect solution would be to completely raze churches and rebuild ruins in their place. The solution proposed in the first place was chosen solely for reasons of economy.

Lastly, Jacques Fillon wished to transform churches into *haunted houses*. (Use their current atmosphere by accentuating its panic-inducing effects.)

Everyone agrees to reject the aesthetic objection, to silence the admirers of the portal of Chartres. Beauty, *when it is not a promise of happiness*, must be destroyed.[5] And what could better represent unhappiness than this sort of monument built to everything in the world that is not yet mastered, to life's immense inhuman fringe?

Keep the railroad stations as they are. Their rather moving ugliness adds to the atmosphere of travel, which provides what slight attraction these buildings possess. Gil J. Wolman demanded the complete suppression or falsification of all information about departures (destinations, times, etc.). This would encourage *dérive*. After a lively debate, the opposition that had been expressed gave up its argument and the project was accepted without reservation. Heighten the acoustic environment of train stations by broadcasting recordings from a large number of different stations—and certain ports.

Suppression of the cemeteries. Total destruction of dead bodies, and of these sorts of memories: neither ashes nor remains. (Attention should be drawn to the reactionary propaganda that this hideous survival of a past filled with alienation stands for, by the most automatic of association of ideas. Is it possible to see a cemetery without thinking of Mauriac, Gide or Edgar Faure?)

Abolition of the museums, and the redistribution of their artistic masterpieces in bars (the work of Philippe de Champaigne in the Arab cafés of rue Xavier-Privas; David's *Sacre* in the Tonneau in Montagne-Geneviève).

Free and unlimited access to the prisons for everyone. Allow people to use them for vacations. No discrimination between visitors and prisoners. (To add humor to life, lots could be drawn twelve times in the year, so that visitors might find themselves rounded up and sentenced to real punishment. This in order to accommodate imbeciles who absolutely must run some interesting risk: today's spelunkers, for example, and all those whose *need for games* is satisfied by such poor imitations.)

Monuments whose ugliness cannot be put to any use (such as the Petit or Grand Palais) should make way for other constructions.

Removal of the remaining statues whose significance has become

---

5 An appropriation of Stendhal's famous statement, "beauty is the promise of happiness." [Ed.]

outmoded—whose potential aesthetic renovations are condemned by history to failure in advance. The presence of statues could usefully be broadened—during their final years—by changing titles and inscriptions on their plinths, either in a political direction (THE TIGER CALLED CLEMENCEAU on the Champs-Elysées) or in a baffling direction (DIALECTICAL HOMAGE TO FEVER AND QUININE, at the intersection of boulevard Michel and rue Comte; THE GREAT DEPTHS, in the cathedral square on Île de la Cité).

Stop the cretinizing effect on the public of current street names. Erase town counselors, heroes of the Resistance, the Emiles and Edouards (55 streets in Paris), the Bugeauds, the Gallifets, and more broadly all foul names (rue de l'Evangile).

In this regard, the appeal launched in *Potlatch* no. 9 for the non-acknowledgement of the word *saint* in place names is more than ever valid.

EXCERPTS FROM *PARIS AND THE PARISIAN REGION*[6]

PAUL-HENRY CHOMBART DE LAUWE

The study of social space

[...] From a methodological point of view, for all of our frequent references to English and American human ecology, we place ourselves within a different point of view. American ecologists in particular have singled out (with reference to biology) a "symbiotic order," in which sub-social life unfolds, within the larger "cultural order" where the world of symbols is located. The relations of inter-attraction and competition dominate the symbiotic order and play a preponderant role in social life. Though symbols might have an influence on sub-social life, they are less important than factors peculiar to the latter. The entirety of our psychic life is thus dominated by the influence of ecological processes that direct spatial distributions and structures. Two spaces come in this way to be distinguished: ecological space and socio-cultural space, which must be studied independently. In his commentary on Sorokin's book *Sociocultural Causality, Space, Time*,[7] bearing in part on the study of socio-cultural space, Georges Gurvitch points out that the latter—as envisaged by the American sociologist—"simply no longer has anything to do with space" and that "certain levels of social reality like the

---

6   Paul-Henry Chombart de Lauwe, "Paris et l'agglomération parisienne" (1952), in *Paris: Essais de sociologie, 1952–1964* (Paris: Éditions ouvrières, 1965), 19–101. [Ed.]
7   Pitrim A. Sorokin, *Sociocultural Causality, Space, Time: A Study of Referential Principles of Sociology and Social Science* (Durham: Duke University Press, 1943).

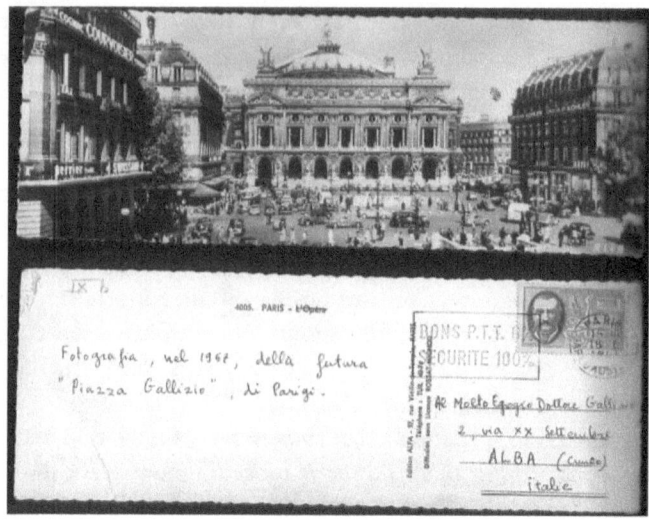

Fig.3.2.1 Postcard from Guy Debord to Pinot Gallizio, 1957. Debord's inscription reads: "Photograph, c. 1957, of the future 'Place Gallizio,' Paris."

morphological and ecological basis, technological models, organized superstructures, behaviors and practices visibly belong to a spatial framework not very far from that of common sense."[8]

However it is precisely in order to grasp these levels of social reality, especially practices and behaviors, that we must define a simultaneously ecological and cultural space, without effecting a dissociation between the two orders of phenomena. Under these conditions, we could not in our studies remain within the limits that Quinn, in a recent book, fixes for a human ecology concerned with the relations between humanity and the merely material and spatial environment.[9] Nor can we study the facts of psychic life by referring solely to an abstract space in which social roles are located. No mathematical space replaces for us the concrete spaces in which individuals and groups evolve, nor the social space that is the synthesis of them.[10]

We are closer to the conceptions of certain specialists in human geography. For them, as Maximilien Sorre has said, human ecology consists first of all "in the study of humanity considered as a living organism subject to determinant conditions of existence and reacting to the stimulations received

---

8 Georges Gurvitch, in *Cahiers internationaux de sociologie* 4 (1947): 170.
9 James Alfred Quinn, *Human Ecology* (New York: Prentice-Hall, 1950), introduction.
10 A discussion, which cannot be undertaken in this chapter, must be opened with reference especially, on one hand, to Kurt Lewin's studies in topological psychology and, on the other, to work on child psychology by Henri Wallon and Jean Piaget.

from its milieu,"[11] on condition that this first definition is completed by this remark that he makes later on: "What we place at the very center of the picture is humanity with all its powers of invention, with all its schemes."[12] The milieu that we envisage, with the space in which it is inscribed, is one transformed by technology as defined by Georges Friedmann for industrial civilization. In a metropolis like the Parisian region, we must verify if the technological milieu is "specifically linked to the relations of production structuring capitalist society," if its differentiations are "coextensive with those of the economic and social milieu."[13] So many problems we will get to the bottom of later, but whose spatial aspect we must grasp right away. If the space of the industrial economy dominates the social space in which the Parisian worker or intellectual develops, to what extent could residential space, cultural space, or political space be planned without it being necessary to first intervene in economic structures? To what extent may collective representations act upon social space so that our entire lives are not dominated by that economic competition that American ecologists, in their analysis of a laissez-faire capitalist society, have completely naturally placed in a prominent position? In short, this comes back to a more general question: to what extent can we freely build the framework for a social life in which we might be guided by our aspirations and not by our instincts?

In order to try to find other elements of a response to these questions, it is toward morphology, after ecology, that we will now turn. Introduced by Auguste Comte and expressed by Durkheim, it attained its full depth in the work of Maurice Halbwachs. "The material forms of societies," wrote the latter, "reflect the entire order of preoccupations peculiar to each of them."[14] Up to now, we have been close to ecological perspectives as expressed recently by certain American authors.[15] But Halbwachs goes one step further; according to him,

> social morphology, like sociology, rests above all on collective representations... For ... in the representations derived from its spatial conditions, the thought of the group discovers a principle of regularity and stability, just as individual thought needs to perceive the body and space to maintain its equilibrium.[16]

---

11 Maximilien Sorre, *Les Fondements de la géographie humaine*, vol. 1 (Paris: A. Colin, 1948), 6.
12 Sorre, *Les Fondements de la géographie humaine*, vol. 2, 5.
13 Georges Friedmann, *Où va le travail humain?* (Paris: Gallimard, 1951), 369.
14 Maurice Halbwachs, *La Morphologie sociale* (Paris: A. Colin, 1936), 18.
15 Emma Llewellyn and Audrey Hawthorn, "Human Ecology," in *Twentieth Century Sociology*, eds. Georges Gurvitch and Wilbert E. Moore (New York: Philosophical Library, 1945, 466–98.
16 Halbwachs, *La Morphologie sociale*, 18.

One of the goals we are pursuing precisely by trying to provide an exact representation of social space in the Parisian region is to better allow the populations living there to become conscious of it. The impossibility of the inhabitants of a metropolis to *place themselves* in a concrete space is not the least cause for disequilibrium in our society. In the study of relations between the material forms of a society and its representations and aspirations, we see appear a third element of social space, which is the very idea of them that the groups and persons who live there have. Thus an urban quarter is not determined only by geographic and economic factors, but by the representation that its inhabitants and those of other quarters have of it.

[...] If we are to summarize our view of social space, we could just say that it is determined by the complex outline of a group of points caught in a whole series of other spaces: topographic space (determined by physical conditions), biological space (determined by ecological conditions), anthropological space (determined by distribution of anthropological types), temporal space (determined by rapidity of communications), economic space (determined by production, consumption, and exchange), total geographic space (which includes all the changes exercised by nature and by humanity on topographic space), demographic space (determined by volume, density, and distribution of populations), cultural space (determined by collective representations having a material expression in concrete space), etc. Social space is determined, for example, by the points of attraction and the symbols that the Stock Exchange, a church, etc. represent, by the surface limits of distribution of individuals belonging to a particular profession, etc.—all this in connection with the forms of the terrain, industrial concentration, nature of the habitat, or the frequency of people of a certain height.

Once social space has been in this way determined, we can return in a more efficient manner to properly ecological enquiries. We better understand why the fact of inhabiting such or such an area of the Parisian region (wide milieu: habitat) or such a kind of house (limited milieu: housing) commands certain habits, certain comportments. If material facts of this sort are far from determining all an individual's manners of thinking and movements of a group, they must nevertheless be placed in a prominent position in researching the entirety of causes.

Taking these remarks into account, we could say that spatial structures, such as they appear to us, are determined in part by material conditions and technologies and in part by collective representations. On the other hand, milieu and spatial structures may be spontaneously altered in step with the material and moral needs of populations. In a word, humanity comes profoundly under the influence of the milieu and humanity can, with the help of means currently at its disposal, alter this milieu just about however it wishes. The current drama stems from the fact that it is rarely the same people who most strongly come under these influences of the milieu that dispose of the means to change it. In examining this problem closely, we will see anew that it is the economic structures that are here involved. [...]

Urban sectors and quarters

[...] The delimitation of geographic sectors accomplished primarily with the help of aerial views calls on two other ideas: that of the *urban tissue or fabric* and that of *breaks*. The first, created by urbanists and ecologists, is very useful so long as comparisons (which may nevertheless be fruitful) with the tissues of vegetal and animal organisms aren't pushed carelessly. A series of divisions, exchanges, and relations effectively exist that are the manifestation of a more or less intense life. These exchanges seem to be made between poorly differentiated units and are regrouped around nodes (centers of attraction), but here the comparison must presently stop for us.[17]

Centers of attraction may be made up of different elements. The essential (not the ideal) center in the present-day structure of a city like Paris is the group of shops that constitute the indispensable equipment for daily life. The variety of trades in metropolises and dispersion of certain categories of them make us lose sight of their regroupings. For others, this regrouping becomes evident above all on comparative maps (like those drawn up for the 12th and 16th arrondissements) upon which shops are indicated by category. The existence of small economic nuclei allows the outline of the true elementary units of quarters to be discerned. But rather than seeing them neatly separated as distinct cells, they reveal themselves here in the form of complex tissues where the nuclei seem to be irregularly distributed as in an energide tissue.

Moreover these economic centers are far from being the only ones. The social life of quarters is controlled by the attraction of the approaches to a large factory, by a school, by a neighborhood cinema, by a metro station, by a church. These points of attraction are at the centers of circles of dispersion of individuals who gravitate around them, and all these circles blend unequally. We should add here also long-distance centers of attraction, completely outside the quarters, such as first-run cinemas, large halls for public meetings, department stores, etc. One could then think that this network, in which the individual is drawn by such varied centers, is inextricable. But

---

17   Quoist's analysis of a quarter of Rouen provides an interesting example for a mid-sized city ("Une unité résidentielle de type prolétarien," *Idées et forces* [November 1949]).

against these positive forces are posed other elements, having this time a negative function, which will allow us to distinguish clearer separations.

Indeed there exist breaks with quite precise characteristics. To obstacles that delimit geographic sectors by making pedestrian circulation impossible or difficult (elevated railway, canal, group of factories…), may be added secondary breaks such as very large arterial roads, and intermittent breaks such as secondary arteries. The same avenue may be, at two different places, a link and a separation depending on the buildings lining it. A first cutting-up of the urban tissue is thus directed by more or less distinct breaks.

Social space and urbanism in the metropolises

[…] The social repercussions of the development of a large region have often been evoked, but seldom demonstrated with arguments that would allow us to judge them. We know with some exactitude what the percentages of certain illnesses for each administrative sector are, but the development of mental illnesses, for example, still escapes us. We possess measurements for individuals' weight and height, but more precise anthropological measurements that would allow us to understand the influence of the urban milieu on city-dwellers are missing. We know that a city like Paris is a place where populations of diverse origins mix, but studies of the present-day composition of such or such social class are still at the early stages. We know that technological evolution and economic concentration have a decisive influence simultaneously on the transformation of the living environment and on the evolution of social structures, but we do not yet know the new structures that have sometimes scarcely been sketched out. We know that certain living conditions imposed upon marginalized populations generate not only poverty, but delinquency and crime as well; and nevertheless, we find ourselves incapable of saying how this state of affairs might be abolished. We know that the development of metropolises promotes the concentration of cultural resources and we are flattered by Paris' reputation in this regard, but we still have no idea what segment of the population profits from this and, what's more, what might make this culture accessible to all.

[…] Currently urbanists classify the principle problems facing the planning of cities according to human needs into four points of view: living, working, recreation for body and mind, and circulation.[18] But if we think in terms of future plans, there is one concern that is preponderant: the

---

18   Here we take up the divisions of *The Athens Charter* (published 1943) and reaffirmed by the C.I.A.M. groups during their VI Congress (London, 1947) on the proposal of the ASCORAL association (*Grille C.I.A.M. d'urbanisme* [Boulogne: Éditions del' Architecture d'aujourd'hui, 1948]).

location and valorization of monuments that have a symbolic function and that provide a sense of direction. Before all else, a plan must be popular, it must incite the enthusiastic devotion of all categories of the population. There is no great work or harmonious life without an animating faith. This faith must be expressed in monuments whose forms and placement in the city correspond to their function and their symbolic value. Around them are distributed the social spaces that Maurice Halbwachs emphasized in his study of collective memory: juridical space, economic space, religious space.[19]

However in a metropolis like the Parisian region, we often see the most important public monuments placed in areas set aside for only a fraction of the population. These monuments should be surrounded by welcoming and familiar spaces approached by wide and well-conceived roads that facilitate access for even the most distant populations. Le Corbusier's plan for Paris, however exaggerated it may be from certain points of view, takes account of this need to aerate and highlight essential symbolic monuments. If the new plan for Warsaw, conceived after the destruction of a large part of the city during the war, has met with such success, it is in part because of this concern.[20] We need, then, to study the position of populations in the Parisian region like those of the suburban allotments, who find themselves cut off from the vital centers and because of this feel pushed to the margins of national life. This is a problem of social cohesion for which ecological analyses can provide important clarifications.

THEORY OF THE DÉRIVE[21]

GUY DEBORD

In 1953 Ivain had recommended that the inhabitants of his future city undertake what he called a "CONTINUOUS DÉRIVE," noting that "the changing of landscape from one hour to the next will result in complete disorientation." Three years later Debord would return to this subject in an attempt to theorize the practice. In this important article he began by defining dérive—*as "a technique of swift passage through varied environments"—and noting its relation to the concept of "psychogeography"; he then described it as a kind of dialectical wandering, in which the subject's trajectory was both determined*

---

19 Halbwachs, *The Collective Memory* (1950), trans. Francis J. Ditter, Jr. and Vida Yazdi Ditter (New York: Harper & Row, 1980).
20 Cf. P. George, "Varsovie 1949: Reconstruction ou naissance d'une nouvelle ville," *Population* no. 4 (1949): 718.
21 *Les Lèvres nues* no. 9 (November 1956): 6–10. [Ed.]

by the city's "*psychogeographic relief*" *and brought under control by that relief's objective mapping. While acknowledging its indebtedness to the field of urban sociology—then in its relative infancy in France—Debord also aligned* dérive *with a Marxist-inspired insistence on the absolutely historical (and hence mutable) nature of the city. He then went on to divide the practice into two variants, one devoted principally to "studying a site," the other to "bewildering affective results," each with their own character and aims. Debord concluded on a note that looked back to Ivain's original text, predicting "one day, cities will be built for* dérive.*"*

Among various modes of Situationist conduct, *dérive* is defined as a technique of swift passage through varied environments. The concept of *dérive* is indissolubly linked with the recognition of effects of a psychogeographic nature, and with the assertion of a ludic-constructive comportment, which contrasts it on all points with classical ideas of the journey and the stroll.

One or more persons indulging in *dérive* give up, for a greater or lesser duration, their familiar reasons for movement and action, their own acquaintances, jobs, and forms of leisure, to release themselves to the solicitations of the site and of the encounters suiting it. The place of the aleatory here is less determinant than is thought: from the point of view of *dérive*, there is a psychogeographic relief of cities, with constant currents, fixed points, and vortexes that make approaching or exiting certain zones very difficult.

But *dérive*, in its unity, includes at the same time this release and its necessary contradiction: the control of psychogeographic variations by the knowledge and calculation of their possibilities. In this latter regard, the data highlighted by ecology (however narrow may be, a priori, the social space that this science proposes to study) usefully supports psychogeographic thought.

The ecological analysis of the absolute or relative character of breaks in the urban tissue, of the role of micro-climates, of the completely distinct, elementary units of administrative quarters, and above all of the predominant effect of centers of attraction, must be utilized and completed by the psychogeographic system. The objective field of passion in which *dérive* is propelled must be defined at the same time according to its own determinism and according to its relations with social morphology.

In his study on *Paris and the Parisian Region*, Chombart de Lauwe notes that "an urban quarter is not determined only by geographic and economic factors, but by the representation that its inhabitants and those of other quarters have of it;"[22] and he presents in the same work—to show "the narrowness of the real Paris in which each individual lives ... geographically

---

22   See Paul-Henry Chombart de Lauwe, "Excerpts from *Paris and the Parisian Region*," translated in this volume, 71 [Ed.]

a setting whose radius is extremely small"—the plotting of all the journeys effected in a year by a female student from the 16th arrondissement: these journeys compose a triangle of reduced dimension, without deviations, whose three apexes are the Ecole des Sciences Politiques, the residence of the young woman, and that of her piano teacher.

There is no doubt that such diagrams, examples of a modern poetry capable of inciting sharp affective reactions—in this case indignation that it's possible to live that way—or even the theory, promoted by Burgess about Chicago, of the distribution of social activities in defined concentric belts, will assist in advancing *dérive*.

In *dérive* chance plays a role that is all the more important as psychogeographic observation is still little confident. But the action of chance is naturally conservative and tends, in a new setting, to reduce everything to the alternation of a limited number of variants and to habit. Progress being nothing but the rupture of one of the fields where chance operates, by the creation of new conditions more favorable to our plans, it can be said that the opportunities presented by *dérive* are fundamentally different than those of the stroll, but that the first psychogeographic attractions discovered run the risk of fixating the subject or group on *dérive* around new routine axes, where everything constantly draws them back.

An insufficient distrust of chance, and of its always reactionary ideological use, condemned to a dismal failure the famous directionless ramble undertaken in 1923 by four Surrealists, starting from a city chosen by lot: wandering in the open country is obviously depressing, and the operations of chance are poorer than ever there.[23] But mindlessness is pushed much further in *Médium* (May 1954) by one Pierre Vendryes, who believes he can compare—because they all partake of the same anti-determinist liberation—this anecdote with some probability experiments, such as one on the aleatory distribution of tadpoles in a circular crystallizer, to which he adds the last word by specifying: "of course, such a population must not come under any controlling influence." In these conditions, the prize really goes to the tadpoles, who have the advantage of being "as stripped as possible of intelligence, sociability, and sexuality," and consequently "truly independent from one another."[24]

---

23   In May 1923 Louis Aragon and André Breton, joined by Max Morise and Roger Vitrac, decided to abandon Paris; laying out a map of France on a table, Breton closed his eyes and randomly pointed his finger at the town of Blois. From there the group wandered aimlessly across the Sologne for ten days. In 1952 Breton described the experience: "The absence of any aim very soon cut us off from reality and raised beneath our steps more and more phantasms, ever more disturbing... An exploration on the confines of waking life and dream life, wholly in keeping with our preoccupations of that time." [Ed.]

24   Pierre Vendryes, "Surréalisme et probabilité," *Medium: Communication surréaliste*

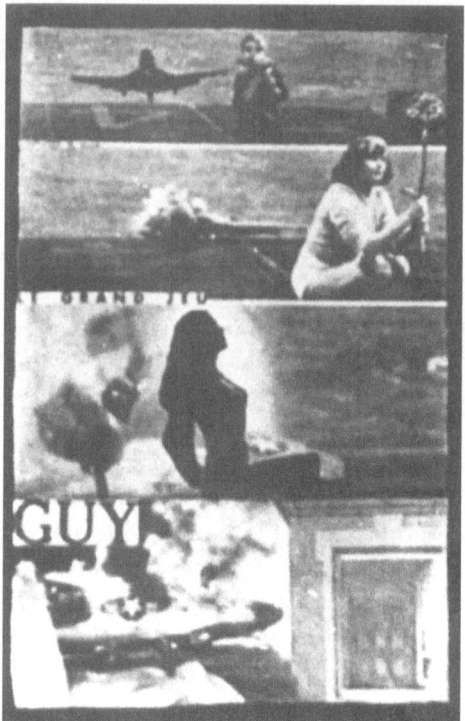

Fig.3.4.1 Still from Guy Debord, *Critique of Separation*, 1961, showing an undated collage by Debord.

At the very opposite of these eccentricities, the chiefly urban character of *dérive*, in touch with those centers of possibilities and meanings that are the metropolises transformed by industry, would correspond to Marx's sentence: "Men can see nothing around them that is not their own image; everything speaks to them of themselves. Their very landscape is alive."

One may undertake *dérive* alone, but everything indicates that the most fruitful numerical allocation consists of several small groups of two or three people who have reached the same awakening of consciousness, the prior crosschecking of these different groups' impressions authorizing the possibility of objective conclusions. It is desirable that the composition of these groups change from one *dérive* to another. Beyond four or five participants, the character peculiar to *dérive* rapidly wanes, and in any case it is impossible to exceed about ten without *dérive* fragmenting into several *dérives* led simultaneously. The experience of this last movement

---

n.s., no. 3 (May 1954), p. 5. At the conclusion of his article, Vendryes cites the same four-person deambulation undertaken by Breton and his colleagues in 1923 mentioned above by Debord. [Ed.]

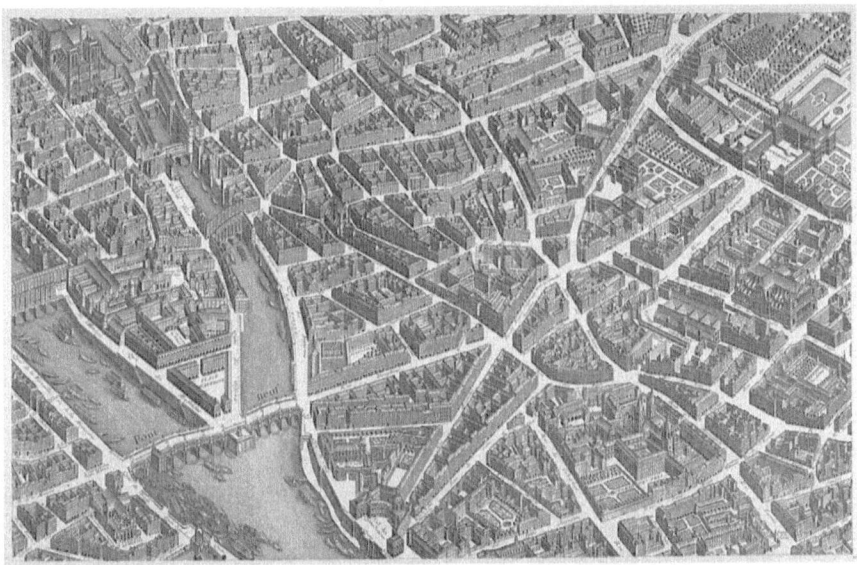

Fig.3.4.2 Plate from Michel Turgot's large-format atlas *Plan de Paris*, 1739; Louis Bretez, cartographer.

is moreover of great interest, but the difficulties it entails have until the present not allowed it to be organized to the extent desired.

The average duration of a *dérive* is one day, considered as the interval of time contained between two periods of sleep. The starting and finishing points in time, in relation to the solar day, are unimportant, but it should be noted however that the last hours of the night are generally unfit for *dérive*.

This average duration of *dérive* only has a statistical value. First, it rather rarely occurs in all its purity, the interested parties avoiding with difficulty at the beginning or end of this day stealing one or two hours to spend on banal tasks; at the end of the day, fatigue contributes greatly to this withdrawal. But above all *dérive* often unfolds in a few, deliberately fixed, hours, or even fortuitously during fairly brief moments, or on the contrary over several days without interruption. In spite of the interruptions imposed by the need for sleep, certain *dérives* of a sufficient intensity have been extended three or four days, or even longer. It is true that in the case of a series of *dérives* over a rather long period, it is almost impossible to determine with any precision the moment when the state of mind peculiar to one given *dérive* gives way to another. One series of *dérives* had continued without notable interruption for around two months, which doesn't occur without bringing about new objective conditions of comportment that entail the disappearance of a good number of the old ones.

The influence on *dérive* of weather conditions, though real, is determinant only in the case of prolonged rains, which almost certainly suspend it. But storms or other types of precipitation are rather propitious to them.

Dérive's spatial field is more or less precise or vague according as this activity is aimed sooner at studying a site or at bewildering affective results. The fact that these two aspects of *dérive* present multiple interferences and that it is impossible to isolate one of them in a pure state must not be overlooked. But finally the use of taxis, for example, can furnish a clear enough dividing line: if in the course of a *dérive* a taxi is taken, either to a precise destination, or to be moved twenty minutes to the west, one is concerned above all with self-disorientation. If direct exploration of a site is adhered to, one is advancing the search for a psychogeographic urbanism.

In all cases the spatial field depends first on all on the starting base represented, for isolated subjects, by their residences, and for groups, by selected gathering points. The maximum extent of this spatial field does not exceed the entirety of a metropolis and its suburbs. Its minimum extent may be limited to a small unitary ambiance: a single quarter, or even a single block of houses if it's worthwhile (the far limit being the day-long static-*dérive* without leaving the Lazare station).

The exploration of a fixed spatial field thus presupposes the setting up of bases, and the calculation of directions of penetration. It is here that the study of

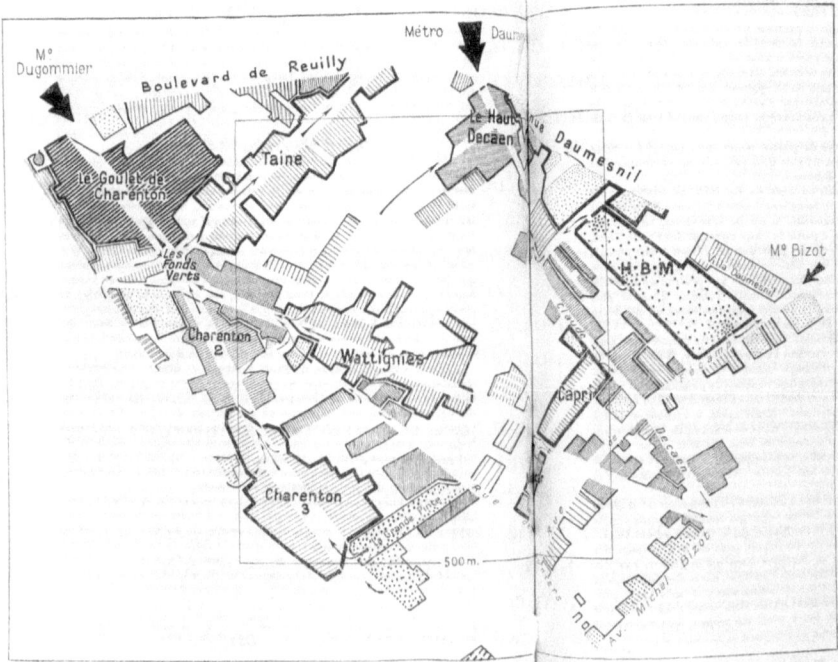

Fig.3.4.3   "The sector's residential units: The social life that grows on a daily basis within an urban sector underlies a familiar framework that exceeds the narrow dimensions of housing." From Paul-Henry Chombart de Lauwe, *Paris and the Parisian Region*, 1952.

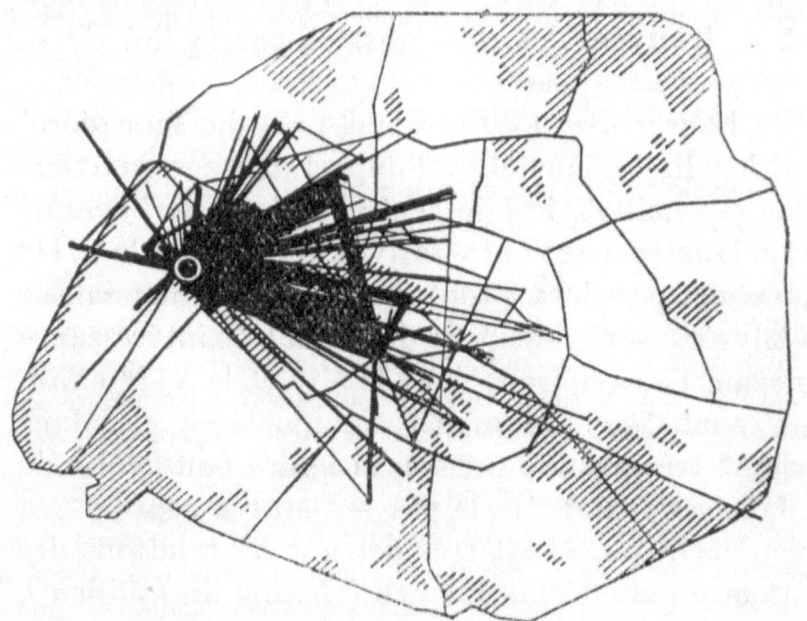

Fig.3.4.4   "Commutes during the course of a year by a girl in the 16th arrondissement. The central triangle has for vertices: home, piano lessons, and courses in Political Science." From Paul-Henry Chombart de Lauwe, *Paris and the Parisian Region*, 1952.

maps, as much standard ones as ecological or psychogeographic ones, intercedes, along with the correction and improvement of these maps. Is there any need to say that the taste for an unknown, never-before surveyed quarter is by no means involved? Beyond its unimportance, this aspect of the problem is completely subjective, and does not last long. This criterion has never been used, and if it has, only occasionally when it has been a matter of finding psychogeographic outlets from an area by systematically straying from all routine points. In that case one may lose oneself in quarters already amply surveyed.

On the contrary the place of exploration is minimal, compared with that of a bewildering comportment, in the "possible rendezvous." The subject is asked to go alone at a specified time to a chosen place. He is freed of the tedious obligations of the ordinary rendezvous, since there is no one to await. However this "possible rendezvous" having led him unexpectedly to a place he may or may not know, he observes his surroundings. One could at the same time assign another "possible rendezvous" at the same place to someone whose identity he cannot anticipate. He may never have even seen the other person, which will incite him to strike up conversation with various passersby. He may meet no one, or even meet by chance the person who has decided on the "possible rendezvous." In any case, and particularly if the place and time have been well chosen, the subject's use of time will take an unexpected turn. He may even ask via telephone for another "possible rendezvous" from someone who doesn't know where the first has taken him. The virtually infinite resources of this pastime are obvious.

Thus, certain stunts in so-called dubious taste, which I have always highly esteemed among my circle—as for example entering nightly into the floors of houses being pulled down, traveling without interruption through Paris by hitchhiking during a transport strike, on the pretext of increasing confusion by having oneself driven anywhere, wandering in those catacomb tunnels forbidden to the public—arise from a more general sentiment that is nothing other than the sentiment of *dérive*.

Dérive's lessons permit the drawing up of the first surveys of the psychogeographic articulations of a modern city. Beyond the reconnaissance of unitary ambiances, of their main components, and of their spatial localization, their principal axes of passage, their exits, and their defenses would be perceived. The central hypothesis of the existence of psychogeographic rotating platforms is arrived at. The distances that effectively separate two regions of a city are measured, distances that cannot be gauged with what the approximate vision of a map may have you believe. By means of old maps, aerial photographic views, and experimental *dérives*, a cartography of influences can be drawn up that has so far been lacking, and whose current uncertainty—inevitable before an immense amount of work has been done—is no worse than that of the first portulans, the only difference being that it is no longer a matter of accurately fixing the boundaries of solid continents, but of changing architecture and urbanism.

Today, the different unitary atmospheres and habitations are not precisely divided, but are surrounded with more or less extensive bordering edges. The most general change that *dérive* leads to proposing is the constant reduction of these bordering edges, until their complete suppression.

In architecture itself, the taste for *dérive* leads to proposals for all sorts of new labyrinthine forms, which modern possibilities of construction promote. Thus, the press reported in March 1955 on the construction in New York of a building in which the first signs of an opportunity for *dérive* inside an apartment may be glimpsed:

> The helicoidal house's accommodations will have the form of a slice of cake. They may be enlarged or reduced at will by the removal of movable partitions. Gradation by half-floor avoids limiting the number of rooms, the tenant being able to request the use of the next slice overhanging or lower down. This system permits the transformation in six hours of three four-room apartments into one apartment of twelve rooms or more.

The sentiment of *dérive* is naturally linked with a more general manner of living, which it would nevertheless be clumsy to try to deduce from it mechanically. I will dwell neither upon *dérive*'s precursors—which may be rightfully recognized, or improperly appropriated [*détourner*]—in the literature of the past, nor upon the specific notions of passion that this activity entails. *Dérive*'s difficulties are those of freedom. Everything leads us to believe that the future will precipitate the irreversible transformation of current society's comportment and setting. One day, cities will be built for *dérive*. Certain areas that already exist may be used, with relatively light touching up. Certain people that already exist may be used.

DEBORD'S PARIS AND BILL'S CINEVOX[25]

The anathema pronounced on routine town-planning concepts by Asger Jorn in his *Fin de Copenhague* is only part of a general onslaught on urbanism by Jorn's connection, an onslaught that has been pursued in another direction by his colleague Guy Debord [...]. [His map of Paris] shows "quartiers d'états d'âme" and "gradients of psychogeographical drift"—factors not generally taken into account by the average planning authority. Nevertheless, this microclimatology of the psyche is something to which every town-dweller can testify, and in a city like Paris, whose very street-names are part

---

25 *Architectural Review* (July 1958): 1. [Ed.]

of Western culture, it is a more than personal affair—that pioneer document of psychogeography, André Breton's *Nuit du Tournesol*, which ought on the face of it to be an entirely private exercise in erotic topography, can be read with understanding, even by those who have never visited Paris.

In fact, Debord's program of cultural dislocation is remarkably objective, and his celebrated anti-film *Hurlements en Faveur de Sade* is chiefly notable for the fact that the uproar it creates is designed and predictable. Something like motivation research underlies most of the "Situations" that it is his aim to precipitate, and snap judgments on the publications of the Situationist International had best be restrained until the documents have been frisked for hidden persuaders. What looks like a revival of the rather amateur techniques of the Dadaists may well be only protective coloring for something that is subversive in a more up-to-date manner.

Thus the first proclamation of the German section of the Situationist International, dedicated to Jackson Pollock, Nicolas de Stael, Wols, Dylan Thomas and James Dean, contains at one point the slogan *Max Bill muss nach Ulm zurück*, which may well come as surprise in view of the known hostility to Bill and his New Bauhaus of the Situationists and the Bauhaus Imaginists. But the present administration at Ulm, under Tomás Maldonado, may yet prove a bigger situation-provoker than they in the world of product design, and in the meantime, Max Bill has produced a situation that is unusually and subtly subversive of "established culture," by designing the *Cinevox* cinema at Neuhausen in an idiom of such impeccable rectitude that it must seem downright anti-visual design by comparison with the wide-screen, Technicolor extravaganzas seen inside.

EXCERPT FROM *ALL THE KING'S HORSES*[26]

MICHÈLE BERNSTEIN

I hadn't seen much of Gilles during this period. When I met him afternoons, he was most often tired from having walked the whole night with Carole, between les Halles, Maubert, and Monge. He hardly took her to Saint-Germain, I think, nor around Pigalle, and even less to Montparnasse (which we hated), in none of those quarters of Paris where the night drags on like the day with the same people always met with again and again. I knew Gilles's taste for passing the night in long march, when a café still open became a precious port of call in the streets where the night-prowlers are no longer plentiful. After two in the morning, the rue Mouffetard is

---

26   Michèle Bernstein, *Tous les chevaux du roi* (1960) (Paris: Éditions Allia, 2004), 21–22 and 25–26. [Ed.]

empty. You have to go back up to the Panthéon to find a bar, on the rue Cujas. The next halting-place is near the Sénat, then rue du Bac, if ever one would have the good taste to bypass what we still call the Quartier. Here, I can imagine Carole relating the story of her life (she must not have much of one yet). And the morning twilight dawning at les Halles, a rite.

Finally, the day after, exhausted perhaps by these rambles, Gilles would bring Carole home. I would be surprised, upon her arrival, at the satisfaction that she betrayed about recent quarrels that she had caused, or suffered. I would show her nothing but the greatest cordiality, and it seemed to me that she took some comfort in it. [...]

The rum had slowly dulled us.

"I'm tired," she explained. "I'm used to getting to bed late but now, it's much worse. And I'm not even painting anymore."

I saw that she was looking at her canvas on the wall, pleased with the place it had found among the others.

"And isn't it the same with Gilles? When does he work?"

And turning round toward him:

"What exactly are you interested in? I don't really know."

"Reification," answered Gilles.

"It's serious research," I added.

"Yes," he said.

"I see," Carole observed, admiringly. "It's very serious work, with heavy books and lots of papers spread out across a big table."

"No," said Gilles, "I go for walks. Mainly, I go for walks."

4.

Consolidation

EXCERPT FROM "ON THE PASSAGE OF A FEW PEOPLE THROUGH A RATHER BRIEF MOMENT OF TIME"[1]

GUY DEBORD

Voice 2: The era had reached a degree of knowledge and technological means that made possible and—more and more—necessary, a *direct* construction of all aspects of a liberated affective and workaday existence. The appearance of these superior means of action, still unused on account of delays experienced in liquidating the commodity economy, had already condemned aesthetic activity, whose ambitions and powers had both been left behind. The decay of art, as well as of all the values of former conduct, had formed our sociological foundation. The dominant class's monopoly on the instruments we had to control in order to realize the collective art of our time had placed us outside even a cultural production officially devoted to the illustration and repetition of the past. An art film on this generation could only be a film on the nonexistence of its oeuvres.

    Others unthinkingly followed the paths learned once and for all, toward their work and their home, toward their predictable future. For them duty had already become a habit, and habit a duty. They did not see the insufficiency of their city. They thought natural the insufficiency of their life. We wanted to get out of this conditioning, in search of different uses of the urban landscape, of new passions. The atmosphere of a few places made us conscious of the future powers of an architecture that had to be created as the support and setting for less mediocre games. We could expect nothing from what we ourselves had not altered. The urban milieu declared the

---

1   Guy Debord, "Sur le passage de quelques personnes ..." (1959), in *Oeuvres*, ed. Jean-Louis Rançon (Paris: Éditions Gallimard, Coll. "Quarto," 2006), 476–479. [Ed.]

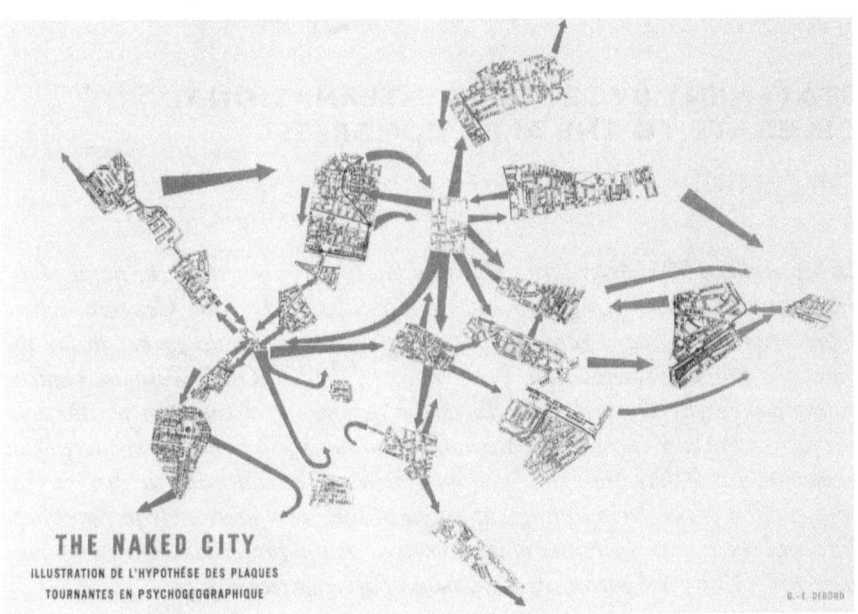

Fig.3.4 5   Guy Debord, *The Naked City*, 1957.

orders and tastes of the ruling society with a violence equal to that of the newspapers. It is humanity that makes the unity of the world, but humanity has scattered everywhere. Human beings can see nothing around them that is not their own image; everything speaks to them of themselves. Their very landscape is alive. There were obstacles everywhere. There was coherence in the obstacles of all kinds. They maintained the coherent reign of poverty. Everything being linked, it was necessary *to change everything* by a unitary struggle, or nothing. It was necessary to link up with the masses, but round us was nothing but sleep.

Voice 3: The dictatorship of the proletariat means a persistent struggle—bloody and bloodless, violent and peaceful, military and economic, educational and administrative, against the forces and traditions of the old society.[2]

STATEMENT BY LETTRIST INTERNATIONAL DELEGATE TO THE ALBA CONGRESS[3]

GUY DEBORD

In September 1956, Asger Jorn and Pinot Gallizio convened, in the name of the International Movement for an Imaginist Bauhaus, the Alba Congress, where representatives of avant-garde groups of eight nations would gather to lay the bases of a unified organization. In the name of the L.I. Gil J. Wolman, reading a text written by Debord, underlined the necessity of a common platform in the face of the ever-increasing potential for humanity to mold the entirety of its environment. If "creation can now only be a synthesis aiming at the integral construction of the surroundings, of a style of life," this necessarily put architecture and the city at the center of any renewed avant-garde. Hence the emphasis here on "unitary urbanism" as a synthesis of art and technology.

Comrades,

A general movement determines the parallel crises that are currently affecting all modes of artistic creation, and the fulfillment of these crises can only be reached through a broad perspective.

The process of negation and destruction that, with growing speed, has manifested itself against all the old conditions of artistic activity, is irreversible: it is the consequence of the appearance of superior possibilities of action upon the world.

---

2   V. I. Lenin, "'*Left-Wing' Communism – An Infantile Disorder*" (1920), in *Collected Works*, Vol. 31 (Moscow: Progress Publishers, 1966), 44. [Ed.]
3   From *Documents relatifs à la Fondation d'Internationnale situationniste*, ed. Gérard Berreby (Paris: Éditions Allia, 1985).

The existence of these possibilities has been reflected, in different ways, for a century in political struggles or the technological organization of everyday life. As these possibilities are themselves rapidly developing, they have definitively condemned the retreat or the continuation of the old order in all intellectual disciplines. But their development presents, because of economic and social resistances, great unevenness from one domain to another. It is easy to understand, for example, that nuclear physics, because its applications are temporarily useful to the ruling class, reaches further in its results than the search for a thought or a manner of life that would be at the level of all present potentialities, since such a search is harmful for the ruling class, and is openly opposed to the stinking ideologies that it supports.

Nevertheless, whatever credit the bourgeoisie wishes today to grant to fragmentary, or deliberately retrograde, artistic efforts, creation can now only be a synthesis aiming at the integral construction of the surroundings, of a style of life.

Starting from these considerations, we are led to work for a truly modern urbanism, of which until the present only a few chance predecessors can be identified.

We know that the material forms of societies, the structure of cities, express the order of concerns peculiar to those societies. And if temples have been, even more than written laws, the means to express the representation of the world that a defined historical community was able to form, it remains to build monuments that express, with our atheism, the new values of a new manner of living whose triumph is certain.

To whatever extent possible, the settings and comportments of an era that is beginning must be tested. The nothingness of a so-called "proletarian" literature no longer allows us to doubt the fatal consequences of the distinction—in itself highly suspect—between an art engaged in urgent propaganda and an art oriented toward the non-immediate renewal of themes of life. In reality, these two viewpoints are necessarily complementary, and any exclusive extolling of a single one among them must be considered reactionary.

A unitary urbanism—the synthesis, appropriating arts and technologies, that we are demanding—must be built in step with certain new life-values, that it is from the present a question of singling out and spreading.

It must be well understood that everything that may be undertaken from now on, in urbanism, in architecture, or elsewhere, can only be of value to the extent that one had first answered this question of the style of life, and had answered it correctly.

It is not worthwhile to go looking further to condemn Le Corbusier and Company's architecture, which means to establish a definitive harmony from a Christian and capitalist style of life, rashly thought to be immutable.

If one thinks, following a broad and demystified analysis of the movement of social relations, that the family such as we know it is happily destined to soon disappear, one understands that it is unfortunate for an architecture that wishes to be oriented toward the future to have linked its fate to the family's preservation.

Since Le Corbusier has made of his work an illustration of and a powerful means of action for the worst oppressive forces, this work—certain of whose lessons should however be incorporated into the next phase—is promised a complete bankruptcy.

Of this future style of life, whose circumstances must be anticipated in order to provide a direction to the present, we may say, without advancing anything too specific, that it will principally be determined, as opposed to the current one, by freedom and forms of leisure.

The experimental urbanism that we must undertake should already be situated in this direction. "New chaotic jungles must be discovered," writes Asger Jorn at the end of his essay "Immagine e forma," "through useless, senseless experiments." And Marcel Mariën announced in *Les Lèvres nues* no. 8 that: "For pre-stressed concrete, you will see the winding road, the sunken path, the impasse, taking its place. The wasteland will be the object of quite particular studies and competitions will be launched to find the best projects."

We will not be opposed to what in this urbanism is called baroque, at least in its first efforts, since it will be turned completely toward life, and opposed to functional classicism. But it will not remain baroque. It will master the old baroque-classical contradiction. Unitary urbanism must become, by every means, the setting of and occasion for thrilling games.

The Lettrist International considers it possible to agree with other progressive tendencies on a precise program of joint action for architecture and urbanism; and that this agreement may be founded at present within the International Movement for an Imaginist Bauhaus, in which the Lettrists have been represented since May 1956.

However, the Lettrist International emphasizes the necessity of concretely agreeing on a minimum of positive statements; of unequivocally denouncing the old ends of art or writing; of radically excluding backwards factions.

Failing this, no joint action could be supported.

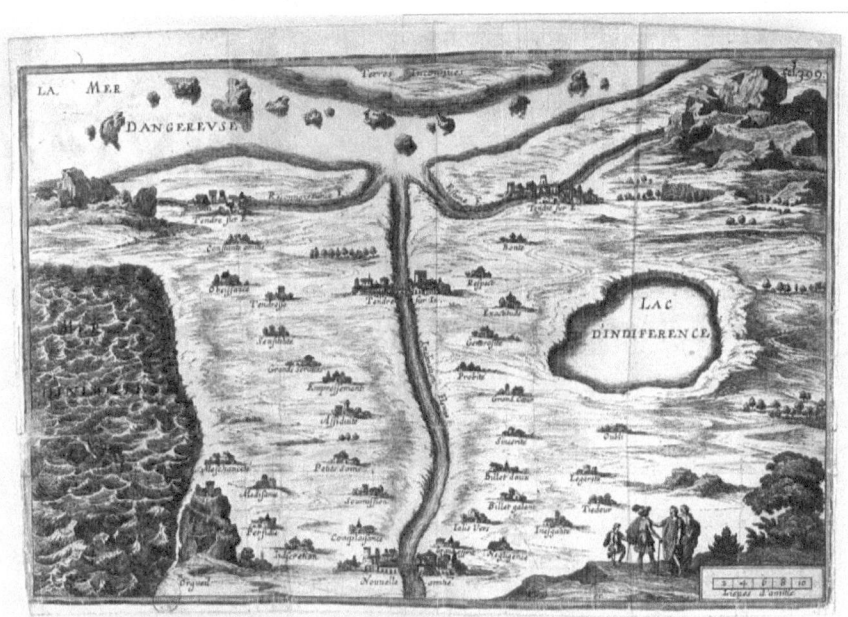

Fig.4.4.1   Carte de Tendre, from Madeleine de Scudéry, *Clélie*, 1654-60.

TOWARD A SITUATIONIST INTERNATIONAL[4]
GUY DEBORD

In 1957 Debord published the Report on the Construction of Situations and on the International Situationist Tendency's Conditions of Organization and Action. *Beginning with historical accounting of past avant-gardes, and a synthesis of the first results of Lettrist experimentation, this text expresses the fundamental perspectives from which the Situationist International would evolve. In this excerpt, the construction of situations was named the central idea that would determine the program of the S.I.; unitary urbanism, in collaboration with styles of comportment, was deemed the only level at which "integral art" could be realized; and the need for a new sort of play was announced. Debord then developed a critique of the subjective dimension of alienation (a dimension largely ignored in revolutionary politics at the time) by introducing the concept of "spectacle," here still closely linked to theatricality, as a means to criticize the passivity of the spectator—but this was, of course, a concept destined to continually grow in significance, until it came to be understood as the very essence of contemporary society.*

Our central purpose is the construction of situations, i.e. the concrete construction of temporary settings of life and their transformation into a higher passionate nature. We must develop an intervention, directed by the complicated factors of two great components in perpetual interaction: the material setting of life and the behaviors that it incites and that overturn it.

Our prospects for action on the environment lead, in their latest development, to the idea of a unitary urbanism. Unitary urbanism first becomes clear in the use of the whole of arts and techniques as means cooperating in an integral composition of the environment. This whole must be considered infinitely more extensive than the old influence of architecture on the traditional arts, or than the current occasional application to anarchic urbanism of specialized techniques or of scientific investigations such as ecology. Unitary urbanism must control, for example, the acoustic environment as well as the distribution of different varieties of drink or food. It must take up the creation of new forms and the appropriation [*détournement*] of known forms of architecture and urbanism—as well as the appropriation [*détournement*] of the old poetry and cinema. Integral art, about which so much has been said, can only materialize at the level of urbanism. But it can no longer correspond with any traditional definitions of the aesthetic. In each of its experimental cities, unitary urbanism will work through a certain

---
4 From *Documents relatifs à la Fondation de l'Internationale situationniste.*

number of force fields, which we can temporarily designate by the standard expression district. Each district will be able to lead to a precise harmony, broken off from neighboring harmonies; or rather will be able to play on a maximum breaking up of internal harmony.

Secondly, unitary urbanism is dynamic, i.e. in close touch with styles of behavior. The most reduced element of unitary urbanism is not the house but the architectural complex, which is the union of all the factors conditioning an environment, or a sequence of environments colliding at the scale of the constructed situation. Spatial development must take the affective realities that the experimental city will determine into account. One of our comrades has promoted a theory of states-of-mind districts, according to which each quarter of a city would tend to induce a single emotion, to which the subject will consciously expose herself or himself. It seems that such a project draws timely conclusions from an increasing depreciation of accidental primary emotions, and that its realization could contribute to accelerating this change. Comrades who call for a new architecture, a free architecture, must understand that this new architecture will not play at first on free, poetic lines and forms—in the sense that today's "lyrical abstract" painting uses these words—but rather on the atmospheric effects of rooms, corridors, streets, atmospheres linked to the behaviors they contain. Architecture must advance by taking as its subject emotionally moving situations, more than emotionally moving forms, as the material it works with. And the experiments drawn from this subject will lead to unknown forms. Psychogeographical research, the "study of the exact laws and precise effects of the geographical environment, consciously organized or not, acting directly on the affective comportment of individuals," thus takes on its double meaning of active observation of today's urban areas and establishing of hypotheses on the structure of a Situationist city. Psychogeography's advancement depends to a great extent on the statistical extension of its methods of observation, but principally on experimentation through concrete interventions in urbanism. Until this stage, the objective truth of even the first psychogeographical data cannot be ensured. But even if these data should turn out to be false, they would certainly be false solutions to a genuine problem.

Our action on comportment, in connection with other desirable aspects of a revolution in customs, can be defined summarily as the invention of a new species of games. The most general aim must be to broaden the non-mediocre portion of life, to reduce its empty moments as much as possible. It may thus be spoken of as an enterprise of human life's quantitative increase, more serious than the biological processes currently being studied. Even there, it implies a qualitative increase whose developments are unforeseeable. The Situationist game stands out from the standard conception of the game by the radical negation of the ludic features of competition and of its separation from the stream of life. In contrast, the Situationist game does not appear distinct from a moral choice, deciding for what ensures the future reign of freedom and play. This is obviously linked to the certainty of the continual and rapid increase of leisure, at a level corresponding to that of our era's productive forces. It is equally linked to the recognition of the fact that a battle of leisure is taking place before our eyes whose importance in the class struggle has not been sufficiently analyzed. To this day, the ruling class is succeeding in making use of the leisure that the revolutionary proletariat extracted from it by developing a vast industrial sector of leisure that is an unrivalled instrument for bestializing the proletariat through byproducts of mystifying ideology and bourgeois tastes. One of the reasons for the American working class' incapacity to become politicized should likely be sought amidst this abundance of televised baseness. By obtaining by collective pressure a slight rise in the price of its labor above the minimum necessary for the production of that labor, the proletariat not only enlarges its power of struggle, it also widens the terrain of the struggle. New forms of this struggle then occur parallel with directly economic and political conflicts. Revolutionary propaganda can be said until now to have been constantly dominated in these forms of struggle in all countries where advanced industrial development has introduced them. That the necessary transformation of the base could be delayed by errors and weaknesses at the level of superstructures has unfortunately been proven by some of the twentieth century's experiences. New forces must be hurled into the battle of leisure, and we will take up our position there.

A first attempt at a new manner of deportment has already been achieved with what we have designated *dérive*, which is the practice of a passionate uprooting through the hurried change of environments, as well as a means of studying psychogeography and Situationist psychology. But the application of this will to ludic creation must be extended to all known forms of human relationships, and must for example influence the historical evolution of emotions like friendship and love. Everything leads to the belief that the main insight of our research lies around the hypothesis of constructions of situations.

A human being's life is a sequence of chance situations, and if none of them is exactly similar to another, at the least these situations are, in their immense majority, so undifferentiated and so dull that they perfectly present the impression of similitude. The corollary of this state of affairs is that the singular, enchanting situations experienced in life strictly restrain and limit this life. We must try to construct situations, i.e. collective environments, ensemble of impressions determining the quality of a moment. If we take the simple example of a gathering of a group of individuals for a given time, and taking into account acquaintances and material means at our disposal, we must study which arrangement of the site, which selection of participants, and which incitement of events suit the desired environment. Surely the powers of a situation will broaden considerably in time and in space with the realizations of unitary urbanism or the education of a Situationist generation. The construction of situations begins on the other side of the modern collapse of the idea of the theater [*spectacle*]. It is easy to see to what extent the very principle of the theater—nonintervention—is attached to the alienation of the old world. Inversely, we see how the most valid of revolutionary cultural explorations have sought to break the spectator's psychological identification with the hero, so as to incite this spectator into activity by provoking his capacities to revolutionize his own life. The situation thus is made to be lived by its constructors. The role of the "public," if not passive at least a walk-on, must ever diminish, while the share of those who cannot be called actors but, in a new meaning of the term, "livers," will increase.

Let us say that we have to multiply poetic objects and subjects (unfortunately so rare at present that the most trifling of them assumes an exaggerated emotional importance) and that we have to organize games of these poetic subjects among these poetic objects. There is our entire program, which is essentially ephemeral. Our situations will be without a future, they will be places where people are constantly coming and going. The unchanging nature of art, or anything else, does not enter into our considerations, which are in earnest. The idea of eternity is the basest one a human being could conceive of regarding his or her acts.

Situationist techniques have yet to be invented, but we know that a task presents itself only when the material conditions necessary for its realization already exist, or are at least in the process of formation. We must begin with a small-scale, experimental phase. Undoubtedly we must draw up blueprints for situations, like scripts, despite their unavoidable inadequacy at the beginning. Therefore we will have to introduce a system of notation whose accuracy will increase as experiments in construction teach us more. We will have to find or confirm laws, like those that make Situationist emotion dependent upon an extreme concentration or an extreme dispersion of acts (classical tragedy providing an approximate image of the first case, and *dérive* of the second). Besides the direct means that will be used toward precise ends, the construction of situations will require, in its affirmative phase, a new implementation of reproductive technologies. We could imagine, for example, live televisual projections of some aspects of one situation into another, bringing about modifications and interferences. But more simply cinematic "news"-reels might finally deserve their name if we establish a new documentary school dedicated to fixing the most meaningful moments of a situation for our archives, before the development of these elements has led to a different situation. The systematic construction of situations having to generate previously non-existent feelings, the cinema will discover its greatest pedagogical role in the diffusion of these new passions.

Situationist theory resolutely asserts a non-continuous conception of life. The idea of consistency must be transferred from the perspective of the whole of a life—where it is a reactionary mystification founded on the belief in an immortal soul and, in the last analysis, on the division of labor—to the viewpoint of moments isolated from life, and of the construction of each moment by a unitary use of Situationist means. In a classless society, it might be said, there will be no more painters, only Situationists who, among other things, make paintings.

Life's chief emotional drama, after the never-ending conflict between desire and reality hostile to that desire, certainly appears to be the sensation of time's passage. The Situationist attitude consists in counting on time's swift passing, unlike aesthetic processes that aim at the fixing of emotion. The Situationist challenge to the passage of emotions and of time will be its wager on always gaining ground on change, on always going further in play and in the multiplication of moving periods. Obviously it is not easy for us at this time to make such a wager, however even were we to lose it a thousand times there is no other progressive attitude to adopt.

The Situationist minority was first formed as a trend within the Lettrist left wing, then within the Lettrist International, which it eventually controlled. The same objective impulse is leading several contemporary avant-garde groups to similar conclusions. Together we must discard all the relics of the recent past. We deem that today, an agreement on a unified action among the revolutionary cultural avant-garde must implement such a program. We do not have formulas or final results in mind. We are merely proposing an experimental research, which will collectively lead in a few directions that we are in the process of defining, and in others which have yet to be defined. The very difficulty of arriving at the first Situationist achievements is proof of the newness of the realm we are entering. What alters the way we see the streets is more important than what alters the way we see painting. Our working hypotheses will be reconsidered at each future upheaval, wherever it may come from.

We will be told, chiefly by revolutionary intellectuals and artists who for reasons of taste put up with a certain powerlessness, that this "Situationism" is quite disagreeable; that we have made nothing of beauty; that we would be better off speaking of Gide; and that no one sees any clear reason to be interested in us. People will shy away by reproaching us for repeating a number of viewpoints that have already caused too much scandal, and that express the simple desire to be noticed. They will become indignant about the conduct we have believed necessary to adopt on a few occasions in order to keep or to recover our distances. We reply: it is not a question of knowing whether this interests you, but rather if you yourself could become interesting under new conditions of cultural creation. Revolutionary artists and intellectuals, your role is not to shout that freedom is abused when we refuse to march with the enemies of freedom. You do not have to imitate bourgeois aesthetes who try to bring everything back to what has already been done, because the already-done does not make them uncomfortable. You know that creation is never pure. Your role is to search for what will give rise to the international avant-garde, to join in its program of constructive critique, and to call for its support.

UNITARY URBANISM AT THE END OF THE 1950s[5]

This essay is an attempt to summarize the achievements of unitary urbanism following an initial stage of its development. It is defined in largely negative terms: "unitary urbanism is not a doctrine of urbanism but a critique of urbanism," "it is not a reaction to functionalism, but rather a move past it," and so forth. Once again, functionalism is discussed, although no longer in wholly disapproving terms—some positive contributions are admitted, but on the whole this architecture is seen as having aligned itself with the most steadfast of conservative doctrines (most damnably, religion). As opposed to this, unitary urbanism is allied to "the interests of a complete subversion" and the envisioning of cities as playing fields for new, participatory games.

In August 1956, a tract signed by the groups preparing the founding of the S.I. called for the boycott of a would-be "Festival of Avant-garde Art" being held in Marseilles at the time, an event that the tract called the most complete, official selection of "what in twenty years will represent the idiocy of the 1950s."[6]

And indeed, the modern art of this period turns out to have been dominated by, and almost exclusively composed of, camouflaged repetitions, that is, a stagnation that bespeaks of both the definitive exhaustion of the entire old theater of cultural operations as well as of the incapacity to discover a new one. Nevertheless, at the same time certain movements have constituted themselves underground. Such is the case for the origins of unitary urbanism (U.U.), discovered as of 1953 and first named as such at the end of 1956 in a tract distributed on the occasion of a demonstration by our Italian comrades in Turin ("Obscure statements," wrote *La Nuova Stampa* on 11 December,

---

5 *Internationale situationniste* no. 3 (December 1959): 11–16. [Ed.]
6 See "Failure of the Marseille demonstration" (1956), trans. Gerardo Denís, in *Theory of the* Dérive *and Other Situationist Writings on the City*, eds. Libero Andreotti and Xavier Costa (Barcelona: Museu d'art contemporani and ACTAR, 1996), 61–62. [Ed.]

in the style of the following warning: "Your children's future depends on it: demonstrate in favor of unitary urbanism!").[7] Unitary urbanism is one of the central concerns of the S.I. and despite any delays and difficulties that might arise in its application, it is entirely correct (as the opening report of the Munich conference confirms) that unitary urbanism has already begun the moment it appears as a program of research and development.[8]

The 1950s are about to come to a close. Without trying to predict whether the idiocy of this decade in the art and practice of life—itself a function of more general causes—will diminish or intensify in the short run, it is time to examine the current state of U.U. following the first stage of its development. A number of points need to be clarified.

First of all, unitary urbanism is not a doctrine of urbanism but a critique of urbanism. By the same token, our participation in experimental art is a critique of art, and sociological research ought to be a critique of sociology. No isolated discipline whatsoever can be tolerated in itself; we are moving toward a global creation of existence.

Unitary urbanism is distinct from problems of housing and yet is bound to engulf them; it is all the more distinct from current commercial exchange. At present it envisages a terrain of experimentation for the *social space* of the cities of the future. It is not a reaction to functionalism, but rather a move past it; it is a matter of reaching—beyond the immediately utilitary—a thrilling functional environment. Functionalism—which still has avant-garde pretensions because it continues to encounter outdated resistance—has already triumphed to a large extent. Its positive contributions—the adaptation to practical functions, technical innovation, comfort, the banishment of superimposed ornament—are today banalities. Yet although its field of application is, when all is said and done, narrow, this has not led functionalism to adopt a relative theoretical modesty. In order to justify philosophically the extension of its principles of renewal to the entire organization of social life, functionalism has fused, seemingly without a thought, with the most static conservative doctrines (and, simultaneously, has itself congealed into an inert doctrine). One must construct uninhabitable ambiances; construct the streets of real life, the scenery of daydreams. The issue of church construction provides a particularly illuminating criterion. Functionalist architects tend to agree to construct churches thinking—if they are not stupid deists—that the church, an edifice without function within a functional urbanism, can be treated as a free exercise of plastic form. Their error is that they fail

---

7   The tract, entitled "Manifestate a favore dell'Urbanesimo Unitario," is reprinted in facsimile in the documents section of Mirella Bandini, *L'estetico il politico: Da Cobra all'Internazionale situazionista, 1948-1957* (Rome: Officina Edizioni, 1977), 275. [Ed.]
8   Constant, "Inaugural Report to the Munich Conference" (1959), trans. in this volume, 106–109. [Ed.]

to consider the psycho-functional reality of the church. The functionalists, who are the expression of the technological utilitarianism of an era, cannot successfully build a single church if one considers that the cathedral was once the unitary accomplishment of a society that one has to call primitive, given that it was much further embedded than we are in the miserable prehistory of humanity. In the very era of the technologies that gave rise to functionalism, the Situationist architects, for their part, are searching to create new frames of comportment free of banality as well as of all the old taboos. The Situationist architects are thus absolutely opposed to the construction and even to the preservation of religious buildings with which they find themselves in direct competition. Unitary urbanism merges objectively with the interests of a comprehensive subversion.

Just as unitary urbanism cannot be reduced to questions of housing, it is also distinct from aesthetic problems. It opposes the passive spectacle, the principle of our culture (where the organization of the spectacle extends all the more scandalously the more the means of human intervention increase). In light of the fact that today cities themselves are presented as lamentable spectacles, a supplement to the museums for tourists driven around in glassed-in buses, U.U. envisages the urban environment as the terrain of a game in which one participates.

Unitary urbanism is not ideally separated from the current terrain of the cities. It is developed out of the experience of this terrain and based on existing constructions. As a result it is just as important that we exploit the existing settings—through the affirmation of a ludic urban space such as is revealed by *dérive*—as it is that we construct completely unknown ones. This interpenetration (employment of the present city and construction of the future city) entails the deployment of architectural appropriation [*détournement*].

Unitary urbanism is opposed to the temporal fixation of cities. It leads instead to the advocacy of a permanent transformation, an accelerated movement of the abandonment and reconstruction of the city in temporal and at times spatial terms. We are thus able to envisage making use of the climatic conditions in which two major architectural civilizations arose—in Cambodia and in southeast Mexico—in order to construct moving cities in the jungle. The new quarters of such a city could be constructed increasingly toward the West (which would be gradually reclaimed as one goes along) while to the same extent the East would be abandoned to the overgrowth of tropical vegetation, thereby creating on its own layers of gradual transition between the modern city and wild nature. This city, pursued by the forest, would offer not only the unsurpassable zone of *dérive* that would take shape behind it; it would also be a marriage with nature more audacious than the attempts by Frank Lloyd Wright. Furthermore, it would have the advantage of a *mis-en-scène* of passing time over a social space condemned to creative renovation.

Unitary urbanism is opposed to the fixation of people at certain points of a city. It is the foundation for a civilization of leisure and of play. One should note that in the shackles of the current economic system, technology has been used to further multiply the pseudo-games of passivity and social atrophy (television) while the new forms of ludic participation also rendered possible by the same technology are regulated by all sorts of police: amateur radio operators, for example, are reduced to technological boy scouts.

Since the Situationist experiment of *dérive* is simultaneously a means of study of, and a game in, the urban milieu, it is already on the track of unitary urbanism. If U.U. refuses to separate theory from practice, this is not only in order to promote construction (or research on construction by means of models) along with theoretical ideas. The point of such a refusal is above all not to separate the direct, collectively experienced ludic use of the city from the aspect of urbanism that involves construction. The real games and emotions in today's cities are inseparable from the projects of U.U. just as later the realized projects of U.U. should not be isolated from games and emotions that will arise within these accomplishments. *Dérives* that the Situationist International is committed to undertake in the spring of 1960 in Amsterdam using quite powerful means of transportation and telecommunication are envisaged as both an objective study of the city and as a communication game.[9] In fact, beyond its essential lessons, *dérive* furnishes only knowledge that is very precisely dated. In a few years, the construction or demolition of houses, the relocation of micro-societies and of fashions, will suffice to change a city's network of superficial attractions—a very encouraging phenomenon for the moment when we will come to establish an active link between *dérive* and Situationist urban construction. Until then, the urban milieu will certainly change on its own, anarchically, ultimately rendering obsolete *dérives* whose conclusions could not be translated into conscious transformations of this milieu. But the first lesson of *dérive* is its own status as a game.

We are only at the beginning of urban civilization; it is up to us to bring it about ourselves using the pre-existing conditions as our point of departure. All the stories that we live, our life's *dérive*, are characterized by the search for—or the lack of—an overarching construction. The transformation of the environment calls forth new emotional states that are first experienced passively and then, with heightened consciousness, give way to constructive reactions. London was the first urban result of the industrial revolution and English literature of the nineteenth century bears witness to an increasing awareness of the problems of atmosphere and of the qualitatively different

---

9   For a description of the Amsterdam *dérive*, see the final section of "Die Welt als Labyrinth" (1960), trans. Gerardo Denís, in *Theory of the* Dérive *and Other Situationist Writings on the City*, 98–99. [Ed.]

possibilities in a large urban area. The love between Thomas de Quincey and poor Ann, separated by chance and searching for one another without ever coming upon each other "through the mighty labyrinths of London; perhaps even within a few feet of each other ..." marks a turning point in the slow historical evolution of the passions.[10] In fact, Thomas de Quincey's real life from 1804 to 1812 makes him a precursor of *dérive*:

> Seeking ambitiously for a *northwest passage*, instead of circumnavigating all the capes and headlands I had doubled in my outward voyage, I came suddenly upon such knotty problems of alleys ... I could almost have believed, at times, that I must be the first discoverer of some of these *terrae incognitae*, and doubted, whether they had yet been laid down in the modern charts of London.[11]

Toward the end of the century this sensation is so frequently expressed in novelistic writing that Robert Louis Stevenson presents a character who, in London at night, is astonished "to walk for such a long time in such a complex décor without encountering even the slightest shadow of an adventure."[12] The urbanists of the twentieth century will have to construct adventures.

The simplest Situationist act would consist in abolishing all the memories of the *employment of time* of our epoch. It is an epoch that, up until now, has lived far below its means.

THE AMSTERDAM DECLARATION[13]

CONSTANT AND GUY DEBORD

This is a preparatory text for the third S.I. conference, held in Munich in April 1959. In it, unitary urbanism is deemed the Situationists' "minimum program," and the conditions of its application are specified. Unitary urbanism is considered to be above all a dynamic approach not only to the traditional problems of architecture (as defined, for example, by functionalist manifestoes like the Athens Charter*), but to the style of living itself; as such, it is less a utopian program for the post-revolutionary future than a task to be undertaken in the present as a step toward "the development of the construction—both joyful and solemn—of situations of a freer society."*

---

10   Thomas de Quincey, *Confessions of an English Opium Eater* (1821) (Harmondsworth, U.K.: Penguin Books, 1971), 64. [Ed.]
11   de Quincey, *Confessions of an English Opium Eater* (1821), 81; first emphasis in citation not in original text. [Ed.]
12   Robert Louis Stevenson, *New Arabian Nights* (1882) (Boston: Shambhala Publications, 1986). [Ed.]
13   *Internationale situationniste* no. 2 (December 1958): 31–32. [Ed.]

The eleven points below, offering a minimum definition of Situationist action, are to be discussed as a preparatory text for the third S.I. conference.

1st. Situationists must at every opportunity resist retrograde ideologies and forces, in culture and everywhere that the question of the meaning of life is expressed.

2nd. No one should consider his or her membership in the S.I. as a simple agreement of principle; this implies that the most important part of the activity of all participants must correspond with perspectives elaborated in common and with the necessity for disciplined action—as much in practice as in public stands.

3rd. The possibility of a unitary and collective creation is already foretold by the disintegration of individual arts. The S.I. cannot shelter any attempt at renewal of these arts.

4th. The S.I.'s minimum program is the testing of complete settings, which must be extended to a unitary urbanism, and the search for new compartments in conjunction with these settings.

5th. Unitary urbanism is defined in the complex and ongoing activity that consciously re-creates humanity's environment according to the most developed conceptions in all fields.

6th. The solution to problems of housing, traffic, and recreation may only be considered in accordance with social, psychological, and artistic perspectives working to achieve the same proposed synthesis, at the level of the style of living.

7th. Unitary urbanism, independently of any aesthetic consideration, is the fruit of a collective creativity of a new sort, and the development of this creative intellect is the preliminary condition of a unitary urbanism.

8th. The creation of ambiances favorable to this development is the immediate task of today's creators.

9th. All means are usable, on condition that they serve a unitary action. The coordination of artistic and scientific means must lead to their total fusion.

10th. The construction of a situation is the building of a transient micro-ambiance and of the play of events for a unique moment of a few persons' lives. It is inseparable from the construction of a general, relatively more lasting ambiance, in unitary urbanism.

11th. A constructed situation is a means of approaching unitary urbanism, and unitary urbanism is the indispensable basis of the development of the construction—both joyful and solemn—of situations of a freer society.

Amsterdam, November 10th, 1958

5.

The Architectural Interlude

EXCERPT FROM "EXPERIMENTAL UTOPIA: TOWARD A NEW URBANISM"[1]

HENRI LEFEBVRE

[…] Consciously or spontaneously, the project's authors have employed the investigative procedures of programmatic thought, which operates upon virtual (possible) objects and compares them with experience because it wishes to make the imagined or conceived object vanish into practice—in a word, to realize it. This thought wishes to invent forms, but concrete forms. It does not therefore dispense with an appeal to the imagination, but is provoked and verified by practical givens. The method employed is then that of *imaginary variations* on themes and exigencies defined by the real as understood in the broadest sense: by the problems posed by reality and by the virtualities held within it. This method navigates between two dangers; it avoids two impasses. On one hand, it avoids the purely empirical (or what believes itself to be the purely empirical) finding that is content with recording and then extrapolating what is accomplished when it is doing its best to conceive the possible. On the other hand, it avoids a priori construction, in the present case the abstract utopia that attends to the ideal city without connection to definite situations. The method thus navigates between pure practicality and pure theorization. To designate these operations of rational thought, to employ them in a coherent fashion, do we not need to introduce a vocabulary, concepts, and a methodology? We could give the name "transduction" to reasoning irreducible to deduction and induction, reasoning that constructs a virtual object from information about reality and a definite problematic (the eminent information theorist

---

1 *Revue française de sociologie*, no. 3 (July–September 1961) 191–198. [Ed.]

Benoit Mandelbrot, moreover, employs this term in an analogous sense).[2] We could also give the name "experimental utopia" to the exploration of human possibilities, with the help of the image and the imagination, accompanied by a ceaseless criticism and a ceaseless reference to the given problematic in the "real." Experimental utopia exceeds the customary use of hypotheses in the social sciences.

INAUGURAL REPORT TO THE MUNICH CONFERENCE[3]
CONSTANT

Since the experiment by the Lettrists, around 1953, of a game in comportments allowed by the current urban milieu, the notion of a conscious construction of the surrounding milieu—in relation to a life, and its changing habits—has led to the idea of a unitary urbanism. If we are speaking of urbanism here, it must be understood that the conception of a conscious creation, and its relation to a higher form of life, spur us to break definitively with standard notions of urbanism.

If we are to begin studying and putting into practice a creative change of the urban milieu, linked to a qualitative change of comportment and way of life, it will be a question of a true collective creation, at the level of art.

Current conditions within culture—the disintegration of individual arts and the impossibility of renewal or prolongation of these arts—have produced a creative void that could work to the advantage of our endeavor. The disappearance of traditional artistic forms and the gradual regulation of social life entail a growing lack of ludic possibilities in everyday life. Our refusal of this state of affairs not only drives us to look for new play conditions, but also compels us to reconsider the whole problem of culture, to finally arrive at a ludic general theory and a conscious practice of the construction of ambiances.

We know that collective work is a necessity for the realization of our ideas, and we are counting on the creative dissatisfaction of the most advanced present-day artists, a dissatisfaction that links us together. Creation only exists within our perspectives.

The idea of a unitary urbanism had been drawn up on one hand by experiments like *dérive* and psychogeography, invented and practiced by the Lettrists; and on the other, by research into construction guided by a few modern architects and sculptors. On both sides, the need to reach the planning of

---

2 Cf. *Lecture de l'expérience* (Paris: Presses Universitaires de France, 1955), 43, especially "psychological transductors."
3 *Internationale situationniste* no. 3 (December 1959): 25–27. [Ed.]

THE ARCHITECTURAL INTERLUDE 107

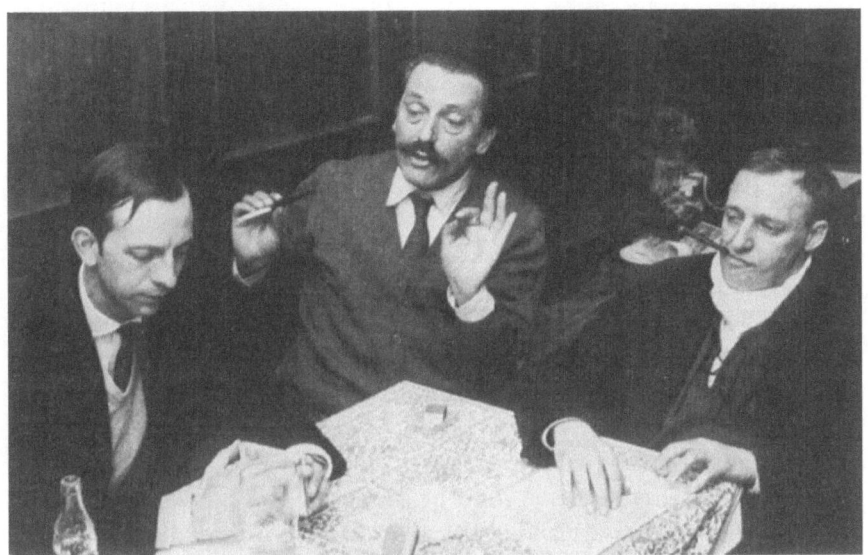

Fig.5.2.1 Munich Conference of the Situationist International, April 1960; from left to right: Constant, Pinot Gallizio, and Asger Jorn.

complete settings, the integral unity of comportment and surroundings, led to a common action.

In 1958, in a declaration made in Amsterdam, we established a few points by trying to define unitary urbanism and our current task in light of this perspective.[4] This declaration will propose the testing of complete settings, which must be extended to a unitary urbanism, and the search for new comportments in connection with these settings, as the minimum program of the Situationist International. Therefore, according to the Amsterdam Declaration, we should consider the Situationist program as having failed if we cannot carry out a practical activity in this domain.

A Situationist praxis within the perspective of a unitary urbanism must be our first task, and the principal goal of our current meeting. We must not leave each other without having examined in common the possibilities that already exist for practical experiments.

Unitary urbanism, states the Amsterdam Declaration, is defined in the complicated and ongoing activity that consciously re-creates humanity's environment according to the most developed conceptions in all fields. This ongoing activity must not be transferred to a future more favorable than the present, but it is our immediate task to set in motion this activity by the efficient execution of our program. Within this program we can distinguish three tasks that we can undertake right away, or that we have already begun:

Firstly: The creation of ambiances favorable to unitary urbanism's promotion. We must tirelessly denounce the decay of individual arts, and oblige artists to make their choice and to change profession;

Secondly: We must carry out a collective creative work by forming teams and putting forward actual projects;

Thirdly: Collective creation must be supported by ongoing study of the problems that we envisage and of the solutions that we will discover.

The architect, like other workers in our endeavor, is facing the inevitability of a change of profession: he [sic] will no longer be a builder of forms alone, but a builder of complete ambiances. What makes contemporary architecture so boring is its principally formal preoccupation. Architecture's problem is no longer the function/expression opposition; that question has been surpassed. While using existing forms, and creating new forms, the architect's principal concern must become the effect that all this will have on the inhabitants' comportment and existence. All architecture will thus belong to a more extensive and more complete activity, and finally, architecture—like other present-day arts—will disappear to the benefit of this unitary activity.

The new urbanism will find its first animators in the poetic field and that of theater, among practitioners of the plastic arts and architecture,

---

4 Constant and Guy Debord, "The Amsterdam Declaration" (1958), trans. in this volume, 103–104. [Ed.]

within the ranks of advanced urbanists and sociologists. However, none of the forme—even while perfectly collaborating in teams—will be capable of entirely realizing our vision. The assistance of everyone, of all those who will live and build this life that we consider the very matter of future creation, will be required.

If we are putting forward such ambitious perspectives as those to be introduced, this is not to say that we want to limit ourselves to predictions and prophecies. That idealist attitude is the greatest danger that we run at the present time. It makes us run the risk of missing the transition to practice, which is essential for advancing.

The life that we are currently leading must already make plans for all the possible conditions for the development and the realization of our ideas. However, unitary urbanism is a work of culture, but an ongoing activity, and this activity began at the very moment when the notion of a unitary urbanism was born. We also declare that unitary urbanism has been materializing for years. Everything we have considered—the *dérive* experiments, the psychogeographical studies and maps, the models of ambiance—has contributed from the start to its launch. We will hasten its course through appropriate measures.

To this end, we have agreed on the foundation, in Amsterdam, of a research bureau for unitary urbanism, which will be charged with carrying out teamwork and the study of practical solutions. This work must strictly stand out from teamwork as it already exists among individual contemporary architects, collective creation being for us not a unity, but rather an infinite quantity of variable elements. The research bureau for unitary urbanism must as a first stage arrive at elaborated projects, grounded in reality, which, while illustrating our ideas, must at the same time constitute the micro-elements of what unitary urbanism is to become.

The bureau's activity will succeed to the extent that we are able to attract qualified collaborators who understand the spirit of our enquiries, and to the extent that we are able to carry out projects that will test the efficacy of our chosen route.

CONTRIBUTION TO *FORUM* SPECIAL ISSUE ON FUSION OF THE ARTS AND "INTEGRATION? ... OF WHAT?" (1959)[5]

CONSTANT

For a half century, the best and most advanced artists have posed the problem of the integration of the arts into everyday life, and a number of theories and experimentations have been devoted to it. Nevertheless, during this entire period, we have not been able to progress toward the realization of integration. The reason for this is the impossibility of fusing two phenomena that historically have developed in a contradictory fashion: the creative poverty of contemporary industrial designers enslaved to industry shows it. A complete change of social structure and of artistic creativity must come before integration.

As is well known, the Situationists believe that individual arts, because of their historical function, are unable to be integrated into everyday life such as it appears today. The revolutionary destruction of these arts that has been taking place for a few decades is a direct consequence of this fact. The Situationists oppose to this the idea of unitary urbanism that, as a collective creation merging all aspects of life, can recapture the social and psychological role of the dying arts. In the present phase, the production of artworks can only be of value as preparation for unitary urbanism; outside this perspective, any attempt at integration or synthesis is doomed to fail in advance. Consequently, explaining what unitary urbanism is is the sole valid content of a publication on the integration of life and art.

The cultural crisis that began during the second half of the nineteenth century has reached a dramatic threshold.

The arts have been withered on account of the individualism upon which they rest. Architecture and the construction of cities have been reduced to simple utilitarian activities deprived of all artistic meaning.

Neither the retreat into ornamentation at the beginning of the twentieth century nor the aesthetic dictatorship of industry has produced the much-awaited cultural renewal. And the monstrous coupling of functional architecture and the individual arts so discussed today has not demonstrated any viability.

The integration of art and life, upon which a culture rests, cannot be realized with traditional means. A revolution in our existence and our

---

5   Originally published in *Forum* no. 6 (1959), this translation made from the French version published in *Archives situationnistes*, vol. 1, ed. Luc Mercier (Paris: Contre-Moule and Editions Librairie Parallèles, 1997), 25–28. [Ed.]

thought is required first. The construction of new situations is our first, most indispensable task.

These new situations can become the nuclei of a new construction of our environment. The separated arts would no longer have any role to play in it. Our life and the environment within which it unfolds can only make up an indissoluble unity, which merges everything that at present we collect here and there in a still fragmentary fashion.

A unitary urbanism . . .

Unitary urbanism's point of departure is the changeableness of our aspirations and our activities. We know that neither eternal truth nor absolute beauty exist and that, for this reason, ideal form does not exist. Form that is in constant modulation and in agreement with the unceasingly changing aspects of our existence, such as we will produce it. The environment in which we live influences our activity, but reciprocally this environment is a product of our creative activity.

This is why we must arrive at a conscious production of our environment with all the means that give rise to it.

Integration is thus the condition for unitary urbanism, which we imagine as a dynamic style of living, characterized by the perpetual creation and recreation of our environment. Unitary urbanism comprises more than a creation, it is the culture of creative activity itself, in which no stagnation is possible.

It constitutes more than the integration of arts and technology with urbanism, it is the enlarging of the notion of urbanism to a universal art of a completely new type.

It constitutes more than an art, it is the collective expression of a new society.

It is not a frozen expression, like present-day individual arts, but an ongoing game with life, inspired by the changing events that we ourselves will provoke.

UNITARY URBANISM[6]

CONSTANT

TRANSLATED BY ROBYN DE JONG-DALZIEL

The postwar years have witnessed tremendous activity in the field of urban development: villages have become cities, cities have turned into metropolises, metropolises have spread into such immense conglomerations that people have started devising ways of limiting the concentration of buildings, of decentralizing the city. In the underdeveloped regions of Asia, Africa, and South America, industrialization has entailed the erection of a growing number of wholly new cities. But even in the already industrialized countries of Western Europe and North America, the continuing mechanization of life on one hand, and population growth on the other, have resulted in a drastic change in the appearance of the big city. The huge influence over everyday life that this state of affairs gives to urbanism accords it a central place in contemporary culture. Or rather: causes it to play a key role in the cultural crisis that characterizes the present age. For although urbanism has become a more important factor in culture than ever before, it cannot be said to have enriched everyday life or culture. On the contrary, we must begin by stating that the influence urbanism currently exerts on people's lives appears to be of a negative character, that the cultural crisis has intensified and that urbanism has contributed to this, that the great deficiency of culture, of social life, is felt more acutely than ever. I would even go so far as to claim that the continued existence of culture currently depends on a revolutionary intervention in our everyday environment and in our way of life. For one of the prime causes of the cultural crisis is the manifest discrepancy between the prevailing way of life and humanity's biological development. The city, as the foremost exponent of this way of life, provides the clearest illustration of this discrepancy.

The failure of modern urbanists can be attributed to their opportunism, their passive attitude to the problems confronting them, their uncritical deference to an obsolete cultural convention, to the existing image of society. What nowadays counts for urbanism confines itself to the more or less aesthetic solution of current socio-economic problems; for the most part housing and traffic problems. For pragmatic reasons, that is for the sake of a quick provisional solution, urbanists isolate these problems from the totality of social life, they see them as detached from the cultural issue. The result is that urbanists lag behind their times, that they are forever out of step with developments. For example, in looking for solutions to the

---

6   Lecture delivered at the Stedelijk Museum, Amsterdam, December 20, 1960. Originally published in Mark Wigley, *Constant's New Babylon: The Hyper-Architecture of Desire* (Rotterdam: 010 Publishers, 1998). [Ed.]

housing issue, urbanists almost invariably take the family as their starting-point. Yet the family has long ceased to be the most important binding factor in society, and changing morals are leading to the formation of new social groupings that are unable to assert themselves adequately in today's urban environment. This must certainly be seen as one aspect of the anarchism of today's youth, of the gangs of disaffected young people prowling our city centers, etc. Another function of urbanism, traffic, is so dominated by the needs of the private car that no consideration is given to the possibility, indeed, one can already say the necessity, of socializing traffic. After New York, Paris too is finding itself forced to close off large sections of the city center, perhaps even the entire center, to private traffic, and to replace it with a dense network of small public transport vehicles. While urbanists continue to attach exaggerated importance to the interests of private cars, Paris bus stops have in recent years carried a request to motorists from the Préfecture de police urging them to make more use of the buses so as to ease traffic congestion in the city center. But the most telling example of the extent to which the urbanists' pragmatism has distanced them from the reality of life, and stands in the way of a creative approach to urbanism, is undoubtedly the Athens Charter. In this declaration drawn up in 1933 by the CIAM (with Le Corbusier in the lead) and since then neither updated nor amplified, urban planning is summed up in four functions: living, working, transport, and recreation, with total disregard for everything to do with culture. Here is a very clear demonstration of the urbanists' deferential attitude to the mechanistic and commercial tendencies dominating this age. Here is the proof that today's urbanists are indeed to blame for the failure of the modern city as a human habitat, for the disappearance of a social space in which a new culture could arise.

Are they perhaps aware of this? Is this why they are so intent on making up for the huge deficiency of the built environment with green belts and landscaping? Do they imagine that human beings, whom they have helped to rob of their living space, are to be fobbed off with a few bits and pieces of pseudo-nature? Where does this idea of the "garden city" come from anyway?

When we examine the origins of this idea, we find that it is connected with such phenomena as the reform movement, vegetarianism, naturism, nudism, and so on, that it developed as a nineteenth-century reaction to mechanization, a manifestation of fear of the machine. A certain Ebenezer Howard thought he could curb the pauperization of the proletariat in the slums of the emerging English industrial cities with his garden allotments movement. This was the time when groups of laborers sought to defend their daily bread, which they earned with their own hands, by smashing machinery to smithereens. The time, too, of the new art, *art nouveau* or Jugendstil, which had its roots in the utopian socialism of John Ruskin and William Morris, which felt compelled to hark back to a past that had more to offer than the machine. But even though the machine has not let itself be checked, even though it has survived the ideas of Morris and Ruskin, even though it is presently opening up unlimited perspectives for humanity, for culture, the garden city idea lives on. Not Ebenezer Howard's garden city, however: the nineteenth-century rural garden city degenerated under the pressure of events into the traffic city, embellished with parks and trees, where social contacts became increasingly difficult, where human beings grew lonely. All that remains of the garden city in our own day are traffic-free enclaves, islands in a sea of traffic where the pedestrian leads a legally protected but languishing existence, comparable to that of the North American Indians on their reservations. What is understood by "garden city" is a mere fiction! In reality the modern urbanist regards the city as a gigantic center of production, geared to the efficient transport of workers and goods, to the accommodation of people and the storage of wares, to industrial and commercial activity. The rest, that is to say creativity, life, is optional and comes under the heading of recreation and leisure activities.

The fact that the constant growth in leisure time in this age of automation poses an acute problem, that young people are protesting more and more vociferously against the interminable boredom of present-day life, must in itself be sufficient reason for us to overhaul those famous urban planning functions and to resist a view of the city as a machine for living, a "machine à habiter" as Le Corbusier put it. Human beings are more than machine fodder; life is more than well-oiled participation in the production process. The slavish existence of living, working, and recreation cannot possibly constitute the starting-point for building our living environment, the starting-point for a creative urbanism. These functions, however essential they may be, are subordinate to the all-embracing function of life: creativity, the urge to manifest oneself, to turn life into a unique event, to realize life as such. Urbanism is not industrial design, the city is not a functional object, aesthetically "sound" or otherwise; the city is an artificial landscape built by human beings in which the adventure of our life unfolds. Rather than comparing it to a workman's tool, therefore, it would be better to compare it to an artist's plaything. But a plaything is not really appropriate either because the city is, or should be, an active and integral part of our game of life. I deliberately refer to the "game of life" here—thinking of Huizinga's *Homo Ludens*—rather than to "culture," because culture could easily be misunderstood; it has already been too much compromised by the disintegration of the traditional cultural forms of recent centuries and the attendant phenomenon of mass pseudo-culture. Literature, painting, music—these typically individual forms of creative play—are in the process of losing their meaning, together with the individualism that gave rise to them. But where should one expect new cultural forms to come from in this century of "massification," if not from the masses—lacking traditions, neither heir to worn-out cultural patterns nor prey to delusions of superiority? The city has produced the masses, only the masses can give shape to the city.

Who exactly are the masses? Are they the nineteenth-century proletariat, underpaid and dulled by mind-numbing labor and with nothing to lose but their chains? Or are they the people of the future, robbed of their occupations by automation and cracking up from boredom, who are already a source of serious worry for sociologists? No, if we wish neither to resign ourselves to the deficiencies of the present, nor to abandon ourselves to fear of the future, we must rely on the enormous creative potential that still lies dormant in the masses. We must see the so-called masses as those who have succeeded in defeating nature, who have won unprecedented social freedom for themselves, who possess virtually unlimited resources. What I am going to propose as an alternative to the functional city where culture, a new culture, has no chance, is based on faith in humanity, in these elusive masses to whom everybody seems to feel superior but who are nonetheless destined to be the bearers of the coming culture. Culture can no longer rely on the exception.

The new culture will either be a mass culture, or there will be no culture at all. It is the masses, the burgeoning masses, who are becoming increasingly influential, who hold the future in their hands and who are also the main victims of the current state of affairs; it is these masses, to whom we all belong, who must achieve the unity between lifestyle and environment that is absolutely essential for a new culture—for unitary urbanism.

What is unitary urbanism? Unitary urbanism is neither urbanism, nor art, nor style; nor does it correspond to concepts like integration and the synthesis of cultural forms, which are much discussed nowadays, not even when this integration concerns the totality of social life. For this integration presupposes the presence in contemporary culture of useful practices, of directly applicable concepts, like architecture, poetry, social ties, moral principles.

Yet there is nothing to integrate, because there is nothing! Which is why at this stage I would prefer to define unitary urbanism as a very complicated, very changeable, ongoing activity, a deliberate intervention in the praxis of daily life and in the daily environment; an intervention aimed at bringing our lives into lasting harmony with our real needs and with the new possibilities that will arise and that will in turn transform these needs. So I am not simply opposing a different aesthetic, a different kind of "form-giving" to static, material functionalism, to the aesthetic of the modern city. Unitary urbanism is flexible, it respects our freedom to change our way of life, it adapts to every situation, to every need, to every technical, geographical, or psychological possibility, it is the objectification of the creative urge, the collectivization of the artwork, the materialization of a dynamic lifestyle. A lifestyle, in other words, which recognizes no goal in life, which is not intent on giving life a meaning, but which makes life itself the goal, which looks for the fulfillment of this life in daily praxis, a lifestyle, which aims to be the creation of our life. This conception of life is essential to unitary urbanism, just as the conception that places the meaning of life beyond this life, in the super-terrestrial, the abstract, is essential to that fragment of human history that is determined by the struggle for material existence and that seems to be nearing its end.

There are consequently two distinct aspects to unitary urbanism: a transformation of our habits, or rather of our way of life or lifestyle, and, connected with this, a profound change in the way our material environment is produced, a dynamic urbanism. Since the first-mentioned condition is bound up with a process that takes time, it follows that the second cannot be realized immediately either. Hence, the New Babylon project, which you will have an opportunity to see after the interval, is an imaginary project; it anticipates history, it is a futuristic project; it is based on a desirable course of history and is therefore also in a sense a utopian project. Nonetheless, I prefer to call it a realistic project because it distances itself from the present condition that has lost touch with reality, and because it is founded on what is technically feasible, on what is desirable from a human viewpoint, on what is inevitable from a social viewpoint. Because it is a reaction to a declining culture and a response to facts that signal a crucial change in the notion of culture.

Let us take a closer look at these facts in relation to urbanism. Human beings inhabit the earth's surface and exploit it; they change the earth from nature into culture. What are the circumstances under which they currently operate; what is the result, up to now, of humanity's presence, of its interventions? Where will those interventions lead? If we calculate the average habitability of all points on the earth's surface, the correlation between nature and human habitation, which so dominates contemporary urbanism, presents a far less attractive picture than when considered exclusively from the relatively favorable climatological and geographical conditions prevailing in a densely populated, highly industrialized region like Western Europe. This picture becomes even less attractive if we take account of climate, of seasonal change, of weather conditions and natural phenomena injurious to human beings. When we try to express the habitability of the earth—under natural conditions and during one seasonal cycle—as a percentage of the total surface area, we are forced to conclude that this figure bears absolutely no relation to the size of the earth's population and that it is most certainly disastrously out of step with the number of people estimated to be populating the earth in 50, 100, or 200 years' time. This disparity already manifests itself today and under the current manner of inhabiting the earth, in the overpopulation of climatologically favorable regions. But faced with the prospect of a world population estimated to exceed 7 billion a century from now, faced too with the prospect of needing to exploit the earth's surface more intensively in order to provide all these people with the basic necessities of life, we can no longer restrict ourselves to these few regions when it concerns urbanism, that is to say, when it concerns not just housing but the very lives of these multitudes. Yet human beings are not simply faced with the necessity of inhabiting less attractive regions; they also have the means to make these regions habitable, to render themselves independent of nature.

The world has acquired a new dimension; nature's role is played out; nature now is simply raw material, controlled by human beings and used in accordance with their needs. And these needs can no longer be met by nature alone; technology already furnishes us with material conditions that are far superior to natural conditions; we are already completely dependent on technology for the bare necessities. And, owing to the force of circumstances, our needs are continually increasing, not just quantitatively, but also qualitatively, in the same measure as our connection with nature is declining. Technology replaces nature, technology becomes nature, becomes the medium, the sense by which we interpret nature. Not only are human beings, with the help of technology, preparing to leave the earth's surface and to go adventuring in outer space; they are even roaming, flying over, the earth's surface itself, in every direction, without omitting a single spot. And wherever they go, which is to say everywhere, nature gives way to technology. As such, the living space of each individual is getting bigger and bigger, their radius of action is extending further and further afield, the tracks they leave behind them form an increasingly complicated pattern. Human beings are leaving the closed community for a nomadic existence that will cover ever-larger areas. Their existence is becoming more adventurous, their impressions more varied, their horizon wider, their need for change, for excitement, greater. Should we deduce from all this, as some urbanists are doing, that the huge urban concentration has had its day? Those who think this forget that population growth keeps pace with the increase in the radius of action of each individual, and that when the inevitable saturation point is reached, individuals will be forced to indulge their greatly increased urge for expansion within a limited area. This will entail the formation of enormous, perpetually expanding conglomerations that, to a limited extent, must nonetheless permit a tremendous spatial expansion.

Taken to its logical conclusion, this means that the city might eventually expand to cover the entire surface of the earth, but also that this surface will have to be far more intensively used. What we lose in geometrical space, we must recover in the form of psychological space. By intensifying the use of space we will be able to increase the living space of every individual, despite the increase in the number of individuals. Where, in such an intensive exploitation of the earth's surface, is the contrast between city and landscape; where can we still expect to find untrammeled nature; where is the outdoor life? Faced with the certainty that nature cannot remain inviolate, we must use the means at our disposal not simply to replace nature, but to surpass her. Our planning must even now take account of a total exploitation of the earth's surface, with unlimited development. But also with an unrestricted freedom to move around, with an undisturbed (and undisturbing), unlimited increase in traffic, on the ground and in the air.

Faced with this prospect, even the prosaic problems of the urbanist—traffic and housing—call for revolutionary solutions. But an even more fundamental and all-embracing question is: how are all these people going to live? How will they be able to express themselves, manifest themselves, develop; in short, what possibilities will they have to realize their lives? Before looking at this question in more detail, we must first mention a factor that is crucial to any attempt to answer it: the so-called second industrial revolution, automation.

It is generally acknowledged that automation (by which we mean the mechanization of all routine work, including regulation and control of mechanical processes), the systematic automation of production, will lead to a colossal increase in so-called free time. Fear of the social consequences of this increased leisure time is one of the reasons why automation is progressing at a slower pace than is technically feasible. We may nonetheless assume that automation will not only remain a technical possibility, but that it will, within the foreseeable future, become a social fact, and urbanism should even now be addressing this fact. Whatever the case, the development of the robot to perform slave labor (Norbert Wiener compares the electronic machine to the imported slaves of antiquity) will sooner or later bring humanity, which is to say the masses, unprecedented freedom, an undreamt-of opportunity for the free disposal of time, for the free realization of life. For it goes without saying that it will no longer be possible to speak of "free time" once essential work is so much in the minority, and so much less monotonous, that it is no longer experienced as an onerous duty. Thus, we also reject all theorizing about the use of leisure that springs from a worn-out ethic stating it a duty to "earn one's daily bread by the sweat of one's brow." When a major part, the greatest portion, of our life is no longer taken up with non-creative work, it no longer makes sense to speak of free time as if it were a matter of spare moments that have to be spent one way or another. For it is in *this* time that the largest part of our life will be realized: this time will *be* our life.

Life is activity. The freedom won as a result of the disappearance of routine work is a freedom to act. Obviously, it will be a creative activity that replaces work. The fulfillment of life lies in creativity. We do not of course see this creativity in the same sense as a contemporary artwork. The individual work of art, seen from the vantage point of an unsatisfied, unfulfilled life, represents higher things, the more fulfilled, the exceptional. The manifestation is based on permanence, on the ideal of eternity. Unsatisfied by the existing situation, it tries to drown it out, to surpass it. The lived artwork, in the sense of unitary urbanism, is exactly the opposite: it exists in time, it is the activation of the temporary, the emergent and transitory, the changeable, the volatile, the variable, the immediately fulfilling and satisfying.

Seen from the vantage point of unitary urbanism, the traditional artwork is no more than a consolation, a surrogate that is no longer necessary. It is quite evident, therefore, that existing cultural forms have no role whatsoever to play in the realization of unitary urbanism. Returning to urbanism, one can not ask: which urban function is essential for the development that we foresee, which urban form corresponds to the changes society is undergoing, how does this unity of lifestyle and environment, unitary urbanism, come about? Answering these questions leads us to a previously neglected function of urbanism that unitary urbanism makes its chief and most characteristic theme: social space. While it is true that in recent years, and particularly in America, social space has been turned into a study—ecology—this study has confined itself to registering facts, to analyzing social space, insofar as it still exists in today's cities. Ecology is a static method that attempts to derive the laws of social space from statistical data. Ecology studies the conglomeration in its present form as if it were a quintessential rather than a fortuitous form of human cohabitation. But ecology takes no account of the fact that the city shapes its inhabitants every bit as much as the inhabitants shape their city. It takes no account of the fact that people are to a large degree determined by the environment in which they live, it disregards the psychological influence exerted by the environment.

For unitary urbanism, however, all this is of overwhelming importance. Indeed, unitary urbanism goes even further: having noted the psychological influence exerted by the environment, it resolves consciously to apply this influence, to use the environment to psychological effect, ultimately to achieve an interplay between environment and life. Which brings us to psychogeography. The concept of psychogeography distinguishes itself from ecology by its creative character. Psychogeography does not merely record facts, it also tries to identify and explain the unconscious influences exerted by the urban atmosphere and ultimately to use them as a means of activating our environment. It turns these influences into an artistic medium by which our environment is created. As an example of the fact that the psychological atmosphere is independent of the ecological definition of an urban district, I mention here St. Germain de Prés. The atmosphere of this bourgeois quarter of Paris was so profoundly altered by a small group of intellectuals, the so-called existentialists, that it acquired international fame and even became a tourist attraction. For ecology this phenomenon is of only minor interest because the inhabitants remain the same and all the action takes place in the streets and in the cafés that are dominated by individuals from other quarters. But if the built environment is included among the psychological influences on ambiance, it becomes clear that unitary urbanism has some pretty powerful resources at its disposal in its construction of social space.

Let us take a closer look at this concept of "social space." Historically, the street was more than a mere traffic artery. Its additional function, which may even have been more important than its role as thoroughfare, was as a collective living space where all the public events—markets, festivals, fairs, political demonstrations—took place, as well as encounters and contacts between smaller numbers of individuals, in short, all those activities that do not belong to the more intimate, private domain. The inn and the café, which sometimes spilled over into the street, were continuations of this collective space, public places where people were able to get away from the traffic on the street. The tremendous increase in traffic robbed the street of this social function. As a final refuge there remained the café, but the street itself became a traffic route and thus a sharp dividing line between isolated units of housing. This might perhaps account for the cultural significance of the café in the last century. The overriding importance that unitary urbanism attaches to social space is related to the role of the frequent personal contacts that it considers vital for culture, for the mass culture that is to come. The realization of life in the sense of unitary urbanism depends to a large extent on the place of social space in urban planning. It is here, after all, that most of the events that influence and determine daily life take place. It is here that a deliberate intervention in the material environment has most effect, only here can this intervention become a collective game aimed at the creation of our environment.

The cultural significance of social space makes it necessary to isolate this function from the purely utilitarian functions, especially those of traffic and production, to which social space has been sacrificed in today's industrial cities. The creation and maintenance of an extensive social space is, given the prospect of mass culture, the prospect of more free time—or rather a freer disposal of life—given also the prospect of an as yet unlimited increase in population and traffic, an absolute prerequisite. This is why I based New Babylon on a strict separation of traffic and industrial space on one hand and residential and social space on the other. This separation is vertical because I accepted the principle of a covered city, composed of layers and supported on *pilotis*, that leaves the ground level entirely free. The actual urban body containing living spaces and collectively used spaces is consequently raised above the ground, inaccessible to traffic, which for its part has 100% of the ground level at its disposal. Unconstrained by buildings, the traffic is free to take the shortest route, but visitors to the city will have to leave their vehicles and take one of the numerous elevators to the top. The factories, fully automated, are for the most part built underground. The plan of New Babylon reveals a decentralized, reticular structure consisting of an irregular stringing together of numerous sectors, each covering an area of 12 to 24 acres, which stretches for hundreds of kilometers in every direction and in which a population of on average 10 million people resides. Each sector consists of several levels topped by a flat roof that may contain a runway, a heliport, or sports fields. In view of their huge size, the levels are largely inaccessible to sunlight, so the interior of the city is artificially lit, ventilated, and air-conditioned. There is no attempt to effect a faithful imitation of nature, however; on the contrary, the technical facilities are deployed as powerful, ambiance-creating resources in the psychogeographical game played in the social space.

The typically linear structure of the plan means that inhabitants are never further than a few hundred yards from free, undeveloped space. Yet it is also possible to spend days, even weeks, traveling on foot through the endless expanse of the urban body, from space to space, from ambiance to ambiance, experiencing the adventure of New Babylon, finding accommodation in the residential precincts that are present in every sector; or traveling by vehicle at ground level from one quarter to another, traversing bits of landscape or passing beneath the city and coming up again somewhere else. Only 15% of the internal space of the urban body is taken up by permanent housing or hotels; the rest is social space. These social spaces must be thought of as gigantic halls, one above the other, hundreds of yards long, which can be subdivided into bigger and smaller spaces, varying in size from a room to a public square, highly diverse and differing in atmosphere. The movable walls are an active element of the psychogeographical game referred to earlier. They are used to construct veritable labyrinths of the most heterogeneous forms in which one finds special halls for radiophonic games, film games, psychoanalytical games, erotic games, games based on chance and on coincidence. Even a short trip through the social space of New Babylon is more fruitful than a long journey through the unified world we know. A long sojourn in New Babylon would surely have the effect of brainwashing, erasing all routine and custom. There are no customs in New Babylon; it is obvious that a culture based on a dynamic game with life, that takes this life itself as its theme, that uses the activities of life as raw material for creativity, precludes all routine, all custom, all convention. The New Babylonian culture is based on the ephemeral, on the transience of an experience, and the contrast between this and new experiences. For this reason, even living and traffic cease to be purely utilitarian functions and become part of the game. Living becomes rest, the pause after a climax, the bridge between two activities; traffic becomes a means of increasing the pace, of accelerating action, of intensifying the contrast. New Babylonians play a game of their own devising, against a backdrop they have designed themselves, together with their fellow city-dwellers. That is their life, therein lies their artistry. They realize that it is the non-utilitarian element of play that is important for life; their ethics are based on freedom.

As I was under no obligation to adapt my city to given socio-economic conditions, an obligation that has wrecked the plans of modern urbanists, I have reversed the roles and painted my city against the background of a society based on freedom. I have therefore taken no account of land subdivision, of land and home ownership, of the many speculative and commercial elements that play a role in the construction of a city. I have excluded everything that prevents a city from becoming a work of art. Nonetheless, New Babylon is just as real as any work of art. In essence it is the realization of an old dream, a dream that figures in all tendencies, all movements, all endeavors in the history of art this century, and which, in its simplest form, one could refer to by its Wagnerian name: *das Gesamtkunstwerk*, the total work of art.

DESCRIPTION OF THE YELLOW SECTOR[7]

CONSTANT

Constant's final participation in the communal activity of the S.I. was this "Description of the Yellow Sector," his scheme for a hanging Situationist city, elevated on pilotis. *Here, various atmospheric effects, the labyrinth-houses, and the moveable partitions all work toward overcoming the separation of play and residence.*

This area, which is situated on the edge of the city, owes its name to the color of a rather large part of its floor, notably on the second level to the East. This particularity adds to the rather joyful atmosphere that predisposes the area to its adaptation as a zone for play. The different levels —three in the East, two in the West—are supported by a metallic construction, disengaged from the ground. For the construction bearing the floors and the buildings within, titanium has been used; for the streets and the covering of partitions and walls, nylon. The lightness of this construction explains not only the minimal use of supports, but also a great flexibility in the handling of the different parts, and the complete suppression of volumes. The metallic structure may be considered as the foundation for an arrangement of interchangeable,

---

7   *Internationale situationniste* no. 4 (June 1960), 23–26. [Ed.]

THE ARCHITECTURAL INTERLUDE 123

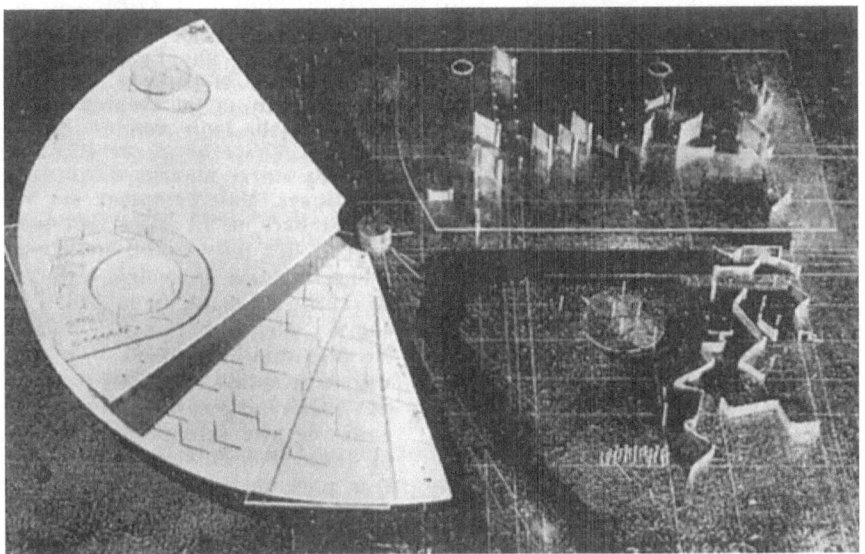

Fig.5.5.1 Constant, model of *Yellow Sector*, from *Internationale situationniste* no. 4 (June 1960).

dismountable element-types (furniture), favoring the setting's ongoing variation. Therefore, the description that follows will be content with the general framework of the arrangement. The configuration in superimposed levels implies that the greatest part of the surface must be illuminated and air-conditioned artificially. Yet nowhere has it been sought to imitate natural conditions, but on the contrary to profit from this circumstance by creating climatologic conditions and forms of lighting. This becomes an integral part of the plays of ambiance that are one of the attractions of the Yellow Sector. It should be noted, furthermore, that in many places one emerges suddenly into the open air.

One can arrive in this part of the city either by air, the flat roof providing for runways; or, at ground level, by car; or, lastly, by underground train—according to the distances to be covered. The ground level, crossed in all directions by freeways, is devoid of buildings, with the exception of a few *pilotis* that support the construction, and a round building of six stories (A), which supports the overhanging terrace. These supports, around which areas for parking of the means of transport have been foreseen, contain the elevators that lead to the upper levels of the city or to its basement. The building (A) that houses the technical services is separated from the rest of the area and accessible only from the terraces or the ground level. All the rest communicates internally and forms a large common space, from which only two buildings on the periphery of the city, containing dwellings (B and C), are separated. Between these two dwelling-buildings, whose windows look out onto the landscape, are to be found, at the city's Northeast angle and extending beyond the upper terrace, the great arrival hall (D), a metallic construction covered in sheet-aluminum of a fairly free form, whose two floors contain the passenger station, and warehouses for the distribution of goods. This hall being situated still in the open, the interior of the area itself is entirely covered.

The Eastern part is divided vertically into two covered floors, plus the part of the terrace where the airdrome is found. By means of moveable partitions, the floors are arranged into a great number of large rooms—communicating horizontally as well as vertically, by stairs—whose varied ambiances are continually changed by Situationist teams, in touch with the technical services. Intellectual games, above all, are practiced here.

The Western part appears right away more complicated. The large labyrinth-house is found here, along with the small one (L and M), which pick up and develop the ancient forces of architectural confusion: water games (G), the circus (H), the great ballroom (N), the white plaza (F) beneath which is suspended the green square, which enjoys a splendid view over the freeway traffic that passes below.

The two labyrinth-houses are formed by a large number of irregularly shaped chambers, spiral staircases, remote corners, wastelands, and blind alleys. They are wandered through at random. One can find oneself in the quiet room, clad in insulating material; the shrill room in vivid colors and with overwhelming sounds; the room of echoes (games with radiophonic transmitters); the room of images (cinematographic games); the room for reflection (games of psychological influences); the room for rest; the room for erotic games; the room of coincidences, etc. An extended stay in these houses has the tonic effect of a brainwashing and it is frequently practiced to erase habits that are liable to take root.

The water games are found between these two houses, in the open, the terrace above having an opening that permits the sky to be seen. Jets of water and fountains are interspersed here with fences and constructions in bizarre shapes, including a heated glass grotto where one can bathe in deepest winter while watching the stars.

By taking passage K that, instead of windows, is equipped with large optical lenses that greatly magnify the view of the neighboring area, one arrives at the grand ballroom. Or else one passes over the terraces surrounding the water games; these roofs overhang the white plaza, visible below, where demonstrations are held, and also give access to the green square on the floor below. In descending below this square the public transport may be found that lead to other district.

THESES ON UNPREMEDITATED ARCHITECTURE (1958)[8]

GÜNTHER FEUERSTEIN

The inclusion of architecture among the arts is not self-evident. Its amalgamation with technology, and especially the valuable and decisive impulses it has received from structural engineering, have drawn it into the stream of the applied sciences. Rationalist considerations of function, material, methods of building, completely dominate it. The upshot of this tendency is computer planning, where specifications, financing, setting, shoe size, and date of birth of the client are inserted into the electronic brain; in a few seconds appears the perfect floor plan and elevation, together with a guaranteed psychologically correct color scheme. The creative, the spiritual, the emotional qualities have no longer any place. The architect submits to the rationalist decree and counts himself fortunate to have discovered a court of appeals that will acquit him of the charge of bad architecture and faulty inspiration. "It was technologically necessary"—an explanation to silence all objections.

---

8 *Landscape* 14, no. 2 (Winter 1964–1965), 33–37. [Ed.]

Grid

The external symbol of contemporary classical rationalism is the grid floor plan, above all the grid façade. Here is displayed in all clarity the drive toward an elaborate geometry and an architecture that arouses no positive emotions—unless the grid is enlarged to gigantic proportions, and then its overpowering size inspires awe, but also alarm.

The irregular, asymmetrical façade, forgotten for thirty years, is once more in style. It comes from honest building; it represents a breakthrough for anti-rationalist principles.

In the floor plan the grid, being a convenient system for the architect and the structural engineer, serves as the dominating principle of the design. In a house built with a grid of say 2 meters, I can never have a room of 3 meters 30 centimeters, or one which measures five paces, though this might fit some special circumstance or satisfy my humor. The ancient rule whereby the processes transpiring within a house should also be expressed on the exterior seems now to be completely ignored. The aesthetic grid, like a geometrical leprosy, is superimposed on conference rooms, stairwells, broom closets, exhibition halls, toilets, storage space.

Therefore any such measure as the irregular façade that destroys the grid is to be welcomed even though the results are not beautiful in the accepted sense.

Oblique Angle

The recent introduction of the emotional ingredient in architecture brings with it systems using the oblique angle. It is impossible today to span wide distance using rectangular elements alone; at the least a connecting diagonal is needed. Often the arch proves the most suitable form, and with increasing frequency some form of shell construction. Shell construction, to be sure, derives from calculation, not emotion, yet it is very congenial to it and indicates the necessity for incorporating the curve in architecture.

The complexities of calculating bearing surfaces in modern construction lead to a kind of theoretical incalculability. Nervi designs buildings of reinforced concrete that satisfy his intuition, and then proves their feasibility by means of models. Many new buildings are in fact the result of extensive experiments with models. In this manner the art of building reverts, after having gone through the most extreme phases of rationalism, to empirical methods, and, in so doing, produces forms in which we can emotionally participate, whose process we can in a sense recall; and it also produces forms that are freely modeled.

Every architect dreams of the American ideal of total, all-inclusive planning, and in today's classical architecture this has in fact become a necessity: to have the house "down to the last nail" on paper, and only then to begin building—a completely mechanistic-rationalistic design. The imaginative powers, both of the client and of the architect (who dares not admit it, however) are grievously overburdened. Models are built in the scale of 1:1000 all the way up to 1:1, instead of producing a house which is elastic and alterable during the time of construction and afterwards. An immense amount of time that might have been spent in developing a feeling for spaces, in becoming familiar with materials, in developing a sense of simplicity, is squandered on planning. The architect becomes a dictator, the client becomes the slave of the plan, never willing to confess that it is all quite different from what he had imagined. The last resort of his individuality lies in putting those structural features invented by the architect to some inappropriate use.

Superperfection

The building originally conceived of in superperfect terms should also be produced—insofar as possible—in a superperfect manner. It matters not at all whether it provides an outlet for the carpenter or mason; the constant overtaxing of the hand and the eye—both of them still very important tools in European building methods—leads to complicated constructions that in the last analysis are still inaccurate.

The ideal, then, would be the superperfect house so smooth in functioning that one ceases to be aware of it; much as in a well-drawn bath, one has neither the sensation of heat or cold. A dwelling of this sort would be described as "comfortable" or "practical"; one has no further contact with it. We grow quickly accustomed to whatever is practical or pleasant; the experience of "dwelling," of living in a place, is no longer real, because there have ceased to be surfaces of friction.

So what we must foster is the impractical dwelling: a few corners that one knocks against, a roundabout path between bed and closet so that one walks more often through the home; a door that squeaks, a lock that refuses to turn, a table that wobbles, an uncomfortable chair. It is easy, nowadays, to produce a house with every technological refinement. What is by no means so easy is to answer the question: What does a person really need in his home? For instance, an air-conditioned and completely self-sufficient house is looked upon as the *ne plus ultra* of modern construction. Yet aside from the higher costs that affect the much more important factor of the amount of space, we ought to ask ourselves what particular qualities (whether or not people desire them) are lost in this type of house. We cannot open the windows, we cannot feel that it is warm outside and that the trees smell green. Far worse, we cannot get the stench of cars nor hear their noise. In a word, we have no lasting communication with the world we live in, the city. Naturally this is held to be unhealthy, but simply because physical health is all that seems to count. Once the window is opened, the airspace in which we live becomes part of the airspace of the whole world. Between us and the cosmos nothing intervenes but air. It is well for us to sweat a little in our house when summer comes, and in winter when we sit near the window we need to feel the cold air coming from the panes. This is how the city dweller, every hour of his existence, learns about the passage of the seasons.

Poverty

Therefore unpremeditated architecture proposes: no air-conditioning, merely ordinary heating, no tiled bathrooms, no costly window construction, no expensive flooring, no unnecessary machines in the home, no totally washable surfaces. To what use could the savings be put? Larger rooms, more land, more pictures, more books, more music, more traveling, more children, more presents, more help. The less money spent on architecture, the better that architecture will be. The best architecture of all thrives on poverty and frugality, given the right state of mind. At present the dwelling has to be totally planned down to the last corner by the architect, because people bring nothing with them to furnish a bare and simple living space: no genuine life, no imagination, none of those things which have a true relationship to them such as pictures, plants, books, children, music, friends. Space and the designing of space has become an end in itself, no longer a container for people.

Good Kitsch

Objects that have not been through the hands of the architect or designer are stigmatized as *kitsch*. But kitsch is a relative thing. We produce enchantingly beautiful kitsch for the Triennale and for exhibits of industrial design.

Beautifully designed objects are not better simply because they are agreeable. Sometimes kitsch is to be preferred because it can be inspired by the honest emotion of a simple person. The attitude of a person who turns out by formula dishonest objects with snob appeal is worse than the naïve but honest attitude that frequently is back of so-called kitsch. The act of creating this kind of object can elicit emotions of a stronger and more valuable sort than can that of creating objects of recognized art.

Most do-it-yourself objects are thought of as kitsch; quite without warrant. One of the justifications of the do-it-yourself movement is the emotional recall that resides in everything we make ourselves. This recall comes not merely from looking at the object you have made, but from remembering, from knowing exactly what the whole process was. The ideal would be for everyone to build his own house—and this of course would make the architect superfluous. Every house is a blend of the image of the architect and the image of the client; but a house corresponding entirely to the client's image can only come into being when the architect is eliminated.

Nineteenth century classical aestheticism must be considered as obsolete. Architects of the twentieth century still design according to its tenets, to be sure. Just as in the seventeenth, eighteenth and nineteenth centuries, contemporary public buildings and houses are designed according to classical principles of proportion, symmetry, rhythm. The fact that they display no capitals or architraves is of minor consequence.

For a brief period in the 1920s there were signs of a breaking away. The elementary principle that windows should be placed where needed is actually a genuine element in unpremeditated architecture. But usually the logical consequences failed; new aesthetic rules were formulated. Genuine tensions (as with windows in a façade placed according to need or accident or whim) were destroyed by a revived formalism. Even the influence of a technological aesthetic could scarcely change the classical, for the technological aesthetic also operates according to proportions and relationships and harmony. The one great chance of devising a new aesthetic, or better yet of applying the emotional qualities of disharmony and tension in technology and industry was allowed to slip by. Mondrian was drastically watered down by architects, his tense compositions reduced to pleasant, stylish structural tricks, formalism without conviction. Mies van der Rohe managed to bring this technical structuralism to its highest possible perfection, but Mies van der Rohe is near his end and can already be viewed as a grandiose historical phenomenon. His disciples—and who among modern architects is not one?—are simply marking time. Aesthetic superperfection has reached the end of its rope.

The manner in which our apparatuses and machines are produced is something we cannot imagine; something, in other words, we cannot emotionally recall. We succumb to the fascination precisely for the reason that we do not understand them.

Our feeling for cause and effect suffers; it has nothing to work on. There is no sense in trying to understand a television set, for example, or in trying to recall emotionally the way in which it was assembled. The results are all that matter. The same holds true for houses. Brilliance, smoothness, size, technical perfection are enough in a building. For the initiate perhaps the proportions are also interesting, but the methods of construction hold nothing for us. In most cases a curtain-wall façade does not produce emotional recall. The assembly process involved in such a building, even its basic structure, is quite beyond our comprehension. On the other hand everything that is painstakingly joined as in carpentry, laid up as in masonry, built in the traditional sense, lends itself to emotional recall. Even when an occupant has not built his house himself—which would be most desirable—he can at least understand how it arose, and he thereby acquires an extraordinarily close relationship with it.

The most private sphere of an individual cannot be assembled, readymade. Even the readymade rental unit or cooperative apartment is as much a monstrosity as the prefabricated house. In cooperative apartment houses no occupant with any individuality fails to try to alter the partitions and openings as far as possible. But there is far too little that can be done. When prefabrication brings the house straight from the factory, emotional recall is at best limited to bolting it together. It never includes the building of the house, the walls, the roof.

A milder form of prefabrication is confined to small parts of the house, like the wall surfaces, sections of the roof, and so on. The smaller the prefabricated elements, the greater freedom in construction, and it is greatest when we deal with the smallest prefabricated element: the brick; and with the brick unpremeditated architecture becomes possible once more.

Alterations

Contemporary classical architecture strives to present an unchanging appearance to the world. Everything is so designed that no alteration, either by man or any other cause, is allowed. The much-touted "flexible" architecture is flexible only in terms of function, not in terms of changes produced by emotion. At all events, changes resulting from weathering or the passage of time are outlawed.

Unpremeditated architecture, on the contrary, allows of change, allows of history, invites such changes. The age of a house should be legible not only through its style; we ought to be able to read it in the amount of rust, the fading of the concrete, the cracking of the plaster. Modern classical houses become shabby with time; unpremeditated buildings acquire patina, like those of the Middle Ages.

Men must be able to make alterations; not simply shove the furniture about but make windows and doors or holes in the walls according to their pleasure; and they must of course be able to paint the walls. So it is not only the actual process of building that we ought to be able to read but the process of its whole existence, its being lived in and altered. This is how a building acquires the quality of history.

The Suppression of History

Yet at the same time we must be free to do away with the traces of this micro-history when we choose to; for instance, when a dwelling survives a generation of inhabitants or when for emotional reasons a new outward appearance is in order. Here a paint job seems the best method. The character of the painting should be recognizable, i.e. in the brush stroke. Ships acquire a characteristic surface when they have been painted repeatedly, and the blurring of the forms does not disturb us.

Most designers can think only in two dimensions. First the floor plan is sketched, based on considerations of function. This plan is then multiplied by the economically acceptable number of stories and a form of sorts is thus produced; a form which is not the result of any metaphysical occurrence but simply of utility. It possesses no true corporeality since it is actually nothing more than a stacking up of surfaces.

What exists between these several surfaces are holes, small or large, not spaces; not spaces which are restful or exciting or provocative or livable; each of these holes is totally noncommittal, without significance, deriving from no emotion and sparking none. It can never become a symbol. Likewise the building itself never becomes a symbol, a monument. It came into existence as a graphic concept. It was thought up, not created. The act of building is decisive; only one thing takes precedence over it, and that is vision. Let us build without detours: from vision to forms and space, without recourse to drafting paper.

The Hierarchy of Materials

The scale of value in materials depends on two things. First, their power to elicit emotional recall and second, their changeability. There are certain materials whose origin and quality are easily decipherable, like wood or stone. They are infinitely superior to artificial materials that are utterly impersonal, homogenized, and unstructured. There are other materials that have a greater natural capacity for change. Iron rusts, copper develops a patina and is therefore superior to aluminum. Natural wood warps, stone decomposes, neither of which is the case with ceramics. Yet unglazed ceramics, especially those of so-called inferior quality, tend to fade and ooze. Concrete has a great variety of structural forms and shows change.

The skillful use of these findings could bring about a new kind of architectural appearance; once more there could be such a thing as genuine aging. Classical, superperfect architecture with its emphasis on "uncluttered" neatness deteriorates week by week, for despite all efforts the undesirable process of decay cannot be checked. Thus modern buildings are handsome only when they are being inaugurated. For a little while longer they remain photogenic, but that is because in the picture the deteriorating neatness does not show.

With unpremeditated architecture the case is entirely different. Precisely *because* of the aging processes the building acquires an increasingly intense historicity and sensitivity. Once again the passage of time becomes visible.

What must be avoided is a studied cosmetic elaboration of materials. This destroys the innate qualities of good building materials and in the last analysis prevents us from establishing any contact with them. Materials are to be used as they come, the way they offer themselves, whenever possible, without any alteration at all. If however some alterations are necessary—if, for example, some sort of surface protection is called for—then these too should reveal method and process.

The unit of measurement or the module tells us much about people. The original measures derived from man: the ell, the foot, the pace. These were always available but with great variations: imperfect measures and at the same time the most human of measures. Commercial developments demanded a greater accuracy and a kind of stabilization; still, the basis remained what it had been: the human body.

The Japanese house is still a multiple of the rice straw mat, which in turn derived from the human form. Whenever a man lies down on it, its measure is, as it were, verified once again.

The Greek temple derived its module from an anthropomorphic structural element, the column. The measure was multiplied by aesthetic methods, divided by geometrical methods into parts.

The Gothic cathedral was different. The basic measurement was human, but its multiplication, by means of a complicated mystique of numbers, raised it into the sphere of the divine.

The metric system was typical of the scientific worldview of the nineteenth century. It is a totally arbitrary unit, which in theory—though not in fact—derives from a cosmic premise. It is supposed to be the 4-millionth part of the earth's circumference. It is by no means simply a matter of conservatism that has prevented the universal adoption of the metric system, and there have been many attempts to devise new systems of measurement and new modules.

The best known of these is that of Le Corbusier's *modulor*. This is based on the human form, and this circumstance alone, quite aside from the practicability of the system, is of significance and characteristic of Le Corbusier's attitude.

The German industrial norms (D.I.N.) are of course not based on human measurements but merely aim at simplification in technical (and especially industrial) calculations. All these measurements assume a special importance in the building process. To be consistent, every brick construction should be based on the measurement of the individual brick. In point of fact, however, the bricks widely used in Europe are not integrated into the metric system.

Free Form

It has already been suggested that the introduction of the emotional element in architecture will in turn introduce the free form, and the free form is certainly as valid as the geometrical form.

The freely evolved, plastic form is worthy of the greatest regard, for it expresses a large sector of the emotional scale which is lost when design is confined to the rectilinear. This potential was recognized not only by the architects of the Baroque but also by such important modern architects as Gaudi, Mendelsohn and above all Le Corbusier – all of whom can be looked upon as precursors of unpremeditated architecture.

FUNCTION: PROVOCATION[9]

GÜNTHER FEUERSTEIN

Functional architecture: at the beginning liberation from a muddle (historical forms from which one longed for the new without confessing it) and birth of new conceptions of thought. Afterwards, excuse and embarrassment: powerlessness to create new signs, to erect monuments.

Functioning architecture: triumph of our comfort; mechanical unfolding of existence; liquidation of fantasy, imagination, vision, and intuition. The architect's thought exhausts itself in functional studies of estimates of profitability, of lines of access, and of construction details.

Architecture conforms to function: I eat here, and I sleep there. Here I work, and there I read. The architect has carefully studied it. Everything serves its purpose. Where to laugh or cry? Where to hate or breathe? Where to submit to vastness and limited space, the grandeur of weakness, protection and freedom?

Architecture: not only the place for a part of life. The place for all of life, for the whole person.

"The art of building is found beyond questions of utility." (Le Corbusier)

---

9 *Aujourd'hui* no. 53 ("Espaces sculptés/Espaces architecturés") (May–June 1966): 26–27. Originally published in 1965. [Ed.]

ARCHITECTURE FREE OF FUNCTIONS, then? Architecture, which is not dictated by a material function.

The Pyramid of Cheops has a built volume of 2,580,000 cubic meters. The "used" volume is 296 cubic meters.

The Mayan temple at Chichen Itza has a built volume of 51,000 cubic meters. The "used" volume is 80 cubic meters.

Xpuhie's palace is flanked by three pyramids and temples. The pyramids and temples do not have usable interior volumes. Their steps (80° incline) cannot be mounted. The built volume is 7,500 cubic meters, the "used" volume 700 cubic meters.

The Cathedral of Reims has a built volume of 210,000 cubic meters. To perform its function only 50,000 square meters would be needed.

Piranesi titled a few projects *Carceri* (prisons). These are grandiose rooms, without utilization in the end.

Ledoux designed houses in the form of spheres, pyramids, and rings. Form's symbolic value determined the building. It could be used for anything. Or it could very well not be used at all. This remains architecture.

Taut and Scharoun dreamed of glass. What function did it have? Glass was an idea, one now already historical.

Rietveld enlarged his constellations of panel-fragments. In Utrecht they can be used as a house (Schroder House).

Malevich and Vantongerloo joined interior-less masses. These are exemplars for the compact and differentiated architecture of our era.

Simon Rodia's towers, in Watts, Los Angeles, are not utilizable: a game and a whim, sign and monuments.

Constantino Nivola's monument: streets, formed by interior-less "houses."

The Guggenheim Museum, by F.L. Wright, is a foreigner in its environment. It contains a grandiose space, the paintings are hung up in an unusual manner. It is space that could be used for anything. It is space beyond functionalism.

Louis Kahn's laboratories: the rooms are too small, too little adaptable, difficult to fit up, the parapets are too low, the imposts are stuck on with help of paper, the auditoriums have false windows, narrow corridors, and completely empty "auxiliary" shafts. Despite everything, it is one of the present's strongest pieces of architecture.

ARCHITECTURE FREE OF FUNCTIONS. Function is included in a completely different manner. Architecture is not primarily building for certain definite functions. Architecture does not include function; it is function itself.

Architecture's function: PROVOCATION.

PROVOCATION: creation, invocation, proclamation, animation, excitation, attack, scandal, protest, demonstration, revolution, affirmation, aggression, dispute, question, invitation, incitation, encouragement, exigency.

PROVOCATIVE ARCHITECTURE: people feel it, they have contact with it. They are moved, excited, enchanted, offended, filled up, tortured, confronted. People can create, change, look after, and destroy architecture.

"My house is practical. You have all my thanks. The same thanks as those addressed to the engineers who designed the railways and telecommunications. You haven't touched my soul. But the walls rise in the presence of the sky in an order than moves me. I feel your artistic intention. You were gentle or violent, agreeable or dignified. Your stones relate the story to me. You fascinate me at this spot and my eyes watch. My eyes see something that betrays a thought. With raw materials you created relationships that have touched me deeply. This is architecture." (Le Corbusier)

Provocative architecture: a human architecture? Humane? An idea that's been used to death. Understand well: the kind side, manageable, obliging, to scale, in good taste, and well proportioned? Architecture, in which people feel perfectly at ease.

The human: the reflection of humanity's grandeur, the reflection of its power to bear witness by something.

TO BEAR WITNESS and ERECT monuments.

Let us create monuments (not monumentalism) as reflection of a power (and not of a pre-power) of humanity.

WITNESSES and SYMBOLS for present-day powers (not for the powerful) are to be created. Provocative witnesses.

Witnesses for whom? Symbols to what end?
Symbolized architecture:
STRENGTH (Kahn) and weakness.
POWERS (pyramid) and powerlessness.
IDEAS (Le Corbusier) and lack of ideas.
FAITH (cathedral) and unbelief.
COMMUNITY (Scharoun) and singularity.
POLITICS (Vesnin) and intrigue.
VISION (Saarinen) and aberration.
PASSION (Gaudi) and suffering.

Architecture's true "function"? To reflect, to reflect in a provocative manner mental and social factors (and fictions).

Let us build the monument and space as reflections of strengths and not for the carrying out of functions. Let us use buildings for anything or even for nothing at all.

Let us build witnesses, spaces, and forms for SOCIETY.

Meeting other people—friends, children, enemies, young women, war profiteers, saints, generals—this happens within architecture. Meeting other ideas—this happens within architecture.

How do we meet other human beings? How is an idea reflected? These are the decisive questions for architecture, and not that of knowing if the façade should be striped or plaid, if one will build with exposed concrete or with bricks.

Let us build structures. But let us make room for many human things: NAIVETY, BRICOLAGE, FANCY, CHANCE, ACCESSORY, INSUFFICIENCY, ILLUSION, IMPROVISATION, CHANGE.

Sculpture: symbol of humanity, of the human. Symbol for the categories of the human (Vantongerloo and Malevich).

Architecture: symbol of human coexistence. Symbol of society (Scharoun). Symbol of faith (cathedral). Symbol of power (Le Corbusier).

Sculpture and architecture: the two have symbols in common, the general value. Sculpture and architecture: the two are space (André Bloc).

SPACE: distances, volumes, three-dimensional relationships.

SPACE: relation of the mysterious volume, full of tension, comparable to the tensions of the human community.

SPACE: the room, the house, the square, the city, the earth, the universe are determined by it.

Architecture: PROVOCATION, WITNESS, SPACE.

EXCERPT FROM "SITUATIONIST NEWS"[10]

Not long after the June 1960 publication of Constant's "Description of the Yellow Sector," Constant chose to leave the S.I. Already, earlier in 1960, the other members of the Dutch section, the architects Anton C. Alberts (1927–1999) and Har Th. Oudejans (1928–1992), had been excluded in the wake of their acceptance of a commission to design a church (the Mariakerk, Volendam, The Netherlands, 1962). Constant, this short notice explains, had found himself increasingly opposed to the mainstream of the group as he immersed himself in the study of technical questions related to his visionary designs; this preoccupation with what were seen as formal problems was at the expense of those elements seen as central to the project of unitary urbanism: play and creative freedom in everyday life—the "search for a global culture," not an architectural one. In September 1960, the "research office for a unitary urbanism" was moved from Amsterdam to Brussels, and would henceforth be run by Attila Kotányi (1924–2004).

Pinot Gallizio and G. Melanotte were excluded from the S.I. in June. Through naivety or careerism, they had allowed themselves to be involved in contacts, then in collaborations, in Italy, with ideologically unacceptable environments. A first reprimand (cf. the "Situationist News" in our fourth number, about the critic Guasco, notoriously linked to the Jesuit Tapié) had not corrected their politics.[11] The decision to exclude them was thus made without hearing their case any further.

Constant, however, who had with good reason denounced their conduct, was not pleased with this falling out. Moreover, he disapproved of the fact that we had had to resort to the same measure a few months before against the Dutch section's architects, who hadn't been afraid to undertake the construction of a church. More profoundly, Constant had been in opposition with the S.I. because he was—urgently and almost exclusively

---

10 *Internationale situationniste* no. 5 (December 1960): 10. [Ed.]
11 "Renseignements situationnistes," *Internationale situationniste* no. 4 (June 1960): 12-13. [Ed.]

—attending to structural questions of certain unitary urbanism ensembles, at a time when other Situationists recalled that at the present stage of such a project it was necessary to place the emphasis on its content (play, free creation of everyday life). Constant's arguments thus valorized the technicians of architectural forms as opposed to the search for a global culture. And simple equality of treatment, as to the minimum conduct insisted on for the ones and the others, already seemed to him disproportionate in severity. Constant then declared, in the same month of June, that since he disagreed with the S.I.'s discipline, he wished to take back his freedom in this respect, for a length of time to be determined by the train of events. We replied that, outside any idea of hostility or demerit, the value as a *practical weapon* that we have long insisted quarrels recorded by the S.I. have, allowed only an immediate choice between a definitive resignation or renunciation of this form of pressure. Constant chose to quit the S.I.

6.

The Critique of Urban Planning

CIRCULATIONIST MANIFESTO: DEBORD ON PLANNING FROM *ARCHITECTURAL REVIEW* (1960)[1]

It may well be that the specter haunting town-planning is a Situationist. Certainly, the promise of Guy Debord's early researches into the micro-psychology of towns, his plotting of gradients of psychogeographical drift [...] has been fulfilled in the creation of the concept of Urbanisme Unitaire.

To recapitulate briefly, the Situationist Position (to use one of the movement's pet phrases) is this—that the function of creative activity is to construct situations, that is, the "factual construction of transient ambiences for our existence, and their transformation on to a higher emotional plane" (the translation is rough, but the terminology of the original French is specialized). For example, the function of a work of art is to create a momentary ambiance, or environment, for the beholder, and to raise his responses to a higher plane.

But, equally, there are any numbers of pre-existing constructed environments (a phrase that might almost be used by either Situationists or Italian Neo-Libertarians)[2] which have some emotional effect on those who occupy them, and the various parts of towns are clearly in this class. Thus one finds the Situationists simultaneously manufacturing *machines à épater les bourgeois* (such as Debord's notorious anti-film *Hurlements en faveur de Sade*) and making systematic attempts to map the intangibles

---

1   *Architectural Review* (April 1960): 222–223. [Ed.]
2   Neo-Liberty was the name given to an historicizing trend in postwar Italian architecture that seemed to turn its back on the rationalist principles of the modern movement; it reminded some critics of the "Liberty" style of the Art Nouveau period, hence its name. Prominent examples of this trend include Ignazio Gardella's house on the Zattere in Venice (1957) and Franco Albini and Franca Helg's La Rinascente store in Rome (1961). [Ed.]

of town planning. Much of Paris has been so mapped, and Debord has published the results [...]; an English member of the group, Ralph Rumney, was lost to the cause in an attempt to survey the urbanistic jungle of Venice, and a psychogeographic study of Amsterdam is promised, the fieldwork to be done this spring.

Two main techniques seem to be employed in these explorations—one is clearly a simple mass-observation of the way people behave (*comportement* is a good word among Situationists) in different urban environments, the other, and more publicized technique is the assessment of psychogeographical drift, that is, the way in which an undirected pedestrian tends to move about in a particular quarter of the town, tending to establish natural connections between places, the zones of influence of particular institutions and public services, and so forth. It may well be objected that these techniques are un-scientific, disorderly and too subjective, but the fact remains that the Situationists are studying the actual texture of towns and their relationship to human beings more intensively than most architects and in a more down-to-pavement manner than most town-planners.

For this reason, their positive proposals are worth study. Some of them are only of the nature of a current project to colonize that mysterious eyot in the Seine (the *Allée des Cygnes*) whose main function is to carry the intermediate piers of railway bridges between the fifteenth and sixteenth arrondissements. A gimmick? Possibly, but why should the third isle of Paris be uninhabited, and what a marvelous place to live, anyhow! Of more general application, however, is Debord's formal taking up of a Situationist Position on traffic circulation. The document in question appeared in No. 3 of *Internationale Situationniste*, and though some of the detailed positions may alarm and shock, the general tenor of the argument is close to much that has been said already in the pages of *Architectural Review*.

Debord's point of departure is that the motor-car is not a means of transport but the "supreme good" of a way of life that has gone adrift, and that time spent in traveling is merely extra work. We must rid ourselves of this state of affairs and make transport extra pleasure. To remake architecture in terms of the demands of motor-traffic alone is to be unrealistic; architecture must be re-made in terms of *all* forms of mobility. Even if it were possible to divide a town into zones of work and residence, there would still have to be a third zone, that of life, liberty and leisure; in any case the intentions of Unitary Urbanism are against such divisions. It is not a question of fighting the motor-car, but of preventing it destroying its own function through congestion. The motor-car is not necessarily here to stay, in any case—other forms of transport may supersede it. Thus most of the allegedly practical propositions for dealing with it are quite unreal.

As will be recognized, much of this argument lies close to the lines of thought pursued by *Architectural Review* and the *Architects' Journal*, but the peroration reminds us that we are in another country. "Revolutionary town-planners are not concerned solely with the movement of things, and of men stuck in a world of things. They will attempt to break these topological chains, and experiment with terrains for the circulation of men through a more authentic life."

Rhetoric? Again, not altogether so. A recent edition of the Dutch magazine *Forum* (no. 6, 1959), devoted to the integration of the arts, had a kind of Situationist supplement, expounding the concept of Unitary Urbanism, which is defined, among other things as a "Theory of the employment of *all* the arts and sciences ..." in the construction of urban situations, and here was an example of the creation of such a terrain—a project by the Dutch Situationist who signs himself simply as "Constant," for a Covered City. This would indeed break the topological chains, since it calls for nothing less than the clearance of all the ground surface for vehicular circulation, and the suspension of the rest of the city in a giant space-frame above it. In a characteristically Situationist manner this reverses the normal solution of clearing the ground for pedestrians and putting the vehicles up in the air, as in the expressways of the US.

SITUATIONIST POSITIONS ON TRAFFIC[3]

GUY DEBORD

1.

All urbanists make the same mistake of considering the personal automobile (and its byproducts like the scooter) essentially as a means of transport. It is essentially the principal materialization of a notion of happiness that advanced capitalism tends to spread throughout the whole of society. The automobile as sovereign good of an alienated life, and inseparably as essential product of the capitalist market, is at the very center of the all-encompassing propaganda campaign—this year it is frequently said that American economic prosperity will soon depend on the success of the slogan: "two cars per family."

2.

Transit time, as Le Corbusier rightly understood, is a surplus labor that reduces all the more the so-called free part of the day.

3.

We must go from circulation as supplement of work, to circulation as a pleasure.

---

3 *Internationale situationniste* no. 3 (December 1959): 36–37. [Ed.]

4.

Wanting to remake architecture in step with the current massive, parasitical existence of personal cars shifts the problems with a serious unrealism. Architecture must be remade in step with the whole development of society, by criticizing all transitory values linked to doomed forms of social relations (in the first rank of which is the family).

5.

Even if, during a transitional period, the absolute division between work zones and housing zones may temporarily be permitted, a third sphere at least must be foreseen: that of life itself (the sphere of liberty, of forms of leisure—the truth of life). We understand that unitary urbanism is without borders; it intends to establish a complete unity of the human milieu in which separations like work-leisure or collectivity-private life will finally be dissolved. But beforehand, unitary urbanism's minimum action is the terrain of play extended to all desirable structures. This terrain will be at the level of complexity of an old city.

6.

It is not a question of fighting the automobile as an evil. It is its extreme concentration in cities that is leading to the negation of its role. Urbanism should certainly not ignore the automobile, but even less should it accept it as a central theme. It should bet on its decay. In any case, its interdiction inside certain new complexes, as well as in a few old cities, may be foreseen.

7.

Those who believe the automobile to be eternal are not thinking—even from a strictly technological viewpoint—of other future forms of transport. For example, certain models of individual helicopters that are presently being tested by the United States army will probably have spread to the public within twenty years.

8.

The breaking up of the dialectic of the human milieu in favor of automobiles (the opening of freeways within Paris has been projected, entailing the demolition of thousands of lodgings, at a time when otherwise the housing crisis is continuously worsening) masks its irrationality under pseudo-practical explanations. But its true practical necessity corresponds with a definite social condition.

Those who believe the premises of the problem to be permanent want in fact to believe in the permanence of the present society.

9.

Revolutionary urbanists will not only attend to the circulation of things, and of human beings immobilized in a world of things. They will try to break these topological chains, by experimenting with terrains for the circulation of people through authentic life.

GANGLAND AND PHILOSOPHY[4]
ATTILA KOTÁNYI

> *The* Beijing-Bao *is the oldest daily newspaper in the world. It has come out for over fifteen centuries. Its first number was printed in the fourth century in Beijing. The editors of this paper have often fallen into disgrace in the eyes of the Chinese sovereigns, because they have attacked the infallibility of the State and religion. The paper has nevertheless come out every day, though the editors might have paid for it with their lives. In the course of those fifteen centuries, 1500 editors of the* Beijing-Bao *have been hanged.*
> *– Ujvidéki Magyar Szo* (1957)[5]

The Situationist tendency does not have the purpose of preventing the construction of situations. This first restriction in our attitude has numerous consequences. We are making a definite effort to aid in the development of these consequences.

> The term "protection" is the key word of the Garment Center racket. The process is as follows: one day you receive a visit from a fellow who kindly offers to "protect" you. If you are really very naïve, you ask: "Protection against what?"[6]

---

4 *Internationale situationniste* no. 4 (June 1960): 33–35. [Ed.]
5 Hungarian-language newspaper in Budapest. This quote is likely a coded reference to the oppositional role of the press in the wake of the Soviet suppression of the 1956 Hungarian uprising. [Ed.]
6 Stéphane Groueff and Dominique Lapierre, *Les Caïds de New-York* (Paris: R. Julliard, 1958). Both authors were reporters for *Paris-Match*; Groueff was its New York correspondent beginning in 1956. [Ed.]

If, for example, the boss of existentialism assures us that, for him, adopting a vulgar materialism is very hard because culture is a vital part of us, we could say almost the same thing of culture, but without being sure that this is something to be so proud of. That's one consequence.

How to imagine the building of our culture and of our philosophic and scientific information? Modern psychology has eliminated a large part of the doctrines that surrounded the question. It looks for motives: why do we accept an "idea" or an imperative, why do we refuse it?

> We may consider one of the most important results of the process of socialization to be the development of a system of normative equilibrium, which is superimposed on the system of biological equilibrium. The latter regulates the comportment of needs and requirements (nourishment, defense against cold or against blows, etc.), whereas the first system decides which are the actions that can be considered "feasible" or simply "thinkable."[7]

So, people become aware of Situationist activity. They "understand" it and "rationally" follow our arguments. Despite their momentary intellectual support, they lapse. The next day, they no longer understand us. We suggest a slight modification of the psychological description quoted above, in order to follow the play of forces that have prevented them from considering various things as "feasible" or simply "thinkable," whereas we know them to be *possible*. Let us examine the experimental magnification of this reaction:

> The trial of Dio and his accomplices began. Then an extraordinary and scandalous thing took place. The first witness, Gondolfo Miranti, refused to talk. He denied all the depositions he had made before the F.B.I. The judge lost patience. Furious, he had recourse to the final argument: "I order you to answer. If not, you will get five years in prison," he shouted. Miranti, without hesitating, accepted the five long years of prison. In the defendants' box Johnny Dio, smartly dressed and clean-shaven, smiled ironically.[8]

It is hard not to recognize an analogous comportment in people who do not dare speak of problems as they are, as these problems have been made understood to them. One has to wonder: are they victims of an intimidation racket? Yes, they certainly are. What then is the mechanism common to these two kinds of fear?

Miranti lived in gangland since his youth, and this explains many things for us. "Gangland," in Chicago gangster slang, means the domain of crime, the rackets' sphere of activity. I suggest studying from the ground up the

---

7   Peter Robert Hofstätter (1913–1994), an Austrian social psychologist. [Ed.]
8   Groueff and Lapierre, *Les Caïds de New York*. [Ed.]

functioning of the "bisness," despite the risk of being implicated in the case: "And if any one tried to loose another and lead him up to the light," Plato already stated, "let them only catch the offender, and they would put him to death."[9] Philosophy must not forget that it has always spoken its part among the settings of the Grand-Guignol.

A little *handbook of appropriated* [détourné] *vocabulary* should be developed. I am suggesting that, sometimes, instead of reading "neighborhood" we read: *gangland*. Instead of social organization: *protection*. Instead of society: *racket*. Instead of culture: *conditioning*. Instead of leisure: *protected crime*. Instead of education: *premeditation*.

Systematically falsified basic news and, for example, idealist conceptions of space—whose most glaring instance is commonly accepted cartography—are the first guarantees of the big lie imposed by the racket's interests on the whole gangland of social space.

According to Peter Robert Hofstätter, "a 'scientific' method of modeling the process of socialization cannot as yet be named." We believe, on the contrary, that we are capable of constructing a model mechanism for the production and reception of news. It would suffice us to *examine* by means of a comprehensive survey, for a short period of time, the entire social life of a delimited urban sector, to obtain an exact cross-section of the daily *bombardment of news* that falls in a given period of time on present-day urban agglomerations. The S.I. is naturally aware of all the modifications that its examination would itself immediately bring about in the occupied sector, profoundly disturbing gangland's monopoly of ongoing supervision.

"Integral art, about which so much has been said, can only materialize at the level of urbanism."[10] Yes, it is here that one encounters a limit. At this scale, the decisive elements of conditioning can already be *removed*. But if, at the same time, we expect a result in terms of scale, and not in terms of elimination itself, then we will have committed the greatest possible error.

Neo-capitalism has equally discovered something for its own use in the large scale. Day and night, it talks only of territorial planning. But for it, the obviousness of this point lies in the conditioning of commodity production, which it senses escaping it unless it resorts to the new scale. Urbanistic academicism has in this way defined "malfunctioning regions" from the standpoint of postwar neo-capitalism and in its service. Its technique of territorial reorganization is based on empty, anti-Situationist criteria.

The following critique of Mumford must be made: if the quarter is not considered a pathological element (gangland), it will not be possible to find new techniques (therapies).

The constructor of situations must manage to *read* situations in their

---

9   Plato, *The Republic*, Book VII. [Ed.]
10 Guy Debord, "Toward a Situationist International," in this volume, 94 [Ed.]

constructive and alterable elements. Through this reading, the language spoken by situations will begin to be understood. We will know how to speak this language and we will know how to *express ourselves* in this language; and finally we will know how to say through it what has never been said before, with constructed and quasi-natural situations.

ELEMENTARY PROGRAM OF THE UNITARY URBANISM OFFICE[11]

ATTILA KOTÁNYI AND RAOUL VANEIGEM

This article, developed jointly by Kotányi and Vaneigem, expresses the new direction taken by unitary urbanism in the wake of the elimination of what were understood to be "retrograde tendencies" within the S.I. It opens with a distinction between architecture, imbedded within ideology but "real," tangible, and urbanism, which is nothing but "pure spectacular ideology" and "society's field of publicity-propaganda." Where participation has been rendered impossible, spectacle fills the gap. Unitary urbanism, then, is the subversive rewriting (détournement, in Situationist parlance) of this ideological illusion in the name of de-alienation. But whatever transformations in the definition of unitary urbanism have taken place, the authors restate a premise that had been central at least since the "Amsterdam Declaration" of 1958: that unitary urbanism (now conceived as the "destruction of present-day conditioning") remains identical to the construction of situations.

I. NOTHINGNESS OF URBANISM AND NOTHINGNESS OF SPECTACLE

Urbanism does not exist; it is merely an "ideology," in Marx's sense. Architecture does actually exist, like Coca-Cola: it is a production coated with ideology but real, falsely satisfying a falsified need, whereas urbanism is comparable to the display of publicity around Coca-Cola—pure spectacular ideology. Modern capitalism, which organizes the reduction of the whole of social life into spectacle, is incapable of presenting any spectacle other than that of our own alienation. Its dream-urbanism is its masterpiece.

---

11 *Internationale situationniste* no. 6 (August 1961): 16–19 [Ed.]

THE CRITIQUE OF URBAN PLANNING 147

2. URBAN PLANNING AS CONDITIONING AND FALSE PARTICIPATION

The development of the urban milieu is the capitalist training of space. It represents the choice of one definite materialization of what is possible, to the exclusion of others. Like aesthetics, whose advancing disintegration it will follow, it may be considered as a rather neglected branch of criminology. However, what characterizes it at the level of "urbanism"—compared with its simply architectural level—is its insistence on consent of the population, on individual integration into the unleashing of this bureaucratic production of conditioning.

All this is imposed by means of a blackmail of utility. The full extent of this utility being put in service of rebuilding remains hidden. Modern capitalism causes the renunciation of all criticism through the simple argument that people need roofs over their heads, just as television is promoted on the pretext that people need news and entertainment. Overlooked is the obvious fact that this news, this entertainment, and this manner of habitation are not made for people, but without them and against them.

The whole of urban planning can be understood only as a society's field of publicity-propaganda, that is to say the organization of participation in something in which it is impossible to participate.

3. CIRCULATION, FINAL STAGE OF URBAN PLANNING

Circulation is the organization of the isolation of all. In this regard it constitutes the predominant problem of modern cities. It is the opposite of encounter, the incorporation of energies available for encounters or for any sort of participation. Participation becomes impossible and is made up for in the form of spectacle. Spectacle is manifested in habitation and travel (status of housing and personal vehicles). For, in fact, one does not reside in a quarter of the city, but in power. One resides somewhere in the hierarchy. At the summit of this hierarchy, the ranks may be calculated by the degree of circulation. Power is materialized by the obligation of being present daily at places that are more and more numerous (business dinners) and more and more remote from each other. The modern executive could be characterized as a person who manages to be in three different capitals in the course of a single day.

4. DISTANCIATION BEFORE THE URBAN SPECTACLE

The totality of the spectacle that tends to integrate the population is manifested moreover as development of cities and as permanent net of news. It is a sound framework protecting the existing conditions of life. Our first task is to permit people to stop identifying with the surroundings and with model forms of behavior. This is inseparable from a possibility of freely getting one's bearings in a few initial areas demarcated for human activity. People will still be compelled for a long time to accept the reified era of cities. But the attitude with which they will accept it may be changed immediately. The spread of distrust toward those airy and brightly colored kindergartens that represent—in the East as in the West—the new dormitory cities must be supported. Only an awakening will pose the question of a conscious construction of the urban milieu.

5. AN INDIVISIBLE LIBERTY

The chief success of the current planning of cities is to have shaken off the possibility of what we call unitary urbanism, that is to say a living critique, fueled by the tensions of the whole of everyday life, of this manipulation of cities and their inhabitants. Living critique means setting up bases for an experimental life: the gathering of creators of their own lives on sites equipped to their ends. These bases cannot be reserved for forms of "leisure" separated from the society. No spatiotemporal zone is completely separable. In fact, there is always pressure from the total society on its present vacation "reservations." The pressure will be exerted in the opposite direction in Situationist bases, which will act as bridgeheads for an invasion of the whole of everyday life. Unitary urbanism is the contrary of a specialized activity; and to acknowledge a separate urbanistic domain is already to acknowledge the whole urbanistic lie and the lie permeating the whole of life.

Happiness is the promise of urbanism. Urbanism will therefore be judged on this promise. The coordination of artistic means of denunciation and scientific means of denunciation must lead to a complete denunciation of existing conditioning.

6. THE LANDING

All space is already occupied by the enemy, who has domesticated it for its own use down to the elementary rules of this space (beyond legal authority to geometry itself). The moment of authentic urbanism's appearance will be the creation, in certain areas, of the absence of this occupation. What we call construction starts there. It can be understood with the help of the concept of the "positive void" invented by modern physics. Materializing liberty means first shielding from a domesticated planet a few small fragments of its surface.

7. THE LIGHT OF DÉTOURNEMENT

The elementary exercise of the theory of unitary urbanism will be the transcription of the whole theoretical lie of urbanism, appropriated [*détourné*] with an aim of de-alienation: we must defend ourselves at every moment from the epic poetry of the bards of conditioning—and turn the rhythm of their poems upside down.

8. CONDITIONS OF DIALOGUE

The functional is what is practical. The only practical thing is the resolution of our fundamental problem: the realization of ourselves (our uncoupling from the system of isolation). This is useful and utilitarian. Nothing else. All the rest represents only trivial derivations of the practical, and its mystification.

9. RAW MATERIALS AND PROCESSING

The Situationist destruction of present-day conditioning is already, at the same time, the construction of situations. It is the liberation of the inexhaustible energies contained within petrified everyday life. The present-day planning of cities, which appears as a geology of lies, will make way, with unitary urbanism, for a technique for defending the always threatened conditions of liberty, just as individuals—who do not yet exist as such—will freely construct their own history.

10. END OF THE PREHISTORY OF CONDITIONING

We do not maintain that we must return to some stage before conditioning, but that we must pass beyond it. We have invented the architecture and the urbanism that cannot be realized without the revolution of everyday life, that is to say the appropriation of conditioning by everyone, its unlimited enrichment and triumph.

CRITIQUE OF URBANISM[12]

The exclusion of more conservative tendencies, embodied in the Dutch section of the S.I., allowed for new themes to emerge in the study of unitary urbanism, which—far from simply abandoning prior acquisitions—incorporated them ever more closely into the contestation of the whole of society. This is clear from

---

12 *Internationale situationniste* no. 6 (August 1961): 3–11. [Ed.]

the start of this article, which opens on an intransigent note, claiming that urban planning, so long as it is separated from "general revolutionary praxis," is the very opposite of urban life. To accept urban planning as a specialized field of activity is already to accept all the lies that it entails and, in the final instance, the State itself. Even the most progressive urbanism has as its ultimate project to "perfect the conditioning" that the Situationists sought to abolish, "in urbanism and everywhere else." The so-called "crisis of urban planning" (already in 1961!) was, in fact, a social and political—not an architectural or urban—problem, and all the hand-wringing in the press over the prevalence in the new middle-class suburban housing projects of nervous breakdowns, juvenile delinquency, and casual prostitution by housewives failed to recognize that these symptoms merely revealed "that modern capitalism, the bureaucratic society of consumption, is here and there beginning to shape its own setting." The new towns of the 1950s and '60s were nothing less than the spatial translation of alienation and control and in these cities power increasingly could relinquish the old forms of advertising in favor of "the simple organization of the spectacle of objects of consumption, which will only have consumable value illusorily to the extent to which they will first of all have been objects of spectacle"—to the extent, that is, they have first appeared on the television screen, which henceforth had to be seen as an urbanistic tool in its own right.

The Situationists have always said "unitary urbanism is not a doctrine of urbanism but a critique of urbanism."[13] The project of a more modern, more progressive urbanism, conceived as a corrective to the present specialization of the urbanist, is as false as, for example, in the revolutionary project, the overestimation of the moment for seizing power, which is a specialist's idea that immediately involves forgetting, indeed repressing, all the revolutionary tasks posed, at each and every moment, by the whole inseparable combination of human activities. Until it merges with a general revolutionary praxis, urbanism is necessarily the first enemy of all possibilities for urban life in our time. It is one of those fragments of social power that claim to represent a coherent totality, and which tend to impose themselves as a total explanation and organization, while doing nothing except masking the real social totality that has produced them and which they preserve.

By accepting this specialization of urbanism, one puts oneself at the service of the prevailing social and urbanist lie—of the State—in order to carry out one of the many possible "practical" urbanisms. But the only practical urbanism *for us*, the one we call unitary urbanism, is thereby abandoned, since it requires the creation of quite different conditions of life.

Over the past six or eight months, we have seen a number of moves,

---

13 "Unitary Urbanism at the End of the 1950s" (1959), translated in this volume, 100. [Ed.]

THE CRITIQUE OF URBAN PLANNING 151

chiefly among West German architects and capitalists, to launch a "unitary urbanism" immediately, at least in the Ruhr. Some poorly informed merchants, enamored of quick accomplishments, saw fit to announce, in February 1961, the imminent opening of a U.U. laboratory in Essen (as a conversion of the Van de Loo art gallery). They published a disgruntled denial only when faced with our threat to reveal publicly the watered-down nature of the plan. The former Situationist Constant, whose Dutch collaborators had been excluded from the S.I. for having agreed to build a church, now himself offers *factory models* in his catalog published in March by the Municipal Museum of Bochum. This shrewd operator frankly offers himself, along with two or three plagiarized and misconstrued Situationist ideas, as public relations for the integration of the masses into capitalist technological civilization, and reproaches the S.I. for having abandoned his whole program for reordering the urban milieu, he himself being the only one still concerned with it. Under such conditions, yes! Moreover, one might do well to recall that in April 1959 this same group of former members of the Dutch section of the S.I. was firmly opposed to the adoption by the S.I. of an "Appeal to Revolutionary Intellectuals and Artists," and stated: "For us, these perspectives do not depend on a revolutionary overthrow of present-day society, for which the conditions are lacking."[14] They have thus continued logically on their path. What is more curious is that there should be people who still try to seduce a few Situationists in order to involve them in this kind of enterprise. Are they betting on the taste for glory or the lure of gain? On April 15, Attila Kotányi replied to a letter from the director of that Bochum museum proposing a collaboration with the Unitary Urbanism Office in Brussels: "If you know the original well enough, we do not think you can confuse our critical view with the apologetic view hidden behind a copy with the same label." And he cut off any further discussion.

It is not even easy to know the Situationist theses on U.U. in their original version. In June, our German comrades published a special issue of their journal, bringing together texts devoted to U.U. over several years in the S.I. or the trends leading to its formation.[15] Many of these texts were

---

14 For this debate, see "Discussion sur un appel aux intellectuals et artistes revolutionnaires," *Internationale situationniste* no. 3 (December 1959): 22–24. [Ed.]

15 *Spur* no. 5 (June 1961). This issue included Gilles Ivain (pseudo. Ivan Chtcheglov, "Formulary for a New Urbanism" (1953); André-Franck Conord, "Slum Construction" (1954); "Next Planet" (1954); "Skyscrapers by the Roots" (1954); Guy Debord and Jacques Fillon, "Summary 1954" (1954); Michèle Bernstein, Guy Debord, and Gil J. Wolman, "Lettrist Intervention" (1955); Guy Debord, "Introduction to a Critique of Urban Geography" (1955); Guy Debord, "Statement by Lettrist International Delegate to Alba Conference" (1956); Guy Debord, excerpt from the *Report on the Construction of Situations* (1957); "Unitary Urbanism at the End of the 1950s" (1959); and Attila Kotányi, "Gangland and Philosophy" (1960). All are translated in this volume. [Ed.]

unpublished or had appeared in now-inaccessible publications, and none of them had ever been published in German. The measures taken in Germany against the Situationists to prevent the appearance of these texts, or at least to have them altered, were immediately apparent: from blocking the whole edition at the printers for three weeks to loud threats of prosecution for immorality, pornography, blasphemy, and incitement to riot. The German Situationists have obviously weathered these various attempts at intimidation, and today the managers of respectable unitary urbanism in the Ruhr should begin to wonder if this label is a profitable way to launch their operation.

Contestation of the whole of present-day society is the sole criterion for a genuine liberation on the terrain of cities, and the same goes for any other aspect of human activity. Otherwise, "improvement" or "progress" will always be designed to lubricate the system and perfect the conditioning that we must overturn, in urbanism and everywhere else. Henri Lefebvre, in the third number of the *Revue française de sociologie*, criticizes a number of inadequacies in the plan that a team of architects and sociologists have just published in Zurich, *Die neue Stadt, eine Studie für das Fürttal*.[16] But it seems to us that this criticism does not go far enough, precisely because it does not clearly challenge the very role of this team of specialists in a social framework whose absurd imperatives it accepts without discussion. This means that Lefebvre's article still valorizes too many works that certainly have their utility and their merits, but in a perspective radically inimical to ours. The title of this article, "Experimental Utopia: Toward a New Urbanism," already contains the whole ambiguity. For the method of experimental utopia, if it is truly to correspond to its project, must obviously embrace the totality, i.e. carrying it out would lead not to a "new urbanism" but to a new use of life, a new revolutionary praxis. It is also the lack of a connection between the project for a passionate reordering of architecture and other forms of conditioning, and its rejection in terms of the whole society, that constitutes the weakness of Günther Feuerstein's theses, published in the same issue of the journal of the German section of the S.I., despite the interest of several points, in particular his notion of the unpredictable mass, "representing chance and also the smallest organization of objects comprised by an event." Feuerstein's ideas on an "unpremeditated architecture," which follow the S.I. line, can only be understood in all their consequences, and carried out, precisely by overcoming the separate problem of architecture and the solutions that would be reserved for it in the abstract.[17]

---

16 Henri Lefebvre, "Experimental Utopia: Toward a New Urbanism" (1961), partially trans. in this volume, 105–06. [Ed.]

17 *Spur* no. 5 also included a version of Günther Feuerstein's "Theses on Unpremeditated Architecture" that differs at several points from the one translated in this volume, 125–33. Notably, the version published by the German section of the S.I. concluded with two paragraphs on this concept of the "unpredictable mass," a kind of variant on the Surrealist *objet trouvé*. [Ed.]

Henceforth the crisis of urbanism is all the more concretely a social and political one, even though today no force born of traditional politics is any longer capable of dealing with it. Medico-sociological banalities on the "pathology of housing projects," the emotional isolation of people who must live in them, or the development of certain extreme reactions of rejection, chiefly among youth, simply betray the fact that modern capitalism, the bureaucratic society of consumption, *is here and there beginning to shape its own setting*. This society, with its new towns, is building the terrain that accurately represents it, combining the conditions most suitable for its proper functioning, while at the same time translating in space, in the clear language of the organization of everyday life, its fundamental principle of alienation and constraint. It is likewise here that the new aspects of its crisis will be manifested with the greatest clarity.

In Paris, last April, an exhibition of urbanism entitled "Paris Tomorrow" offered in reality a defense of housing projects, those already built or planned for the far outskirts of the city. The future of Paris would be entirely extra-Parisian. The first part of this didactic presentation sought to convince the public (mainly workers) that Paris, as shown by decisive statistics, was more unhealthy and unlivable than any other known capital. They would thus do well to transport themselves elsewhere, and indeed the happy solution was thereupon offered, failing only to mention the now necessary price for the construction of these regroupment zones: for instance, how many years of outright economic slavery the purchase of an apartment in these projects entails, and what an urbanist life sentence this acquired ownership will come to represent.

Still, the very necessity for this faked propaganda, the need to present this explanation to the interested parties after the administration had independently settled the matter, reveals an initial resistance by the masses. This resistance will need to be sustained and clarified by a revolutionary organization truly determined to know and combat all the conditions of modern capitalism. Sociological surveys, whose most stultifying defect is to present options only between the dismal variations of what already exists, indicate that 75% of the inhabitants of housing projects dream of owning a suburban house with a garden.

It is this mystified image of ownership, in the old-fashioned sense, that led Renault workers, for example, to buy the small houses that dropped in their laps in June, in a whole quarter of Clamart. It is not by returning to this archaic ideology of an obsolete stage of capitalism that the living conditions of a society now becoming totalitarian can ever be truly replaced, but rather by freeing an instinct for construction presently repressed in everyone: a liberation that cannot go forward without the other aspects in the conquest of an authentic life.

Debates in progressive inquiries today, on politics as well as art or urbanism, lag considerably behind the reality taking shape in all industrialized countries, namely, the concentrationary organization of life.

The degree of conditioning imposed on workers in a suburb like Sarcelles, or still more clearly in a city like Mourenx (founded on the monopoly of employment of its population in the petrochemical complex of Lacq), prefigures the conditions with which the revolutionary movement will everywhere have to struggle if it is to re-establish itself on a level with the real crises, the real demands of our time. In Brasília, functional architecture reveals itself to be, when fully developed, the architecture of functionaries, the instrument and microcosm of the bureaucratic Weltanschauung. One can already see that wherever bureaucratic, planned capitalism has already built its setting, conditioning has been so perfected, the individual's margin of choice reduced to so little, that a practice as essential for it as advertising, which corresponded to a more anarchic stage of competition, tends to disappear in most of its forms and supports. You might think that urbanism is capable of merging all former forms of advertising into a single advertisement for itself. The rest will be had below market price. It is also likely that, under these conditions, the political propaganda that has been so strong in the first half of the twentieth century will almost totally disappear, to be replaced by an instinctive aversion to all political issues. Just as the revolutionary movement will have to shift the problem far away from the old field of politics scorned by everyone, the powers-that-be will rely more on the simple organization of the spectacle of objects of consumption, which will only have consumable value illusorily *to the extent to which they will first of all have been objects of spectacle*. In Sarcelles or Mourenx, the theaters of this new world are already being put to the test—atomized to the limit around each television screen, but at the same time extended to cover the whole town.

If unitary urbanism designates, as we would like it to, a hypothesis regarding the use of the means of present-day humanity to freely construct its life, beginning with the urban environment, it is absolutely pointless to enter into discussion with those who would ask us to what extent it is feasible, specific, practical, or carved in concrete, for the simple reason that nowhere does there exist any theory or practice concerning the creation of cities, or the kind of behavior that relates to it. No one "does urbanism," in the sense of constructing the milieu required by this doctrine. Nothing exists but a collection of techniques for integrating people (techniques that effectively resolve conflicts while creating others, at present less known but more serious). These techniques are wielded innocently by imbeciles or deliberately by the police. And all the discourses on urbanism are lies, just as obviously the space organized by urbanism is the very space of the social lie and of fortified exploitation. Those who discourse on the powers of urbanism seek to make people forget that all they are creating is the urbanism of power. Urbanists, who present themselves as the educators of the population, have had to be educated themselves—by this world of alienation that they reproduce and perfect as best they can.

The notion of a center of attraction in the chatter of urbanists is quite the opposite of the reality, exactly as the sociological notion of participation turns out to be. The fact is that there are disciplines that come to terms with a society where participation can only be oriented toward "something in which it is impossible to participate"[18]—a society that must impose the need for objects of little appeal, and would not tolerate any form of genuine attraction. To understand what sociology *never* understands, one need only envisage in terms of aggression what for sociology is neutral.

The "bases" planned for an experimental life, of which the S.I. program of unitary urbanism speaks, are at the same time the places, the permanent elements of a new kind of revolutionary organization that we believe to be inscribed in the order of the day for the historical period we are entering. These bases, when they come to exist, cannot be anything but subversive. And the future revolutionary organization will not be able to rely on instruments less complete.

COMMENTS AGAINST URBANISM[19]

RAOUL VANEIGEM

Vaneigem here adds his own particular polemic flair to the critical analysis of contemporary urban planning: not only is urbanism "all that will be needed to preserve the established order without recourse to the indelicacy of machine guns," but "if the Nazis had known contemporary urbanists, they would have transformed their concentration camps into" the kinds of subsidized housing being built by the French state at the edges of its great cities. But beyond this verbal extremism, he develops the argument that the task of the new towns is above all the imposition of historical and social amnesia, an eradication of the popular memory of the traditional city as a space of social struggle and revolution and, beyond that, of the sense that each everyday life contains its own particular and valuable history.

Expert opinion—that of Chombart de Lauwe—declares, after precise experiments, that the programs proposed by planners create in certain cases unrest and revolt, which might have been partly avoided if we had a deeper knowledge of real comportments, and especially of the motivations for such comportments.

---

18 Attila Kotányi and Raoul Vaneigem, "Elementary Program of the Unitary Urbanism Office" (1961), trans. in this volume, 147. [Ed.]

19 *Internationale situationniste* no. 6 (August 1961): 33–37. [Ed.]

Splendor and misery of urbanism. When we have sniffed the urbanistic planner with suspicious insistence, one turns away as one ought to before such a breach of manners, such impropriety. Here it is not a question of impeaching the popular verdict. The people have long since pronounced themselves with the same rudeness: "silly architect!" has always been an explicit way of speaking in Belgium. But, since such an expert sides today with the opinions of the herd and also starts sniffing the planner, we are saved! Thus, the urbanist is officially convicted of arousing unrest and revolt, arousing them "almost" like a primary provocateur. One can only hope that the public authorities will react promptly; it would be unthinkable for centers of revolt to be openly maintained by the very people whose job it is to reabsorb them. Here is a crime against social peace that only a council of war might cut short. Will we see justice prevail among its own ranks? Unless the expert turns out to be, after all, only an urbanist in disguise.

If the planner cannot understand the behavioral motivations of those he wants to house to the best of their nervous equilibrium, might as well incorporate urbanism without delay into the center for criminological research (to hunt down provocateurs—see above—and allow each to remain tranquilly in the hierarchy); if he can really do it, then the science of suppressing crime loses its raison d'être and changes its social purpose: urbanism is all that will be needed to preserve the established order without recourse to the indelicacy of machine guns. Humanity assimilated to concrete, what a dream or happy nightmare for technocrats, wherein they might lose whatever Higher Nervous Activity they have left, and be protected by the power and durability of concrete.

If the Nazis had known contemporary urbanists, they would have transformed their concentration camps into subsidized housing. But this solution seems too brutal to Chombart de Lauwe. Ideal urbanism should enlist everyone, without unrest or revolt, in the final solution of the problem of humanity.

Urbanism is the most advanced, concrete fulfillment of a nightmare. Littré defines nightmare as "a state that ends when one awakens with a start after extreme anxiety." But a start against whom? Who has stuffed us to the point of somnolence? It would be as stupid to execute Eichmann as to hang the urbanists. It would be like finding fault with the targets when you're on a rifle range!

Planning is a big word, some would say a dirty word. Specialists speak of economic planning, and planned urbanism, then they wink with a knowing air, and everyone applauds so as to play the game. The success of the spectacle is the planning of happiness. The advocates of figures are already conducting their inquiries; precise tests establish the density of television viewers; it is a question of developing the territory around them, of building for them, without distracting them from the concerns that are being fed to them

THE CRITIQUE OF URBAN PLANNING 157

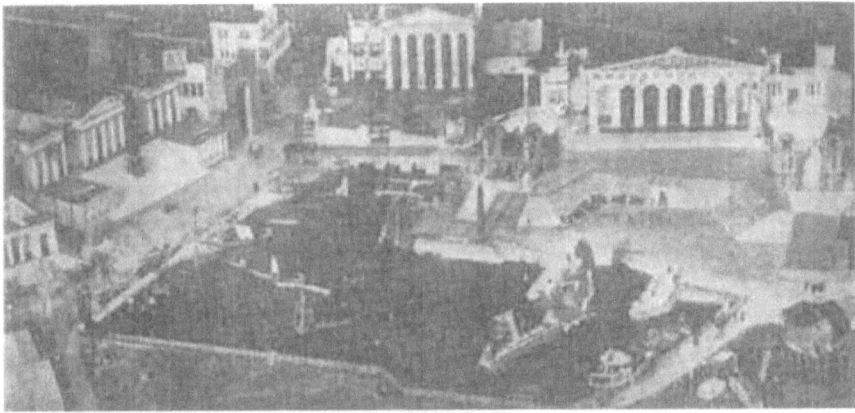

Fig.6.5.2 **Setting and its use**. Four historians and many hundreds of millions, it is said, have been employed this year to reconstruct part of the city of Alexandria on a moor in England. It was all for Elizabeth Taylor to play Cleopatra in. The actress falling ill, the film could not be shot, nor the land put to further use. Finally Alexandria was delivered to the flames. From *Internationale situationniste* no. 6 (August 1961).

through their eyes and ears. It is a question of assuring equilibrium and a peaceful life to all, with that shrewd foresight displayed by comic-strip pirates in their maxim: "Dead men tell no tales." Urbanism and information are complementary in capitalist and "anti-capitalist" societies—they organize silence.

To live in is urbanism's "Drink Coca-Cola." The necessity of drinking is replaced with that of drinking Coca-Cola. To live in means to be at home everywhere, says Frederick Kiesler, but such a prophetic truth grabs nobody by the neck; it's a scarf against the encroaching cold, even if its evokes a flowing knot. We are lived-in; this is the necessary starting point.

As public relations, ideal urbanism is the projection in space of conflict-free social hierarchy. Roads, lawns, natural flowers, and artificial forests lubricate the wheels of subjection and make them enjoyable. In a novel by Yves Touraine, the State even offers retired workers an electronic masturbator; happiness and the economy find it an advantage.[20]

A certain urbanism of prestige is necessary, Chombart de Lauwe claims. This spectacle that it offers us makes Haussmann look quaint, he who could plan no prestige apart from a firing range. This time, it is a matter of scenically organizing the spectacle across everyday life, of letting people live in the frameworks corresponding to the roles that capitalist society imposes on them, of further isolating them by training them, like the blind, to recognize themselves illusorily in a materialization of their own alienation.

The capitalist training of space is nothing but training in a space where you lose your shadow, and end up losing yourself by dint of seeking yourself in what you are not. An excellent example of tenacity for all professors and other licensed organizers of ignorance.

The layout of a city, its streets, walls, and its quarters form so many signs of a strange conditioning. What sign should we recognize there as our own? A few graffiti, words of refusal or forbidden gestures, hastily scrawled, in which learned people only take an interest when they appear on the walls of Pompeii, of some fossil city. But our cities are even more fossilized. We would like to live in lands of knowledge, amid living signs like familiar friends. The revolution will also be the perpetual creation of signs that belong to everyone.

There is an incredible dullness in everything having to do with urbanism. The word "build" is sinking fast, in the water where other possible words float on the surface. Wherever bureaucratic civilization has spread, the anarchy of individual construction has been officially set apart, and taken over by the authorized organisms of power, with the result that the building

---

20 Yves Touraine, *Le Cinquième coup de trompette* (Paris: Arcanes, Coll. "Les Champs magnétiques," 1954). This book is also mentioned in Raoul Vaneigem, *The Revolution of Everyday Life* (1967), trans. Donald Nicholson-Smith (London: Left Bank Books and Rebel Press, 1983), 21. [Ed.]

instinct has been extirpated like a vice and only barely survives in children and primitives (those not held accountable, in administrative parlance). And among all those who, unable to change their lives, spend them demolishing and rebuilding their shacks.

Urbanism knows how to exercise the art of reassurance in its purest form: the ultimate civility of a power on the verge of asserting total mind control.

God and the City: no abstract and nonexistent force would be better able than urbanism to take over from God the post of doorkeeper left vacant by that death we've heard about. With its ubiquity, its immense benevolence, and—perhaps someday—its sovereign power, urbanism (or its project) would certainly have something to frighten the Church, were there the slightest doubt about the orthodoxy of power. But there is none, since the Church was "urbanism" long before power; what could it have to fear from a lay Saint Augustine?

There is something admirable in causing thousands of beings that one deprives of even the hope of a last judgment to coexist in the words "live in." In this sense, the admirable crowns the inhuman.

Industrializing private life: "make your life a business," such will be the new slogan. To propose to people that they organize their vital milieus like little factories to be managed, like miniature enterprises with their substitute machinery, their prestige production, their fixed capital such as walls and furniture—isn't this the best way to make perfectly comprehensible the concerns of those gentlemen who own a factory, a big and real one that must also produce?

Make the horizon uniform: walls and unnatural patches of greenery set new limits to thought and dreaming, for it means poeticizing the desert rather than knowing where it ends.

The new cities will wipe out the traces of the battles between traditional cities and the people they sought to oppress. To root out of everyone's memory the truth that each everyday life has its history and, in the myth of participation, to contest the irreducible character of lived experience—these are the terms in which urbanists would express the goals they pursue, if they deigned to suspend for a moment the air of seriousness that obstructs their thinking. Once the air of seriousness disappears, the sky lightens, everything becomes clearer, or almost; thus, as humorists well know, to destroy one's adversary with H-bombs is to condemn oneself to die in more protracted sufferings. How much longer will one have to go on mocking the urbanists before they grasp the cruel fact that they're preparing the way for their own suicide?

Cemeteries are the most natural areas for greenery that exist, the only ones to be harmoniously integrated within the framework of future cities, like the last lost paradises.

Cost must cease to be an obstacle to the desire to build—so says the leftist builder. May he sleep in peace, for this will soon be the case, once the desire to build will have disappeared.

In France procedures have been developed that turn construction into an erector set (J.-E. Havel).[21] While making the best of things, a cafeteria is never anything but a place where you serve, in the sense that a fork serves for eating.

Combining Machiavellianism with reinforced concrete, urbanism's conscience is clear. We are entering upon the reign of police refinement. Dignified enslavement.

To build with confidence: even the reality of glazed curtain walls does not hide the fictive communication, even the ambiance of public places betrays the despair and isolation of private consciences, even the frantic filling up of space is measured in dead time.

Project for a realistic urbanism: replace Piranesi's staircases with elevators, transform tombs into office buildings, line the sewers with plane trees, turn trash cans into living rooms, stack up the slums, and build all cities in the form of museums; make a profit out of everything, even out of nothing.

Alienation within easy reach: urbanism makes alienation tangible. The starving proletariat experienced alienation in bestial suffering. We will experience it in the blind suffering of things. To feel by groping.

Honest and farsighted urbanists have the courage of stylites. Must we make our lives a desert so as to legitimize their aspirations?

For some twenty years now the guardians of philosophic faith have discovered the existence of a working class. At a time when sociologists are deciding to decree that the working class no longer exists, the urbanists have invented the inhabitant without waiting for either philosophers or sociologists. One must give them credit for being among the first to discern the new dimensions of the proletariat. By a definition all the more precise and much less abstract, they have been able, using the most flexible training methods, to guide almost all of society toward a less brutal but radical proletarianization.

Advice to the builders of ruins: the urbanists will be succeeded by the last troglodytes of the *bidonvilles* and slums. They will know how to build. The privileged residents of dormitory towns will only be able to destroy. We can expect much from such an encounter: it defines the revolution.

By being devalued, the sacred has become a mystery: urbanism is the final decadence of the Great Architect.

Behind the infatuation with technology a revealed truth lies hidden, and

---

21 See Jean-Eugène Havel, *Habitat et logement* (Paris: Presses universitaires de France, Coll. "Que sais-je?," 1957). In his conclusion, Havel calls for a technological solution to the housing problem, favorably citing the rationalized labor processes utilized in the construction of American Levittowns. [Ed.]

as such is unquestionable: we must "live in." Concerning the nature of such a truth, tramps know very well what to cling to. Probably better than anyone else, they are able to measure, amid the garbage cans where they are forced to live and prohibited from "living in," how there is no difference between building their own lives and building their dwellings on the only level of truth that exists—practice. But the exile to which our well-policed world consigns them makes their experience so ridiculous and difficult that the licensed builder could find there an excuse for self-justification—assuming, absurd idea, that the powers-that-be were to cease to guarantee his existence.

It looks like the working class no longer exists. Considerable quantities of former proletarians can today have access to the comfort formerly reserved for a minority—so goes the song. But isn't it rather that a growing quantity of comfort has access to their needs and gives them the itch to ask for it? It seems that a certain organization of comfort proletarianizes in epidemic fashion all those it contaminates by the force of things. Now, the force of things is exercised through the intervention of responsible authorities, priests of an abstract order whose sole privileged members will sooner or later come together to reign over an administrative center surrounded by ghettoes. The last man will die of boredom as a spider dies of inanition in the middle of its web.

So many people need to be housed that we must build in haste, say the humanists of reinforced concrete. The whole of the fatherland must be saved, so we must dig trenches without delay, say the generals. Isn't there some injustice in lauding the humanists and making fun of the generals? In the era of missiles and conditioning, it is still in good taste to make jokes about generals. But to raise trenches in the air with the same pretext!

THE BEAUTIFUL AND THE GOOD[22]

UWE LAUSEN

Perhaps you recall a certain mother who loved her son: she stuffed cotton in his ears, tied disinfected kerchiefs for him to breathe through, never let him out into the street. She protected him from all the dangers of the world, from any risk of suffering or death.

We do not live in a night-watchman State, but in a welfare State.[23] Not only is our sleep protected from the attacks of common murderers, but also

---

22 *Der deutsche Gedanke* no. 1 (April 1963): 13. [Ed.]
23 The "night-watchman State" was a notion of Ferdinand Lassalle (1825–1864), German jurist and socialist political activist. The night-watchman State was the State that only guaranteed its citizens a minimal security. According the Lassalle, it was up to the State to guarantee social justice. [Ed.]

in addition the ugly and the perishable must be caught in the filter of social protection.

Entirely by chance I came across a copy of the *Bavarian Building Regulations* (latest edition). There I read:

> Structures must be designed according to established architectural rules, in order to cause no disfiguring of form, of dimensions, of relation of the whole of the building to its parts, as well as of materials or colors used. Structures must be in harmony with their neighborhood, so that they do not render the appearance of the landscape, the streets, the site, or the projected appearance of the latter, ugly (art. 11).

Established rules . . . Do not *render the appearance ugly*. The bureaucracy of the beautiful and the good does not sleep where we must sleep; the imagination is "arbitrary and anarchic": it terrifies, it disturbs order, and it separates systems that have been assembled with care.

One aspect of the growing social protection is becoming clear. Certain quarters already have the future countenance that cogs are imagined to have: without imagination, a countenance that kills imagination, the faceless countenance of quarters filled with new buildings and of new towns. It would be hard to still point out here the slight, stray impulses of individual conscience. "Can you paint your house red? Can it have more windows? Can you install a glass door instead of wood?" These are examples. Simple facts that echo like excesses. But today, many people really consider success in painting their house such or such a color as a victory and an extraordinary mark of their individuality. In place of personality, *marginal differentiation*.

The majority of architects have given up even when it comes to little things. The wretched remains of their courage, of their imagination, have been smashed in combat lasting months, sometimes even years, against the apparatus, in the cogs of artistic commissions, boards of exam, delivery services, and construction permits. Only construction projects for the State and the Länder—and above all those useful for national defense (art. 103, and see also the federal law on construction § 37)—don't have to pass through the federal cogwheels.

In the welfare States, in the modern metropolises—Stockholm, Copenhagen, New York, Vienna, Berlin, and Hamburg—in the new quarters, in luxury apartments, the rate of suicide is mounting. Here too one doesn't simply fold one's arms, one does something, since "it is impossible to imagine any human situation so unbearable and desperate that healthy people would be driven to kill themselves." An *international working group for the prevention of suicide* will persuade those who lack the will to live that everything isn't all that bad.

We no longer live in misery. Poor quarters have been torn down. We are protected from moldy walls and winding alleys. No more rheumatism in damp spaces. Death and disease, the ugly and the perishable, are held at bay. And yet all this is beautiful and good: no one really wants to go back to mold and rheumatism. It is a matter conversely of finding within the wealth of the technological world, with its enormous resources, new possibilities for the realization of the self. However this only means taking possession of this wealth and these resources, and utilizing them in a different fashion. And what about the negative? Do we need it in order to move beyond the present conditioning? It is there. We are distanced from death, only to find it housed in our hearts. The negative is set aside, yet we encounter it everywhere. Critique and refusal no longer seem to be justified among such wellbeing, but critique has become generalized. This world cohabits with the negative. It will have to look it in the face.[24]

ON THE ROLE OF THE S.I.[25]

At the same time that the S.I. was shedding its "right wing," it also left its readers with no doubt as to its intentions, opening this essay with the promise that the group will dissolve itself "into the population that at every moment lives out" the group's project—an appropriation and transformation of Mao's famous dictum on the nature of guerilla warfare behind enemy lines.[26] If the masses spontaneously think in the same terms as the S.I., however, the French intelligentsia must necessarily be rejected en bloc, and other potential interlocutors are warned that they must either accept or reject the S.I.'s positions as a whole—this global revolutionary theory cannot be chopped into discrete points. All those intellectuals and experts fail to recognize the rising anger of the population: "One day they will all be shocked to see architects being tracked down and hanged in the streets of Sarcelles" (the most infamous of the new towns outside Paris), but the Situationists will be spared the surprise, having predicted the upheaval all along. The S.I. is not a group of specialists, it lays no claim to fields

---

24 This final section contains a (faint) *détournement* of Hegel's "Preface" to *Phenomenology of Spirit*, and in particular of its discussion, in the context of the "Master-Slave" allegory, of the necessary acceptance of the risk of death: "It wins its truth only when, in absolute dismemberment, it finds itself. *Geist* has this power only by looking the negative in the face, and enduring it." See Hegel, *Phenomenology of Spirit*, trans. A. V. Miller (Oxford: Clarendon Press, 1977), 19. [Ed.]
25 *Internationale situationniste* no. 7 (April 1962): 17–20. [Ed.]
26 "Many people think it impossible for guerillas to exist for long in the enemy's rear. Such a belief reveals lack of comprehension of the relationship between the people and the troops. The former may be likened to water and the latter to the fish who inhabit it. How may it be said that these two cannot exist together?" Mao Tse-tung, *On Guerilla Warfare*, chap. 6. [Ed.]

of knowledge; its journal, the record of its "omniscient critique," is the interim report of the coming revolution.

We are completely with the people. We only take into consideration problems that are already in suspense among all the population. Situationist theory is in the people like fish are in the sea. To those who think the S.I. is constructing a speculative fortress, we assert on the contrary: we are going to dissolve ourselves into the population that at every moment lives out our project—living it first of all, of course, as a lack and repression.

Those who have not understood this should return to the study of our program. *Internationale situationniste*, the provisional report on progress toward a supersession, is a journal that makes you realize, after having read the most recent issue, how necessary it is to go back and read the first one.

Specialists perhaps flatter themselves with the illusion that they control certain fields of knowledge and practice, but there is no specialist who escapes our omniscient critique. We recognize to what extent we still lack means, and the lack of our means is first of all our lack of information (as much with regard to the inaccessibility of essential documents where they exist as to the absence of any document on the most important problems that we can designate). But all the same, it should not be forgotten that the technocratic scum also lacks information. Even where it has, by its own standards, the most extensive information at its disposal, it has only 10% of what would be needed to contradict us—a possibility that is sheer extravagance, since the ruling bureaucracy, by its very nature, cannot get very far with quantitative information (it can only remain unaware of how workers *actually* work, how people *actually* live); so therefore it has no hope of catching up with the qualitative. In contrast, the only thing we lack is the quantitative, and in the future it too will be ours, because we grasp the qualitative, which acts from the present as a mathematical exponent that multiplies the quantity of the information we have at our disposal. This example can be extended to the understanding of the past: we are undertaking to investigate thoroughly and reassess certain historical periods, even without having access to the majority of historians' learning.

The raw facts, known by all specialists, repudiate the current organization of reality (say, the setting of Sarcelles no less than the lifestyle of Tony Armstrong-Jones), making an implacable and immediate critique of it.[27] Hired specialists have for too long congratulated themselves on the fact that nobody *represents* these truths that all of reality proffers. How they tremble! Their good times are over. We will knock them down, along with all the hierarchies they shelter.

---

27 Antony Armstrong-Jones (1930–), English photographer and, at the time of the publication of this article, husband of Princess Margaret. [Ed.]

We are capable of contesting every discipline. We will not allow a single specialist to remain master of a single specialty. We are ready to temporarily manage the forms within which calculations and reckonings can be made: what it allows us to know is the margin of error, itself calculable, that inevitably belongs to such calculations. In this manner we ourselves will reduce our results of the factor of error introduced by the use of categories that we know are false. It is easy for us to choose the battlefield each time. If it is necessary to face "models" that are today the points of convergence of technocratic thought (whether it be total competition or total planning), with "models," our "model" is *total communication*. Let no one speak to us any longer of utopia. In that term should be recognized a hypothesis that, obviously, will never be realized exactly in reality, no more than anything else. But we ourselves possess its complementary factor with the theory of potlatch as irreversible expression. There are no more possible "utopias," because all the conditions of its realization already exist. These conditions are being appropriated [*détourne*] to serve the maintenance of the current order, whose absurdity is so dreadful *that it is being realized first*, no matter what the price, without *anyone daring to formulate its theory, even after the fact*. It is the *inverse utopia* of repression: it has at its disposal every power, and nobody wants it.

We are leading as thorough a study of "alienation's positive pole" as of its negative pole. As a consequence of our diagnosis of the poverty of wealth, we are able to establish the world map of the extreme wealth of poverty. These speaking maps of a new topography will be in fact the first realization of "human geography." On them we will replace oil-deposits with the contours of layers of untapped proletarian consciousness.

Under such conditions, it is easy to understand the general tone of our relations with an impotent intellectual generation. We will make no concession. It is clear that, from the crowds who spontaneously think as we do, the intellectuals in their quasi-unanimity must be excluded—that is to say people who, holding the lease on contemporary thought, must inevitably be satisfied with their own thinking about thinkers. Being accepted as such, and therefore as impotent, they then discuss the impotence of thought in general (see the editorial clowns of *Arguments* no. 20, devoted precisely to intellectuals).

From the start of our common action, we have been clear. But now, our activity has become so important that we no longer have to argue with unqualified interlocutors. Our followers are everywhere. And we have no intention of deceiving them. What we are providing is their sword.

As for those who might be valid interlocutors, let them well understand that with us their relations could not be innocuous. Finding ourselves at a decisive turning point, and though we are aware of the proportion of our mistakes, we can nevertheless oblige these possible allies to make a global choice. We have to be accepted or rejected as a whole. We will not allow ourselves to be cut up.

There is nothing surprising in speaking these truths. What is surprising is rather that all the specialists of opinion polls do not know the great nearness of this legitimate, rising anger about so many things. One day they will all be shocked to see architects being tracked down and hanged in the streets of Sarcelles.

The flaw of other groups, which have more or less seen the necessity of the coming change, is their positivity. Whether these groups try to be an artistic avant-garde or rather a new political formation, they all believe in the need to salvage something of the old praxis, and thanks to this they lose their way.

Those who too quickly want to establish themselves as a political positivity do so entirely under the domination of the old politics, in the same way that so many people have urged on the Situationists to establish themselves as a positive art. Our strength is to have never done such a thing. Our dominant position in modern culture has never been emphasized better than by the decision made at the Göteborg Conference to name henceforth all artistic productions by members of the S.I. in the present framework as *anti-Situationist*, so that they will contribute to both destruction and consolidation at the same time.[28]

The interpretation that we are defending in culture can be regarded as a simple hypothesis, and we expect that it will in effect be verified and superseded very quickly; but in every way it possesses the essential characteristics of rigorous scientific verification in the sense that it explains and orders a certain number of phenomena that are, for others, incoherent and unexplainable—which are therefore sometimes even *hidden* by other forces—and in that it allows the *prediction* of certain facts that will be controllable later. We do not fool ourselves for an instant on the so-called objectivity of some researcher whomever it may be, in culture or what is generally called the human sciences. There the rule is, on the contrary, to hide in this objectivity as many problems as answers. The S.I. must reveal the hidden, and reveal itself as the possibility "hidden" by its enemies. We will carry it out—calling attention to the contradictions that others have chosen to forget—by transforming ourselves into the practical force as forecast in the *Hamburg Theses*, drawn up by Debord, Kotányi, Trocchi, and Vaneigem (summer 1961).[29]

The unshakable project of the S.I. is total freedom made concrete in

---

28   See "The Fifth S.I. Conference in Göteborg (excerpts)" (1962), in *Situationist International Anthology*, 88–89. [Ed.]

29   See "Les Thèses de Hambourg en septembre 1961" (1989), in Debord, *Oeuvres*, 585–586. [Ed.]

acts and in the imagination, for freedom is not easy to imagine within the existing oppression. The way that we will win is by identifying ourselves with everyone's most profound desire and giving it free license. The "motivational researchers" of modern advertising find in peoples' subconscious the desire for objects; and we will find the single desire to break life's shackles. We are the representatives of the key idea of the greatest majority. Our first principles must be beyond dispute.

7.

Festival and Urban Revolution

ON THE COMMUNE

GUY DEBORD, ATTILA KOTÁNYI, AND RAOUL VANEIGEM

These Situationist theses set about making conscious the unconscious (or semiconscious) tendencies of the Paris Commune of 1871. Their central claims are that this uprising was "the biggest festival [fête] of the nineteenth century" and that it is precisely the most seemingly reckless acts of the Commune that contemporary revolutionaries must take up as their own.

I.

"We must begin again to study the classical workers movement in a disabused manner, and disabused firstly with regard to its various kinds of political or pseudo-theoretical heirs, for they possess only the inheritance of its failure. The apparent successes of this movement (reformism or the coming to power of a state bureaucracy) are its fundamental failures, and its failures (the Commune or the Asturias rebellion) are so far its honest successes, for us and for the future."[1]

2.

The Commune was the biggest festival of the nineteenth century. One finds, at bottom, the insurgents' impression of having become the masters of their own history, not so much on the level of "governmental" political decision-making as on the level of everyday life in that spring of 1871 (see everyone's *play* with weapons, which means: playing with power.)

---

1 "The Bad Days Will End" (1962), in *Situationist International Anthology*, 84 (trans. modified). [Ed.]

It is *also* in this sense that we should understand Marx: "the great social measure of the Commune was its own working existence."[2]

3.

Engels's saying—"Look at the Paris Commune. That was the Dictatorship of the Proletariat"—should be taken seriously, as the basis of showing what the dictatorship of the proletariat, as a political regime, is not (the various modalities of dictatorship over the proletariat, in its name).[3]

4.

Everyone has been able to make legitimate criticisms of the Commune's incoherence, of the obvious lack of an *apparatus*. But seeing that we now think that the problem of political apparatuses is far more complex than the reprehensible heirs of the Bolshevik-type apparatus claim, it is time to consider the Commune not just as an outmoded revolutionary primitivism, all of whose mistakes are being overcome, but as a positive experiment whose whole truth has not been recovered or realized.

5.

The Commune had no leaders, this in a historical period when the idea that they were necessary absolutely dominated the workers movement. In this way its paradoxical failures and successes are first explained. The official advisers of the Commune were incompetent (if the level of Marx or Lenin, and even Blanqui, is taken as reference). But conversely the "irresponsible" acts of that moment are precisely to be claimed for the continuation of the revolutionary movement of our time (even if circumstances limited almost all of them to the destructive level—the best known example is the rebel saying to the suspect bourgeois, who asserted that he had never been involved in politics: "That's precisely why I'm going to kill you").

---

2 Karl Marx, "*The Civil War in France.—III*" (1871), in Karl Marx and Frederick Engels, *Collected Works*, Vol. 22 ("Marx and Engels: 1870–71") (London: Lawrence & Wishart, 1986), 339. [Ed.]
3 Frederick Engels, "Introduction to K. Marx's *The Civil War in France*" (1891), in Karl Marx and Frederick Engels, *Collected Works*, Vol. 27 ("Engels: 1890–95") (London: Lawrence & Wishart, 1990), 191. [Ed.]

6.

The vital importance of the general arming of the people was manifested, in practice and in signs, from one end of the movement to the other. On the whole the right to impose common will by force was not abdicated in favor of specialized detachments. The exemplary value of this autonomy of the armed groups had its flip side in the lack of coordination—the fact of having at no point, whether offensive or defensive, led the popular force to the rank of military effectiveness in the struggle against Versailles; but it should not be forgotten that the Spanish revolution (and finally the war itself) was lost in the name of such a transformation into a "republican army." It may be that the contradiction between autonomy and coordination depended largely on the technological stage of the period.

7.

The Commune represents, until us, *the one realization of a revolutionary urbanism*, knocking to the ground the petrified signs of the dominant organization of life, recognizing social space in political terms, refusing to believe that a monument could be innocent. Those who reduce this to a lumpenproletarian nihilism, to the irresponsibility of the *pétroleuses*, should acknowledge in return all that they consider as positive and worth preserving in the ruling society (you'll see that it is almost everything). "All space is already occupied by the enemy… The moment of authentic urbanism's appearance will be the creation, in certain areas, of the absence of this occupation. What we call construction starts there. It can be understood with the help of the concept of the 'positive void' invented by modern physics."[4]

8.

The Paris Commune was defeated less by force of arms than by force of habit. The most scandalous practical example is the refusal to resort to cannon to seize the Bank of France at a time when money was so lacking. During the whole of the Commune's influence, the Bank remained a Versaillaise enclave within Paris, defended by a few rifles and the myth of property and theft. Other ideological habits (the resurrection of Jacobinism, the defeatist strategy of the barricades in memory of '48, etc.) were at every turn disastrous.

---

4   Attila Kotányi and Raoul Vaneigem, "Elementary Program of the Unitary Urbanism Office" (1961), trans. in this volume, 148. [Ed.]

9.

The Commune shows how those who defend the old world always benefit, on one score or another, from the complicity of revolutionaries; and above all of those who *think* the revolution. It is on the score where the revolutionaries *think like them*. In this way the old world retains bases (ideology, language, customs, tastes) in the development of its enemies and makes use of them to regain lost ground. (Only the thought in acts natural to the revolutionary proletariat forever escapes it: the Cour des Comptes went up in flames.) The true "fifth column" is in the very minds of revolutionaries.

10.

The anecdote of the arsonists, in the final days, coming to destroy Notre-Dame, and colliding with the armed battalion of Commune artists, is rich in meaning: it is a good example of direct democracy. It also shows, more distantly, problems yet to be resolved within the perspective of councils' authority. Were those unanimous artists right to defend a cathedral in the name of eternal aesthetic values, and in the end the spirit of museums, when other people wanted precisely to have access to expression that very day, in translating by this destruction their total challenge of a society that, in the present defeat, dismissed their entire lives to silence and oblivion? The Commune's partisan-artists, acting as specialists, already found themselves in conflict with an extremist expression of the struggle against alienation. We should challenge the people of the Commune for not having dared to answer the totalitarian terror of power with the use of the totality of their weapons. Everything leads us to believe that the poets who at that moment translated the Commune's fluid poetry *were made to vanish*. The Commune's mass of unaccomplished acts allowed its attempted actions to become "atrocities," and its memory to be censored. The saying "those who make only a half revolution do no more than dig their own graves," also explains Saint-Just's *silence*.

11.

Theorists who restore the history of this movement by placing themselves at the omniscient viewpoint of God, which characterized the classical novelist, easily show that the Commune was objectively doomed and that it did not have a potential transcendence. It must not be forgotten that, for those who lived the events, the transcendence *was there*.

12.

The audacity and inventiveness of the Commune obviously is not measured in relation to our time but in relation to the banalities of that time in political, intellectual, and moral life—in relation to the *interdependence* of all the banalities among which the Commune spread its fire. Thus, considering the interdependence of present-day banalities (on the right or the left), the extent of the inventiveness we can expect of a comparable explosion can be imagined.

13.

The social war of which the Commune was one moment still endures (though its superficial conditions have much changed). In the task of "making conscious the unconscious tendencies of the Commune" (Engels), the last word has not been spoken.

14.

For almost twenty years in France, Christians of the left and Stalinists have agreed, in memory of their anti-German national front, to stress what there was of national disarray and offended patriotism in the Commune, to all speak of "the French people petitioning to be better governed" (according to the current Stalinist "political line"), and finally driven to desperation by the failure of the stateless right wing of the bourgeoisie. It would suffice, to spit out this holy water, to study the role of foreigners who came to fight for the Commune: it was, above all else, the inevitable test of strength to which led, as Marx said, all the activity in Europe by "our party" since 1848.

18 March 1962

EXCERPTS FROM *THE PROCLAMATION OF THE COMMUNE*[5]

HENRI LEFEBVRE

The Paris Commune? It was first an immense and grandiose festival, a festival that the people of Paris—essence and symbol of the French people and of the people in general—gave to themselves and to the world. A spring festival in the city, a festival of the disinherited and the proletarians,

---

5   (Paris: Éditions Gallimard, Coll. "Trente journées qui ont fait la France," no. 26, 1965), 20–23 and 31–33. [Ed.]

a revolutionary festival and a festival of the Revolution, a total festival, the grandest of modern times, unfolding initially in magnificence and joy.

The historic day of March 18, 1871 finished breaking the passivity and resignation that had reigned during the Second Empire, during the war, and even during the siege of Paris, without releasing fundamental forces. These forces would rush in with a grandiose calm. The Parisian people broke its dams and flooded the streets; as a brotherly, animated whole, it enveloped those who were supposed to fight it—the soldiers of the entrenched power. It disarmed them. The collective hero, the popular genius, loomed up in its youth and native vigor. It had vanquished, from the sole fact of having appeared. Surprised by its victory, it metamorphosed it into splendor. It rejoiced, it contemplated its awakening and transformed its power into beauty. It celebrated its rediscovered honeymoon with consciousness, with the palaces and monuments of the city, with the power that had escaped it for so long. And this truly was a festival, one long festival that lasted from the day of March 18 to that of March 26 (elections) and 28 (proclamation of the Commune) and beyond, with a ceremonial and a solemnity that were magnificently arrayed.

Later, or at the same time, the people took pleasure in its own festival and changed it into spectacle. It was mistaken and made a mistake, for the spectacle that it presented to itself diverted [*détourne*] it from itself. Then, as in every true festival, drama in its pure state was foretold and projected. Popular festival apparently changed character. In truth, it continued; it plunged into sorrow. We understand that Tragedy and Dramas are bloody festivals, over the course of which the failure, sacrifice, and death of the superhuman hero who had defied fate is accomplished. Misfortune is there changed into grandeur, and failure leaves a lesson of strength and hope in the purified heart of its cowardly fears. Hercules the tamer of monsters struggles to keep the poisoned shirt from covering his body. He strains all his muscles, in vain. Then he prepares the funeral pyre. Then come death and the triumph of fate and evil, failure and the final holocaust; but the funeral procession does not lose the grandiose meaning of the Festival. Those who fought to the cry of "Liberty or death" preferred death to surrender and the certainty of subjection. They fought on, desperately, madly, with a limitless courage; then with their own hands they lit the pyre on which they wanted to be consumed and disappear. The tragedy ended in a conflagration and a disaster worthy of them.[6] Pursuing until the end and following to its last consequences the titanic challenge, the people of Paris envisaged the end of Paris and wanted to die with what was for it more than a setting and a framework, but its city, its body.

---

6 Let us note right away that we are well aware of the responsibility of the Versaillais for the fires of the Bloody Week.

Thus the Festival became drama and tragedy, an absolute tragedy and a Promethean drama played without a trace of frivolous acting, a tragedy where the protagonist, the choir, and the audience coincided in a unique fashion. But from the start, the Festival held drama; drama recovered its primordial meaning: a collective and real festival, a festival lived by the people and for the people, a colossal festival accompanied by the voluntary sacrifice of the principal actor in the course of his failure, his tragedy.

When we define the Commune's style in this manner, as at once oeuvre and act, we only repeat Liebknecht's formula on "the horrible and grandiose tragedy of the Commune." We will not for all that leave out the other aspects of the events: we will forget neither its antecedents and circumstances, nor the relations between people and groups and the ideas that took part in the action, nor finally the demands of analysis and historical account. But we intend to show how Paris experienced its revolutionary passion. We will see why and how the scattered and divided city became a community of action and how, in the course of the Festival, the community became a communion at the vastest scale imaginable. And how the people acclaimed the symbols of unalienated and unalienating labor, the fall of oppressive power, and the end of alienation. And how it proclaimed the world of labor, that is to say labor as world and creator of worlds. And how, in the course of this immense festival, something here and there pierced through the opaque veils of customary social life, ascended from the lowest depths, passed through the accumulated layers of inertia and gloom, saw the light of day, and opened out. What was it? A fundamental will, to change the world and life as it is, and things as they are, a spontaneity pregnant with the highest thought, a total revolutionary project. A delirious and general "all or nothing." A vital and absolute wager on the possible and the impossible. ...

The Revolution as act had to coincide with the results of the Revolution. One would leap in a single bound from blind necessity to the joyous reign of Liberty, to a grand festival without end. At the same time free labor, labor become a game, came into the world, along with the momentous play with weapons, with life and death.

[...]

Praxis cannot be closed and cannot be considered as closed. Reality and concepts remain open and this opening has several dimensions: nature, the past, human possibility. It is not sufficient to say that the idea of praxis does its best to seize or seizes the complexity of human phenomena. We must add that it, and it alone, seizes their *growing* complexity. Open on all sides, praxis (reality and concepts) for all that does not lose its way in indeterminacy. Only thought of a particular type, namely traditional analytic reason, confuses closure and determination, opening and indeterminacy. To make these ideas comprehensible, let's consider the city in general or better yet a specific city (Paris). It is an oeuvre in the sense that we have taken this term, an oeuvre whose study Marx repeatedly attempted by connecting it—like the other forms and types of human oeuvres—to the general theory of the division of labor. It is obvious that we could pursue this study and that this investigation would be crucial for the writing of a total history. Synchronically, the City is an ensemble, a whole undergoing slow and sudden mutations. Diachronically, the City is the oeuvre of a group, in relation with an all-encompassing society in which it is inserted, as well as with a State that it controls or submits to. A city grows or declines; it succeeds, vegetates, or fails. Why and how? The study of its landscape and position arises from geography, political economy, even vegetal or animal biology. The study of institutions arises from history *stricto sensu* and that of the urban group from sociology. The comprehension of the relation of the City with the all-encompassing society cannot have recourse to these specialized sciences. Does this mean that the City, and the praxis at work in this reality, possess nothing that is concretely distinguishable? To affirm this is to resolve the methodological problem of the human sciences—the relation of these sciences to each other, the assumed or restored unity of their object—by abolishing it by decree.

If we have here used the particular example of the City to illustrate a general thesis, this is obviously not by chance. Not that we pretend to know the total history of Paris, even during a brief period, or to be inspired by it. No. It is a question of a thesis or hypothesis that will navigate the study of the Commune. During the Second Empire, "industrial society" in its *capitalist* form profoundly reordered the *capital*. It cleared its center encumbered by slums, but cut into this center and began to destroy it. The city was enlarged, but already splintered toward its periphery. The Bonapartist State projected itself upon the ground in the reshuffling by Haussmann of the central quarters and streets, as well as by the use of existing monuments and new structures.

In our opinion, the Parisian insurrection of 1871 was the grand and highest attempt of the city to stand as the measure and norm of human reality. That it could be the setting and proof of this reality was a kind of postulate of Western civilization since the Greek *polis* and the Roman *urbs*. The City as human milieu imposed its rational order on the chaos of nature, on rustic barbarism, and on the individuals and groups who made it up. Liberty, inseparable from reason and law, only had meaning within the City.

However, around the middle of the nineteenth century, this model of Western civilization was shaken. Industrialization on the economic level and the State on the political level, mastered the City, reordered it, threatened its center and splintered it toward its peripheries. Disproportion was established. The City would cease providing the measure of humanity and *being* its measure, its reason embodied in a magisterial oeuvre. It became monstrous, the enormous head of a body that no longer belonged to this head, being fastened to rusticity (to the "rural" notables), while the City was mastered and threatened by the facticity of money and Capital.

Did the Parisian proletariat understand this situation? Obviously not. Its historical consciousness and its class consciousness were formulated differently, as we will see. Did a few "leaders" grasp it? Yes, confusedly, partially. It seemed injust and absurd to them that Paris controlled the provinces and that the capital would destroy the vitality of other cities. Who understood the anxious character of centralization and stateification in France? The Commune's Jacobins? No. The Marxists? There were none, and we cannot repeat too many times that the Marxist theory of the withering of the State, in embryo from Marx's earliest writings, followed rather than preceded the experience of the Commune. Only the Proudhonians understood something and inspired a program.

No one could have understood the situation as we can comprehend it today, we who have traversed and continue to traverse terrible experiences: the Revolution of 1917, the semi-failure (to say nothing more) of the transformation of the world by the proletariat, the failures of agrarian socialism, the present-day splintering of the City, etc. We know—because we have lived it and paid dearly for it—that those who make "history" do not do so consciously, that between wills, objectives, and goals, the results, means, and ends, there are peculiar divergences. When these gaps have disappeared, we will enter into a new historical period. Until then, total history must precisely take account of these divergences and gaps, which pose crucial problems.

The insurrection of 1871, accomplished by the entire people of Paris (excepting the lone elements of foul reaction), inspired by the proletarian core, had these paradoxical objectives: maintain Paris against Versailles as capital, while restoring liberty, equality, and fraternity with Paris to all the provincial cities and villages. And this in a way allowing an equal and fair distribution of economic and social progress (let us say, of industrialization). More and better: the city returned to its glory, its beauty, and its reason for being would take part in a festival without end. The day following the revolutionary dawn illuminated a profoundly transformed life, within the powerful, even magical setting of the splendid City, "seat of the West." The appeal to the provincial cities and the federalist program went further than a cry of distress or a political tactic. And this is so even if the advocates and drafters did not suspect it. If they made history, history was also made through them, with its creative inventions, its attempts and detours, its blind heroisms and its tragic conclusions.

THE DECLINE AND FALL OF THE SPECTACLE-COMMODITY ECONOMY[7]

The uprising of American blacks asserted itself with greatest urgency in Los Angeles, during the summer of 1965, by questioning the principle contradictions of advanced capitalism. As the S.I. recalls, thousands of soldiers and police, backed up by tanks, had to be called up to retake—through urban combat—the black neighborhood of Watts, whose population had revolted. Rebels had armed themselves at gun shops (allowing them to shoot at police helicopters) and then commenced the generalized looting of stores before setting them on fire. The suppression of those four days of spontaneous rioting left, according to official figures, 32 dead and 3,000 jailed. The Situationists' analysis is in response not only to these events, but also to the reaction of the worldwide Left, which condemned their irresponsibility and disorder, the looting. This placed the Left at the very opposite pole of the best critical tradition, for example that of Marx and Engels when they wrote: "Far from opposing so-called excesses, instances of popular revenge against hated individuals or public buildings that are associated only with hateful recollections, such instances must not only be tolerated but the lead in them must be taken."[8] The S.I. was the lone revolutionary organization to defend the Los Angeles rebels, by revealing what it saw as the universal meaning of their revolt; so-called excesses like those of Watts express firstly the mutual existence of a critical theory of modern society and that society's critique in acts, which must necessarily enlighten each other. The meaning of the revolt lay in the fact that it was "a revolt against the commodity, against the world of the commodity and of the worker-consumer who is hierarchically *subjected to the standards of the commodity." The black population of Los Angeles had taken modern advertising at its word and demanded the immediate use of all those commodities promised (but seldom delivered) by the propaganda of modern capitalism, so that "real desires" could be communicated "in festival, in ludic assertion, and in the potlatch of destruction." Little surprise these acts called forth the full force of the repressive apparatus of the State, which always stands ready to guard the prerogative of the commodity. In all this, American blacks are shown to be, not an underdeveloped sector within society, but its most developed, "the negation at work." Watts was universal because it was a revolt of humanity against the inhuman life imposed by spectacle, and its lessons would be taken up in the looting practiced by the most extreme fringes of the post-'68 left, most famously in France.*

---

7   *Internationale situationniste* no. 10 (March 1966) 3–11. [Ed.]
8   Marx and Engels, "Address of the Central Authority to League" (1850), in Marx and Engels, *Collected Works*, Vol. 10 ("Marx and Engels: 1849–51") (London: Lawrence & Wishart, 1978), 282. [Ed.]

Between August 13th and 16th, 1965, the black population of Los Angeles rose up. An incident opposing traffic police and pedestrians developed into two days of spontaneous riots. Increasing reinforcements of forces of order were unable to regain control of the streets. By the third day, blacks had taken up arms, looting accessible gun shops, so that they were even able to fire on police helicopters. Thousands of soldiers and police—the military weight of an infantry division, supported by tank—had to be thrown into the struggle in order to encircle the revolt within the Watts neighborhood and then reconquer it over several days at the cost of numerous street battles. The rebels went on to the widespread looting of stores, which they set fire to. According to official figures, there were 32 dead (of whom 27 were blacks), more than 800 wounded, and 3,000 arrested.

Reactions, on all sides, were invested with the lucidity that the revolutionary event—from the fact that it is itself a clarification in acts of existing problems—is always entitled to confer upon its adversaries' diverse shades of thought. The police chief, William Parker, refused all mediation proposed by major black organizations, rightly asserting, "these rioters don't have any leaders." And indeed, since blacks no longer had leaders, it was the moment of truth in each camp. What moreover was one of those unemployed leaders, Roy Wilkins, head of the NAACP, waiting for at that very moment? He declared that the riots "should be put down with all necessary force." And the cardinal of Los Angeles, McIntyre, who protested loudly, did not protest against the violence of the repression, as one might have believed the clever thing to do at the time of the *aggiornamento* of Roman Catholic influence. Rather he protested most urgently in the presence of "a premeditated revolt against the rights of one's neighbor and respect for law and order;" he called on Catholics to oppose the looting and "this violence without any apparent justification." And all those who went so far as to perceive the "apparent justifications" of the anger of Los Angeles blacks (but not, indeed, the real justification), all those thinkers and responsible "authorities" of the international Left—of its nothingness—deplored the irresponsibility and the disorder, the looting, and above all the fact that its first moment had been the looting of stores containing *liquor and weapons*; and the 2,000 counted fires by which the *pétroleurs* of Watts illuminated their battle and their festival. Who then has taken up the defense of the rebels of Los Angeles, in the terms they deserve? We will do so. Leave the economists to grieve over the 27 million dollars lost, and the urbanists over one of their most beautiful supermarkets gone up in smoke, and McIntyre over his slain deputy sheriff; leave the sociologists to bewail the absurdity and drunkenness in this revolt. The role of a revolutionary publication is not only to prove the rebels of Los Angeles right, but also to contribute to *presenting them with their proofs*, to explain theoretically the truth for which practical action expresses here the search.

In the *Address* published in Algiers in July 1965 following Boumedienne's coup d'état, the Situationists—who set forth to the Algerians and to the revolutionaries of the world the conditions in Algeria and the rest of the world *as a whole*—indicated among their examples the movement of American blacks that, "if it could assert itself with effect," would unmask the contradictions of the most advanced capitalist system. Five weeks later, that effect was in the streets. The theoretical critique of modern society, in its most novel forms, and the critique in acts of the same society already each exist—still separated but equally progressing toward the same realities, and speaking of the same thing. These two critiques are explained the one by the other, and each is inexplicable without the other. The theory of survival and the spectacle is illuminated and verified by these acts that are incomprehensible to American false consciousness. In turn, it will illuminate these acts one day.

Until now, demonstrations by blacks for "civil rights" had been kept by their leaders within a legality that tolerated the worst violence of the forces of order and the racists, as in Alabama last March during the march on Montgomery; and even after that scandal, a discreet understanding between the federal government, governor Wallace, and reverend King had led the Selma march, on March 10th, to draw back at the first request, in dignity and prayer. The confrontation expected at that time by the crowd of demonstrators had only been the spectacle of a potential confrontation. At the same time nonviolence reached the absurd limit of its courage: to be exposed to the enemies' blows, and then to push moral grandeur to the point of sparing them the necessity of using their might anew. But the basic idea is that the civil rights movement only posed legal problems by legal means. It is logical to appeal to the law for them legally. What is irrational is to beg legally before obvious illegality, as if it was a meaningless act that would be annulled by being pointed out. It is obvious that the epidermal, outrageously visible illegality still affecting blacks in many American states has its roots in an economico-social contradiction that is not within the scope of existing laws, and that no future *juridical* law will even be able to undo it, faced with the more fundamental laws of the society in which American blacks are finally daring to demand to live. American blacks, in truth, want the total subversion of this society, or nothing. And the problem of necessary subversion emerges of itself as soon as blacks arrive at subversive means; the transition to such means now appears in their everyday life as what is at once the most accidental and the most objectively justified. It is no longer the crisis of the status of blacks in America; it is the crisis of the status of America, posed first among blacks. There was no *racial* conflict here: blacks did not attack whites who were in their path, but only white police; and in the same way, black unity did not extend to black owners of stores, or even to black motorists. Martin Luther King himself had to admit that the limits of his specialty had been crossed, in declaring in Paris in October, "they were not race riots, but class riots."

The Los Angeles revolt is a revolt against the commodity, against the world of the commodity and of the worker-consumer who is *hierarchically* subjected to the standards of the commodity. Los Angeles blacks, like the gangs of young delinquents of all advanced countries—but more radically because at the scale of a class totally without a future, of a part of the proletariat that cannot believe in significant chances of promotion or integration—*take at its word* the propaganda of modern capitalism, its advertising of affluence. They want all the displayed and abstractly available objects *at once*, because they want *to use them*. From this fact they impeach their exchange value, the *commodity reality* that is their mold, rationale, and final aim, and *that has decided on everything*. Through theft and gift, they are recovering a use that immediately denies the oppressive rationality of the commodity, and that makes its relations and its very manufacture appear arbitrary and unnecessary. The looting of the Watts neighborhood showed the swiftest realization of the bastard principle "to each according to his or her false needs" (needs determined and produced by the economic system that looting precisely rejects). But from the fact that this affluence is taken at its word, *rejoined without delay*, and no longer indefinitely pursued in the race of alienated labor and of the increase of deferred social needs, real desires are already being expressed in festival, in ludic assertion, and in the potlatch of destruction. People who destroy commodities show their human superiority over commodities. They will not remain prisoners of the arbitrary forms that the image of their need has assumed. The transition from consumption to *consummation* has been achieved in the flames of Watts. Large refrigerators stolen by people who did not have electricity, or whose homes had had the current cut off, is the best image of the lie of affluence become truth *at work*. As soon as it ceases to be bought, commodity production in all its particular impositions becomes open to criticism and modification. It is only when it is paid for with money, when it is considered as sign of a rank within the order of survival, that it is respected as a wondrous fetish.

The affluent society (not natural and human affluence, but affluence of commodities) finds its *natural* response in looting. And looting, which makes the commodity as such collapse suddenly, also shows the *ultima ratio* of the commodity: force, the police, and other specialized detachments that possess the monopoly of armed violence within the State. What are the police? Active servants of the commodity, people totally subject to the commodity, through whose action such a product of human labor remains a commodity whose magical desire is to be paid for, and not a common refrigerator or rifle—a blind, passive, insensible thing that is subject to the first person to come along and make use of it. Behind the indignity of depending on the police, blacks are rejecting the indignity of depending on commodities. The youth of Watts with no marketable future chose a different *quality* of the present, and the truth of that present was unchallengeable to the point of inciting the whole population – women, children, and even sociologists present on the ground. Bobbi Hollon, a young black sociologist from the neighborhood, declared in October to the *Herald Tribune*:

> Before, people were ashamed to say they came from Watts. They'd mumble it. Now they say it with pride. Boys who used to go around with their shirts open to the waist, and who'd have cut you into strips in half a second, showed up here every morning at seven o'clock. They organized the distribution of food. Of course it's no use pretending the food wasn't looted . . . All that Christian blah has been used too long against the blacks. These people could loot for ten years and they wouldn't get back half the money that these stores have stolen from them all these years . . . Me, I'm just a little black girl.

Bobbi Hollon, who has made up her mind never to wash the blood that splashed on her sandals during the riots, says, "the whole world is watching Watts now."

How do people make history starting from conditions pre-established to dissuade them from intervening in it? Blacks in Los Angeles are better paid than anywhere else in the United States, but there they are even more *separated* than anywhere from the maximal wealth that is shown off precisely in California. Hollywood, the pole of the global spectacle, is in their immediate vicinity. They are promised that they will have access, with patience, to American prosperity, but they see that this prosperity is not a settled sphere but a ladder without end. The higher they climb, the further they get from the top, because they are disfavored from the start, because they are less qualified and thus more numerous among the unemployed, and finally because the hierarchy that crushes them is not only that of buying power as a pure economic fact—it is an essential inferiority that the customs and prejudices of a society in which all human power is aligned with buying power imposes on them in all aspects of everyday life. Just as the human wealth of American blacks is hateful and considered as criminal, monetary wealth will not make them completely acceptable within American alienation: individual wealth will only make a rich *negro* because blacks as a whole must *represent the poverty* of a society of hierarchical wealth. All witnesses heard this cry that appealed to the universal recognition of the uprising: "This is the black revolution and we want the world to know it!" Freedom now[9] is the password of all the revolutions of history; but for the first time, it is not privation but on the contrary material affluence to be mastered according to new laws. Mastering affluence is thus not only altering distribution, it is *redefining all its orientations*, superficial and profound. This is the first step of an immense struggle, of an infinite reach.

Blacks are not isolated in their struggle because a *new proletarian consciousness* (the consciousness of not being in the least master of one's activity, of one's life) is arising in American among strata that reject modern capitalism, and that, because of this fact, resemble them. The first phase of the black struggle has been precisely the signal for a spreading contestation. In December 1964, the students of Berkeley, persistently scolded for their participation in the civil rights movement, initiated a strike that questioned the functioning of this Californian "multiversity" and, through the latter, the entire organization of American society and the passive role intended for them in it. Immediately the profuse drinking or drug taking and the dissoluteness of sexual morals for which blacks have been reproached were discovered among the student youth. This generation of students has since invented a first form of struggle against the dominant spectacle, the teach-in,[10] and this form was taken up again on October 20th in Great Britain, at the University of Edinburgh, on the subject of the Rhodesian crisis. This form, obviously primitive and adulterated, is *the moment of the discussion of problems*, which refuses to be (academically) limited in time, which thus seeks to be pushed to the bitter end, and that end is naturally practical activity. In October tens of thousands of demonstrators against the Vietnam war appeared in the streets, in New York and Berkeley, and they answered the cries of the Watts rioters: "Get out of our neighborhood and out of Vietnam!" Among whites who are becoming radicalized, the notorious frontier of legality has been crossed: "courses" are given on how to cheat draft boards (*Le Monde*, October 19 1965) and draft cards are burned in front of the T.V. In the affluent society disgust for this affluence and *for its price* is being expressed. The spectacle is being sullied by the autonomous activity of an advanced class that repudiates its values. The classical proletariat, to the very extent to which it had been provisionally integrated into the capitalist system, had not integrated blacks (several Los Angeles unions refused blacks until 1959); now blacks are the unification point for everything that refuses the logic of this integration into capitalism, *ne plus ultra* of all promised integration. And comfort will never be comfortable enough to satisfy those who seek what is not on the market, what the market precisely gets rid of. The level attained by the technology of the most privileged becomes an insult, easier to put into words than is the

---

9 In English in the original. [Ed.]
10 In English in the original. [Ed.]

fundamental insult of reification. The Los Angeles revolt is the first in history that could justify itself by deduction from the lack of air conditioning during a heat wave.

Blacks have in America their own spectacle—their press, their magazines, and their stars of color—and they are thus recognizing it and vomiting it up as fallacious spectacle, as an expression of their indignity, because they understand it to be *minoritarian*, a simple afterthought of a general spectacle. They are recognizing that this spectacle of their desirable consumption is a colony of that of whites, and therefore they perceive more quickly the lie of the whole economico-cultural spectacle. By wanting to share effectively and immediately in affluence (which is the official value of every American), they are demanding the egalitarian *realization* of the spectacle of everyday life in America, the putting to the test of the half-heavenly, half-worldly values of this spectacle. But it is in the spectacle's essence to be unrealizable immediately or equally, *even for whites* (blacks act precisely as a perfect spectacular guarantee for this incentivizing inequality within the race for affluence). When blacks insist on taking the capitalist spectacle literally, they are already rejecting the spectacle itself. The spectacle is a drug for slaves. It does not mean to be taken at its word, but followed one tiny step behind (if there is no longer a delay, the mystification becomes evident). As a matter of fact, in the United States, whites are today slaves to the commodity, and blacks are its negators. Blacks want *more than whites*: that is the heart of an insolvable problem, or solvable only with the dissolution of this white society. And so whites that want to get out of their own slavery must first rejoin the black revolt, not obviously as an affirmation of color, but as a global rejection of the commodity, and finally of the State. The economic and psychological gap of blacks in relation to whites allows them to see what the white consumer is, and the legitimate contempt that they have for the white is becoming contempt for any passive consumer. The only chance for whites that also reject this role is to link their struggle ever closer to that of blacks, by discovering them themselves and by supporting their rational motives to the end. If their convergence were to break up in the presence of the struggle's radicalization, a black nationalism would develop, which would condemn each side to confrontation according to the oldest models of the dominant society. A sequence of mutual butcheries is the other current alternative conclusion, when resignation can no longer last.

Attempts at a black nationalism, whether separatist or pro-African, are dreams that cannot match the real oppression. American blacks do not have a native country. In America they are *at home and alienated*, like other Americans, except they know that they are. In this way they are not the lagging sector of American society, but its most advanced sector. They are the negation at work, "the bad side that produces the movement which makes history, by providing a struggle."[11] There is no Africa for that.

American blacks are the product of modern industry, in the same way as electronics, advertising, and the cyclotron. They bear its contradictions. They are people that the spectacular paradise must simultaneously integrate and repel, so that the antagonism of spectacle and people's activity is completely acknowledged in connection with them. The spectacle is *universal* like the commodity. But the world of the commodity being founded upon an opposition of classes, the commodity is itself hierarchical. The obligation for the commodity, and hence for the spectacle that *informs* the world of the commodity, to be at once universal and hierarchical leads to a universal hierarchization. But because this hierarchization must remain *unacknowledged*, it is expressed in unacknowledgable—because *irrational*— hierarchical assessments in a world of *rationalization without reason*. It is this hierarchization that creates *racisms* everywhere: Labour Party England has begun to restrict immigration of people of color; the industrially advanced countries of Europe are again becoming racist while importing their sub-proletariat from the Mediterranean basin, and while exploiting their internally colonized peoples. And Russia does not cease to be anti-Semitic, because it has not ceased to be a hierarchical society in which labor must be sold as a commodity. With the commodity, hierarchy is constantly recomposed in new forms and extended, whether between the director of the labor movement and the workers, or instead between owners of two models of artificially distinguished automobiles. This is the original defect of commodity rationality, the sickness of bourgeois reason, a hereditary sickness within bureaucracy. But the shocking absurdity of certain hierarchies, and the fact that all the might of the world of the commodity is brought blindly and automatically to their defense, reveals—as soon as negative practice begins—the absurdity of all hierarchy.

The rational world produced by the industrial revolution has rationally freed individuals from their local and national limits and has linked them at the global scale; but its folly is to separate them anew, according to a hidden logic that is expressed in mad ideas and absurd assessments. The foreigner everywhere surrounds the person for whom the world has become foreign. The barbarians are no longer at the ends of the Earth, they are *there*, confirmed as *barbarian* precisely by their necessary participation in the same hierarchized consumption. The humanism that cloaks this is the contrary of humanity, the negation of its activity and its desire; it is the humanism of the commodity, the benevolence of the commodity toward the people off

---

11   Marx, "The Poverty of Philosophy" (1847), in Marx and Engels, *Collected Works*, Vol. 6 ("Marx and Engels: 1845–48") (London: Lawrence & Wishart, 1976), 174. [Ed.]

whom it lives. For those who reduce people to objects, objects seem to have all the human qualities, and true human manifestations are transformed into *animal* unconsciousness. "They started acting like a bunch of monkeys in a zoo," William Parker, leader of Los Angeles' humanists, could say.

When authorities in California had declared the "state of insurrection," insurance companies recalled that they do not cover risks—beyond survival—at this level. American blacks, as a whole, are not threatened in their survival—at least if they keep quiet—and capitalism has become sufficiently concentrated and imbricated in the State to distribute "assistance" to the poorest. But by the simple fact that they are *lagging* in the increase of socially organized survival, blacks pose the problems of life, and it is life that they demand. Blacks have nothing to insure that belongs to them; they have to destroy all forms of security and private insurance known up to now. They appear as what they indeed are: the irreconcilable enemies, not to be sure of the vast majority of Americans, but of the alienated way of life of all of modern society—the most industrially advanced country only shows us the road that will be followed everywhere, if the system is overthrown.

Certain extremists of black nationalism, to prove that they cannot accept less than a separate State, have advanced the argument that American society —even if it one day recognizes their total civic and economic equality—will never manage, on the individual level, to permit interracial marriage. *It is therefore this American society that must disappear*, in America and everywhere in the world. The end of all racial prejudice, like the end of so many other prejudices linked to inhibitions (as regards sexual freedom), will obviously be beyond "marriage" itself, beyond the *bourgeois family* (greatly weakened among American blacks), which reigns as much in Russia as in the United States, as a model of hierarchical relations and of stability for an *inherited power* (money or socio-statist rank). It has typically been said for some time now of American youth who, after thirty years of silence, are arising as a force of contestation, that they will find their Spanish war in the black revolt. This time, their "Lincoln brigades" must understand the full meaning of the struggle in which they are engaged and totally support it in its universal aspects. The "excesses" of Los Angeles are no more a political error among blacks than the armed resistance of P.O.U.M. in Barcelona in May 1937 was a betrayal of the anti-Franco war. A revolt against the spectacle is situated on the level of the *totality*, because—even though it indeed took place in the single neighborhood of Watts—it is a protest of humanity against inhuman life; because it begins at the level of the *real single individual*; and because community, from which the individual in revolt is separated, is the *true social nature* of humanity and human nature: the positive supersession of the spectacle.

December 1965

HALL OF MIRRORS[12]

ROBERT CHASSE

The Situationist International circulated a document in 1966 on "The Decline and Fall of the Spectacular-Commodity Economy," which analyzed the conditions of the Watts riot along lines that showed that modern capitalism, even at its most affluent, presents very serious contradictions, and is incapable of resolving them harmoniously. This, at a time when all the apologists of the system claimed—as they continue to claim, though with less assurance—that the system has changed, and transformed the social conditions that it breeds. But the system—we are beginning to realize again—has in effect just sophisticated the methods of repression and, until the riots, offered a perfectly dissimulated portrait of social harmony. Watts —and now Newark and Detroit—have shattered the myth. But how many are aware of it? The word *race* today is being used on all sides to conceal the truth. How will the conscious and unconscious defenders of the system attribute to race—and not class—the *black* woman's proposition that hostages be taken at random from among the rioters, then shot and left to rot in the street?

The Everyday Misery Transfigured

A man is told he works 40 hours a week at three dollars an hour, and that he makes $120. The 40 hours does not include lunch time, time in preparing for work, travel time, so that the real time devoted to the job—which is all the time that cannot be devoted to anything else—is increased by four or five hours a day. He works then about 60 hours a week. He gives his employer 20 hours, he makes two dollars an hour. Before he has spent a cent of what is called his salary, he gives half of it away: taxes are not only federal; there is the city, the state, social security, pensions, sales taxes—city, state, federal—taxes on insurance, insurance itself. If a man works 60 hours a week, he makes about 60 dollars; gives a third of that or more to rent, another third or more to food. He is left with the rest, a rest rarely sufficient for him to buy outright any of the goods offered on the market, but a rest sufficient to make him buy on credit, buy a house for thirty years, a car for 2 or 3 or 5. It is life on the installment plan, lives at the mercy of the things around them, men controlled by their possessions.

But, even so, nearly every man considers his life begins after work, that his real life is the possibilities of pleasure open to him. It begins after 6 or

---

12   (New York: Council for the Liberation of Daily Life, 1967). [Ed.]

7 o'clock; he has four hours a day "for living." But even here he is not left alone. There is every attempt to regiment his pleasure: television, movies, ballgames, organized vacations or the places where they can occur, books—the circus of life.

In contract negotiations between General Motors and the workers' unions, the company expressed the fear that the propositions from the unions would make unemployment more attractive than working, it would be rocking chair dough, fishing money. The problem is not that it couldn't be done but that it would—in the words of management—make unemployment more attractive. The latent avowal that, practically, labor could be eliminated. What stands in the way? if not the world organization of life, institutions that men perpetuate though they have outlived their usefulness?

Should a man wander through the city and see through the busy but aimless throngs, consuming themselves, he would be amazed. It has all the problems of ancient cities: of sanitation and waste disposal, noise, travel and communication, crime and corruption, but aggravated into another dimension by congestion. The results are environmental pollution—of air and outlying waters—mechanized travel reduced to a crawl, homes making way to streets, streets to bridges, highways, tunnels, the soil growing in cost, the buildings allowed to decay; the people living closer and closer to one another in shells that are more and more hollow, whole buildings become sounding boards for the noises in them. There is a choking at all levels of city life. Starting from New York, going north, you must travel over 200 miles—get beyond Boston—before you leave the city. The suburbs are merely the concentric circles of these immense stoneworks. Life, beyond the moviehouse and shopping center, is supposed to reside at the center. In the cities, silence is no longer silence but the memory of a noise. They are hotter than the surrounding countryside, vast amounts of carbon dioxide are produced in them, produce an oxide in combination with lead from motor vehicles, change weather patterns, air currents, bring drought to arable land hundreds of miles away. The prevailing organization of life, in the name of the city, is destroying man's place in nature. The city is a paradise of culture and civilization, some sort of private joke. The world, they say, has never had it so good. The standard of living has never been so high. Men have never been talked to more, communicated to more, in effect, controlled more. The mass media know their power. And if they do not know it, they exercise it. What they are selling is not this or that product—whether it be an approach to city problems, to a governing system, or to soap—but a belief in the viability and soundness—above all the permanence—of the prevailing organization of life. They hold the people in the sorcery of their perverted language. And the language is perverted so long as its use is the concealment of reality. There is a piecemeal and fragmentary approach to questions or problems which is deception. When *The New York Times* attempts to separate the so-called civil rights issue from the war in Vietnam, it is practicing such a deception.

It is common nowadays to condemn the whole system and then systematically attempt to recuperate it in its parts.

The United States has 3,300,000 men in its standing armies, ready at the drop of a hat to enforce freedom and its will anywhere in the world. Such are the imperatives of empire. Beyond that there is probably over a half-million men in the various police forces around the country. New York City alone has money allocated for over 32,000 cops. The law is made to protect property and the cops enforce the law. The size of the police force is no doubt a reflection of the relationship people have to property. The police are the only individuals in the community who, armed to the teeth, watch us in our streets. Theirs is the fundamental illusion that the property they protect is theirs—and must be protected at all cost, against any life. All men are secret thieves. Hence the troubled fraternity between the police and those who confirm their conviction by being outward thieves.

There have been race riots before in America: a hundred years ago, white men turned to Harlem for black skin to lynch, to burn, to drown. In those nights men turned from setting the torch to buildings to a negro hut, resembling the lynching parties on smaller scale that still haunt the south. There is a passion for mutilation, a search for horror. It becomes a frenzy of killing, a madness. I have the vision of the glowing whites of men's eyes around dilated pupils in the torch light. Racism is the expression of the world that turns one man against the other as a matter of course, as a necessity of its own development, and sanctions it.

The riots that are sweeping America today can only be called race riots by an extension of the white man's skin to the businesses he owns. Provoked in every case by the action of the police, people explode out of anger into violence. And in each case—see Watts, Newark or Detroit—they become expressions of joy: people dance in the streets, and feel, like the Governor said, as though they were people laughing at a funeral.

The peaceful demonstrations of the early 1960s expressed the modest desire for a share of the crop. The riot is the expression of the feeling that the system will not give—or give in—and that what we need we want right now, immediately. The enemy is not man but the locked door, the padlock, the grill, the vault. Once broken into and its treasures taken, what can be sensibly done with storehouses if not to burn them to the ground? Beyond the storehouses lies the ghetto, and then, the city. The cry of joy that exploded out of Watts was "Burn, baby, burn." This is not the destruction of property; it is the direct expression that property as possession against every man has had its day.

The violence directed against men in these riots comes from the police. Check the lists of wounded and dead. The police are notoriously trigger-happy, but they are still subject to their chiefs. It might be revealing in New York City to compare the number of people killed by the police under the rule of Commissioner Leary and that of his predecessor Mr. Murphy. No doubt in other cities the game is the same. When people destroy a car, they may beat up the occupant: they are not fundamentally out to kill him. In Newark, a cop—and for the ghetto a cop is first of all his function—was beaten. He took out his revolver and, as the papers described it, accidentally shot one of the youths around him. At this point, they beat him to death. The insanity is to to see the direction of the violence, not to see the action of those youths as a reaction.

But then what can the police do? If it were not that they are armed and dangerous, one could pity them for being victims—and perhaps pity them anyway. The question is not whether there are sensible men who join the police force—or that all cops are pathological killers—but that by becoming a cop, a man either is or is transformed into a willing weapon of the system. Their racism is the racism of the system. But the same unconditional violence met by the black man has been met by the whites. One need only remember police frenzy against white workers in the days when the trade union movement was wracked by the armed violence of the established order. One need only look at police action in the face of wildcat strikes by white workers. The class wars had come to a head. The thing with racism is, it is class war in daily life.

The problem today is not why the black man is rioting but why the white man is not. The riot is the momentary transfiguration of the everyday misery that afflicts us, called "life" by the prevailing organization of it.

The early demonstrations were ignored. The riot must be eliminated, by shot and bayonette if necessary. It is not a fundamental social change but it is an expression too close for comfort—and in the streets—of its need. If the state was the organization of resistance to want, it is now the organization of resistance to plenty. It strives for the continuation of transforming men into things, objects for labor, in a world that can dispense with labor. That even dimly sensed by the rioters is a terrifying prospect for the state. There are men, unfortunately, who are never so much attached to a past as when they feel it passing.

Parody of all tragedies, we are living in a world that enforces want.

"EMERGENCY STATE ENDED IN DETROIT:
Some looters integrated," *The New York Times*, July 27, 1967

> Anti-white feeling ran high on 12th Street in the heart of the city's major Negro ghetto, but elsewhere—and especially in integrated neighborhoods—Negro looters smiled and waved at white policemen and newsmen. Along one section of Grand River Avenue, where Negroes and Southern whites live in adjoining neighborhoods, stores were raided by integrated bands of looters. At Packer's, a blocklong food and clothing center, a Negro looter boosted a white looter through a window. Scores of other Negroes and whites looted and chatted side by side in the store, loading shopping carts, boxes and bags with booty. Negroes, who on Monday were carting off almost everything in sight, milled about the streets yesterday afternoon, waving and smiling at the heavily integrated paratroop units. It was clear, too, that the looting cut across class, as well as racial, lines. One well-dressed Negro filled up the trunk of a new Pontiac convertible with shoes, shirts and suits. Nearby, an emaciated woman pushed a shopping cart heaped high with smoked hams and canned goods. Some Negroes obviously considered the riot a summertime frolic. At 3 am, two Negro couples perched on a fence just off the John Lodge Freeway, alternately kissing and watching firemen battle a major blaze. Once, the couples broke their embrace to shout a warning to firemen. A drunken middle-aged Negro man had staggered from a building and was firing a shotgun into the still night air. Police arrived within minutes and placed the man in handcuffs. "God damn it, shoot me," the man shouted at the policemen.

The Criminal Insurrection, or Laughing at a Funeral

Riots rage through dozens of cities and towns—and tonight as this is being written. Detroit is going up in flames, white looters and snipers have joined in with the blacks, nearly 5,000 paratroopers have moved in with automatic weapons, tanks and a company of 25 helicopters. Yesterday it was New Jersey, today Michigan, and then? Each one of these riots is an enclave; taken together we are in the middle of an insurrection that has been going on for over a month, establishing in the streets a pattern of guerilla warfare that has already required channeling into the ghettoes troops returning from Vietnam.

Understandably, the government hesitated to commit troops to the suppression of domestic unrest: by acting so outwardly it becomes touchy trying to maintain the permanence of its duplicity, the image of its benevolent paternalism. These give way under gunfire and hundreds of millions of dollars worth of property damage to the realities of state: class interest, brute force, total disregard for the lives of all individuals. What matters is sacred property, control of the population, domination. Those who are in government today are perfectly well-aware that their function is not to administer wealth, but to control it—and for the benefit of the ruling class. They will act against the violence of the population to protect their own grounds for violence. They will not tolerate violence in Detroit like they do not tolerate it in Vietnam. And use the same troops.

There has never been a case when the people were not right against the government, against the prevailing organization of life—whether on the job, in their cities, their strikes, demonstrations, insurrections. When they cease reacting to whatever is being done to them and, as the cute phrase goes, assume command of their own destinies, we enter the way to fundamental social change. The sociologists are busily at work trying to muddle the waters: these riots are anarchistic and rise out of the declassed, the workless, the mob—while the workers are growing increasingly away from such people by a greater and greater assumption of the American way of life, which is to work yourself into a heart attack to procure the goods at credit. How fundamental a division is this in the face of cybernation? where the unions struggle to keep workers at the task of production, which can be carried on without them? And in the face of the workers who are beginning to realize that the house they've been paying for 20 years is merely a reflection of their ability to slave away. Out of a job, they discover that the real owner of the house is the bank that holds the mortgage. But even the sociologists will not claim that this is a criminal insurrection, carried on by the criminal element, hoodlums, or, as the Governor of California called them, "mad dogs." The sociologists at least know that those called "criminals" would be slitting their own throats by fighting the state; that the subterranean world of crime is an outgrowth of the prevailing organization of life, that it is a reflection of that life itself, without the frills.

The insurrection—whatever be the future attempts to confuse it, to gloss over it, to gum it up—is a clear sign that between the people and the state no orderly redress of grievances is any longer possible. There are no grievances to be made to the state—there should be no state. We have witnessed an intuitive act of liberation from the prevailing system, beyond the flash of temper that characterizes any riot, no matter how violent. The riot does not show this determination, this persistence. The riot is without joy; and where during the past few weeks in the ghettoes have the people not danced with joy? In Detroit, some of the Uncle Toms complained bitterly that the police allowed a Roman holiday atmosphere to develop. And when the troops arrived the people milled around in the streets, waving and smiling at them, in a carnival atmosphere.

What did the soldiers feel, returning from Vietnam, flying in the same planes, running under the same helicopters, walking behind the same tanks, about the same job of suppression?—only here the joke of fighting for freedom can't take, and the other joke of fighting a world Communist conspiracy must certainly be starting to come through as a transparent piece of buffoonery. In Newark, one of the national guardsmen fingered his weapon nervously and wondered about the first time he has been told to pull the trigger, that it has been to shoot Americans.

The state, the government, the prevailing organization of life—at this clear moment, before we sink back and for how long into the miasma—is isolated: fighting for its life against a population that has revealed through its own action the roots of domination of life upon which the state rests, and for the continuation of which it exists.

The cry of life is being heard in these hours around the country, and the sound of it, in the words of the Governor of New Jersey, is like laughing at a funeral.

Hall of Mirrors

The Black Power Conference a few days after Newark burned established a general consensus around black capitalism. The spirit of opposition to white domination must not be assimilated to the simple desire of replacing it by a black one. A black bourgeoisie would be faced with the necessity of maintaining want and need—of organizing against abundance—in ways no doubt identical to those practiced by the prevailing state. Behind the desire to want to control the means for the organization of *black* wealth as behind the fear of extinction of the blacks (as in excess to the needs of white wealth) lies the same world of imposed poverty, a hoax to keep men struggling for what they already have, theirs for the taking.

There is no need to make elaborate proofs of starvation in America, tumefied bellies from Kentucky to Mississippi, long-range starvation through malnutrition in the ghettoes and scattered through all the communities with high unemployment rates. We have seen photos in the daily press, we have heard Congress be pickeyune over the word they would like to choose up there to designate the condition. And the next day the farmers are paid not to grow wheat. Confusedly perhaps, but surely, all the bureaucrats—from president to welfare worker—realize that the problem of poverty is administrative. Men are not dying because there is not enough food to go around. This is not the older struggle of tearing out of nature enough to feed the living. *The truth of poverty is that it is imposed.* Anything today that does not aim at a total dissolution of society is a return to it, and thereby a re-intensification of its structure.

The project of the bourgeoisie has been to dominate nature, the old enemy, from which nothing could be taken without its being torn away. The past 100 years—and particularly the last 25—have witnessed the victory of this project. But having dominated nature, the system organized for that purpose has merely tilted over into plunder. So we are forced to live as though the ancient struggles were still primary: the victory amounts to nothing. The potential for liberation is denied. The illusion of scarcity drives them into a false opposition, while the true enemy remains, hard at work trying to recuperate the world that made it. It maintains itself by a fragmentation of problems, which it sometimes calls a pluralistic approach.

Besides the question of migration and immigration endemic to American cities, the expansion of population, the desertion of farms for the cities, the city faces a fundamental crisis in kind. It is no accident that the city is de-natured. It has always been a fortress against the ancient enemy, nature. And the enemy is no longer. In the glassbubble cities of the city-planners, we see a vision of the future as a mere extension of the present, a prefabricated environment from which nature has been excluded. The system, as always, can only mirror itself, draw logical extensions of itself, even on the time span of eternity: whether on the morose tones of Spengler or the jubilant ones of McLuhan.

The transformation of historical existence into liberation also involves the destruction of what has been the city. It must be reborn in a new relation with the countryside, lead to a new harmony between man and nature. The rioters wanted to burn down the cities like the wildcat strikers turn to the destruction of cars and homes: intuitively they attack the dead objects that serve to crush them, to maintain them in their servitude. Each saw in the riots the particular realization or premonition of his dream, which could be a nightmare. But how many chose to ignore the direct attack they laid on what is fed to all of us as "life," with its well-defined roads to factory and pool-hall, to work and pleasure, both organized, both shells, both a continuation of existence by forced means, in the shadow of life?

EXCERPT FROM "THE RETURN OF THE REPRESSED"[13]

NORMAN O. BROWN

> My utopia is
> > an environment that works so well
> > that we can run wild in it
> > anarchy in an environment that works
>
> the environment works, does all the work
> > a fully automatic environment
> > all public utilities
> > or communication-networks
>
> (the engineering contribution to unification;
> > unification is also a matter of engineering)
>
> Wasn't there a divinely absurd anticipation in Marx,

---

13   *King Mob Echo* no. 1 (April 1968), 4. [Ed.]

or Engels, saying that the government of persons will
be replaced by the administration of things—[14]

The environment can do all the work
Serious thought,
> thought as work,
> in pursuit of *Wirklichkeit*,
> is about over

Wirklichkeit, the German word for reality, the reality-principle
The reality-principle is about over.
Thought as work can be buried in machines and computers
the work left to be done is to bury thought; quite a job
To put thought underground
as communication-network, sewage-system, power lines
so that wildness can come above ground
technological rationality can be put to sleep
so that something else can awaken in the human mind
something like the god Dionysus
something which cannot be programmed.

The ordering of the physical environment will release
unparalleled quantities and forms of human disorder
The future, if there is one, is machines and madness.
> *What men or gods are these? What maidens loth?*
> *What mad pursuit? What struggle to escape?*[15]

The struggle should not be, is no longer, really, the struggle for existence.

EXCERPT FROM *THE REVOLUTION OF EVERYDAY LIFE*[16]

RAOUL VANEIGEM

The face of happiness has ceased to appear in filigree in works of art and literature since it has been multiplied as far as the eye can see all along walls and hoardings, offering to each particular passerby the universal image in which he or she is invited to recognize him- or herself.

---

14   "State interference in social relations becomes, in one domain after another, superfluous, and then dies out of itself; the government of persons is replaced by the administration of things, and by the conduct of processes of production." Friedrich Engels, "Socialism: Utopian and Scientific" (1880), in *The Marx-Engels Reader*, 2nd ed., ed. Robert C. Tucker (New York and London: W. W. Norton, 1978), 713. [Ed.]
15   Quoted from John Keats, "Ode on a Grecian Urn" (1819). [Ed.]
16   Raoul Vaneigem, *Traité de savoir-vivre à l'usage des jeunes générations* (1967), 2nd ed. (Paris: Éditions Gallimard, Coll. "Folio/Actuel," no. 28, 1992), 85–88. [Ed.]

No more problems with a Volkswagen!
Live carefree with Balamur!
This man is as astute as he is tasteful, he chooses Mercedes Benz.

Happiness is not a myth, so rejoice, Adam Smith and Jeremy Bentham! "The more we produce, the better we shall live," writes the humanist Fourastié,[17] while another genius, General Eisenhower, replies like an echo: to save the economy, "we must buy anything and everything. We must simply buy, buy, buy."[18] Production and consumption are the teats of modern society. Suckled in such a fashion, humanity grows in strength and beauty: rising standard of living, numberless conveniences, varied entertainment, culture for all, dreamed-of comfort. On the horizon of the Khrushchev report, the radiant dawn of communism is finally breaking, inaugurating its reign with two revolutionary decrees: the abolition of taxes and free transport. Yes, the golden age is in sight, within spitting distance.

In all this upheaval, one big thing has gone missing: the proletariat. Has it vanished? Has it gone underground? Has it been relegated to a museum? *Sociologi disputant.* In highly industrialized countries, the proletariat has ceased to exist, some affirm. The accumulation of refrigerators, TVs, Renault Dauphines, subsidized housing, and people's theaters proves it. Others, on the contrary, are indignant and denounce the conjuring trick, pointing the finger at a fringe of laborers whose low wages and wretched conditions undeniably evoke the nineteenth century. "Backward sectors," the first retort, "pockets in process of re-absorption; do you deny that the direction of economic development would be toward Sweden, Czechoslovakia, the Welfare State, and not toward India?"

The black curtain rises: hunting-season for the starving and the last proletarian is open. The prize goes to whoever will sell him his car and his blender, his bar and his library. It goes to whoever will identify him with the smiling character of a quite reassuring poster: "Happy are those who smoke Lucky Strikes."

And happy, happy humanity that will, in a near future, check and sign for the parcels whose delivery orders the rebels of the nineteenth century tore away, at the cost we know so well. The rebels of Lyons and Fourmies certainly have a chance at a posthumous title.[19] The millions of human beings who were gunned down, tortured, imprisoned, starved, brutalized, and knowingly

---

17   Jean Fourastié (1907-1990), French economist who helped to oversee the reconstruction of postwar France. [Ed.]
18   A famous terse comment made by President Dwight Eisenhower when asked what Americans could do to end an economic slump in 1958. [Ed.]
19   Lyons was the site of major uprisings by its silk workers in 1831 and 1834; Fourmies was the site of a massacre on May 1, 1891, when troops fired upon strikers, killing nine and wounding 35. [Ed.]

ridiculed, at least possess—in the peace of their mass burials and communal graves—the historical guarantee of having died so that, isolated in their air-conditioned apartments, their descendants are learning to repeat (on the strength of daily televised transmissions) that they are happy and free. "The Communards were slaughtered to the last man so you too could buy a Philips hi-fi stereo system." A fine future, one that would have delighted the past, no doubt about it.

The present alone is left out of the reckoning. Ungrateful and uncultivated, the younger generation does not want to know anything of this glorious past offered as a free gift to every consumer of Trotskyist-reformist ideology. It claims that making demands means making demands for the here and now. It recalls that the sense of past struggles is fixed firmly in the present of the people who guided them and that this same present—in spite of different historical conditions—is also its own. In short, there has been one steadfast project that inspires radical revolutionary currents: the project of the total person, a *will to live totally* to which Marx was the first to provide a tactics of scientific realization. But these are vile theories that the Christian and Stalinist churches never fail to diligently blast. An increase in wages, in refrigerators, in holy sacraments, and in people's theaters, that will satisfy today's keen revolutionary appetite.

Are we condemned to the state of wellbeing? Levelheaded minds will not fail to regret the form under which is led the contestation of a program that meets with unanimous approval, from Khrushchev to Doctor Schweitzer, from the pope to Fidel Castro, from Aragon to the late Kennedy.

In December 1956, a thousand young people let loose in the streets of Stockholm, setting cars on fire, shattering illuminated signs, tearing advertising billboards, and ransacking department stores. At Merlebach, during a strike triggered to persuade the employers to bring up the bodies of seven miners killed by a cave-in, the workers attacked cars parked in front of the buildings. In January 1961, strikers in Liége sacked the Guillemins railroad station and destroyed the plant of the newspaper *La Meuse*.[20] On the coasts of Belgium and England a few hundred rockers, in a concerted operation, devastated seaside resorts in March 1964. In Amsterdam (1966), workers held the streets for several days. Not a month goes by without a wildcat strike breaking out, pitting laborers against the bosses and union leaders at the same time. Welfare State.[21] The neighborhood of Watts has answered.

---

20 The Stockholm riot is mentioned in "The Sound and the Fury" (1958), in *Situationist International Anthology*, 41; the incidents at Merlebach and Liége are discussed in "The Bad Days Will End" (1962), in *Situationist International Anthology*, 83. [Ed.]

21 In English in the original. [Ed.]

A worker at Espérance-Longdoz[22] summarized as follows his disagreement with the Fourastiés, Bergers, Armands, Moles,[23] and other watchdogs of the future: "Since 1936, I have fought for wage demands; my father, before me, fought for wage demands. I have T.V., a refrigerator, and a Volkswagen. On the whole, my life has never stopped being bloody useless." In words or in acts, the new poetry proves itself to be poorly adapted to the Welfare State.

---

22 A major steelworks in the Liège area. [Ed.]
23 References to Louis Armand (1905–1971), a French engineer who managed several public companies including the state railways and published, with Michel Drancourt, *Plaidoyer pour l'avenir* (Paris: Calmann-Lévy, 1961), in which he wrote about a "second phase" of the industrial revolution that offered "the possibility of affluence"; Gaston Berger (1896–1960), a French futurologist, industrialist, and manager of state concerns, who invented the term "*prospective*"; and Abraham Moles (1920–1992), who taught sociology, psychology, and communications at the university in Strasbourg. He was a target for Situationist-inspired students during the unrest of 1966; see the mention of him in the famous tract, "On the Poverty of Student Life" (1966), in *Situationist International Anthology*, 322n6. [Ed.]

8.

Toward a Synoptic Theory

GEOPOLITICS OF HIBERNATION[1]

The balance of terror that dominated global politics in 1961 was also a balance of resignation, and the two camps prepared less for war than for the indefinite continuation of just that state of equilibrium. There was no better evidence that "the spectacle of the coming war" had begun to "shape the state of peace that we know" than the incredible vogue for atomic shelters that gripped the U.S.A. in that year. The real aim of these shelters was not civil defense and protection of the population in the event of war, but "to test—and thereby reinforce—people's submissiveness" in the present, by producing a whole new array of consumable goods that are, on the face of it, perfectly useless. Survival under these conditions is, the Situationists write, the obverse of life, and in this manner the atomic shelter is just one component of that broader "blackmail of utility" found throughout contemporary society. But the ruling organization of life still meets with resistance, as in the juvenile delinquency that responds to the integration sought by urban planners who want to "humanize" their housing projects. Equilibrium and permanence are illusions that serve only imperfectly to repress "what is absent, forbidden, and hidden, and yet possible, in modern life." Only this "imagination of lack" can unmake the inhuman world in which we live.

The "balance of terror" between two rival groups of States, which is the most visible of the essential themes of global politics at this moment, also means the balance of resignation: each of the antagonists is resigned to the permanence of the other; and within their borders, people are resigned to a fate that escapes them so completely that the very existence of the planet is only a chance privilege, hanging on the discretion and skill of inscrutable strategists. This undeniably involves a generalized resignation to the existing world, to the coexisting powers of the specialists who arrange this fate. The

---

1 *Internationale situationniste* no. 7 (April 1962): 3–10. [Ed.]

latter find an additional advantage in this balance, in that it authorizes the rapid elimination of every novel emancipatory experiment occurring at the edge of their systems, and chiefly in the present eruption of the underdeveloped countries. It is through the same arrangement of neutralizing one menace with another—whichever protector triumphs in the instance—that the Congo's revolutionary outburst found itself crushed with the dispatch of the United Nations expeditionary force (two days after their landing, at the beginning of July 1960, the Ghanian troops, having been the first to arrive, were used to break the transportation strike in Léopoldville) and that of Cuba with the formation of a single party (in March 1962 General Enrique Líster, whose role in the repression of the Spanish revolution is well known, will be named assistant chief of staff of the Cuban army).[2]

The two camps are not really preparing for war, but for the indefinite preservation of this balance, which is the very picture of the internal stabilization of their power. It goes without saying that the latter will have to mobilize huge resources, since it is imperative to rise continually higher in the spectacle of possible war. Thus Barry Commoner, who presides over the scientific committee entrusted by the United States government to estimate the destruction promised by a thermonuclear war, announces that after one hour of this war eighty million Americans would be killed and that the others would have no hope of living normally later on.[3] The chiefs of staff who, in their preparations, no longer count in anything but "*megabodies*" (this unit representing one million dead bodies) have admitted the futility of pushing their calculations beyond the first half day, completely lacking experimental data for further planning. According to Nicolas Vichney, one avant-garde tendency of American defense doctrine already thinks: "the most deterrent conduct would reside in the possession of an enormous thermonuclear bomb buried underground. If the opponent attacked, it would be detonated and the Earth would be blown apart."[4]

The theorists of this "Doomsday System"[5] have certainly found submission's supreme weapon; they have for the first time translated the refusal of history into specific technological prowess. But the strict logic of these doctrinaires merely corresponds to one aspect of the contradictory needs of the society of alienation, whose binding project is to thwart people's

---

2   Enrique Líster (1907–1995) was a Spanish communist who served as an officer in the Republican Army during the Spanish Civil War; after the end of the Civil War he fled to Moscow, and would in 1959 be sent to Cuba as an advisor to the Committees for the Defense of the Revolution. [Ed.]
3   Barry Commoner (1917–), an American academic who became known during the late 1950s as a protester against nuclear testing. [Ed.]
4   Nicolas Vichney, "Les États-Unis face à l'espace: II. – Les épouvantails de la 'dissuasion'," *Le Monde*, January 5, 1962, 3. [Ed.]
5   In English in the original. [Ed.]

lives while arranging their survival.⁶ So that the Doomsday System, in its contempt for a survival that is all the same the indispensable condition for the present and future exploitation of human labor, can only play the role of *ultima ratio* for the reigning bureaucracies—of being, paradoxically, the guarantee of their seriousness. But, on the whole, the spectacle of the coming war—in order to be fully effective—must from now on shape the state of peace that we know, by serving fundamental requirements.

In this respect, the extraordinary spread of fallout shelters over the course of the year 1961 is certainly the Cold War's decisive turning point, a qualitative leap whose immense importance in the process of the formation of a cybernetized totalitarian society on a global scale will be distinguished later. This movement began in the United States, where Kennedy in his state of the union message last January could already assure Congress: "The nation's first serious civil defense shelter program is underway, identifying, marking, and stocking fifty million spaces; and I urge your approval of federal incentives for the construction of public fallout shelters in schools and hospitals and similar centers." This statist organization of survival was rapidly extended, more or less secretly, to other important countries of the two camps. West Germany, for example, first attended to the survival of Chancellor Adenauer and his team, and the divulgence of realizations in this sphere incited the seizure of the Munich magazine *Quick*. Sweden and Switzerland are reduced to the installation of collective shelters hollowed out of their mountains, where workers buried with their factories could continue to produce without let-up until the apotheosis of the Doomsday System. But the foundation of civil defense policy is in the United States, where a number of flourishing companies, such as Peace o' Mind Shelter Company in Texas, American Survival Products Corporation in Maryland, Fox Hole Shelter, Inc., in California, and Bee Safe Manufacturing Company in Ohio, advertise and install a multitude of individual shelters—that is, ones built as private property for planning the survival of each family. We know that a novel interpretation of religious morality is being developed around this fashion, clergymen being of the opinion that duty will clearly consist in refusing access to such shelters to friends or strangers, even by means of arms, in order to guarantee the safety of one's family alone. In fact, morality here had to be adapted in order to cooperate in bringing to its perfection that terrorism of conformity that underlies all the advertising of modern capitalism. It was already hardly tenable, in front of one's family and neighbors, not to have a given car model that a given salary level (always recognizable in American urban housing developments, since the location of the dwelling is precisely in step with that of salary level) allowed one to

---

6   See the contrast of the concepts of life and survival described by Vaneigem in "Basic Banalities" (1962), in *Situationist International Anthology*, 89–100.

acquire by installments. It will be even less easy not to guarantee one's own people the *survival status* accessible according to conjuncture of the market.

It is generally reckoned that in the United States, since 1955, a relative saturation of the demand for "durable goods" has entailed the insufficiency of the spur that consumption should furnish for economic expansion. One can thus understand the enormous vogue for gadgets of all sorts, which represent an easily manipulable development in the semi-durable goods sector. It is easy to see the important role of the shelters in this necessary boost of expansion. With the installation of shelters and their foreseeable offshoots and byproducts, all the appurtenances of life on the surface are to be doubled for the new duplicate life underground. These subterranean investments in layers as yet unexploited by the affluent society are boosting the sale both of semi-durable goods already in use on the surface—as with the boom in canned foods, of which each shelter needs a maximum stock—and of particular new gadgets, such as plastic bags for the bodies of people who will die in the shelter and, naturally, continue to lay there with the survivors.

It is undoubtedly easy to see that these already widespread individual shelters are never effective, if only for such gross technical oversights as the absence of an independent oxygen supply; and that even the most perfected collective shelters would offer only the slightest possibility for survival if thermonuclear war was actually accidentally unleashed. But here, as in every racket, protection is only a pretext. The real use of the shelters is to test—and thereby reinforce—people's submissiveness and to manipulate this submissiveness in a way favorable to the ruling society. The shelters, as a creation of a new consumable commodity in the affluent society, prove more than any presumable commodity that people can be made to work to satisfy highly artificial needs, needs that most certainly "remain needs without ever having been desires" and without having the slightest chance of becoming desires.[7] This society's strength, its formidable involuntary genius, can be measured by this borderline case. If it happened to matter-of-factly proclaim that it imposes an empty and heartbreaking existence to such a degree that the best solution for everyone was apparently to go and hang themselves, it would still succeed in running a sound and profitable business with the production of standardized ropes.[8] But, in all its capitalist richness, the concept of survival signifies a *suicide postponed* until final exhaustion, a renunciation of *all the days* of life. The network of shelters (which are not intended to be used for a war, but right now) outlines the image, still

---

7   Pierre Canjuers and Guy Debord, "Preliminaries Toward Defining a Unitary Revolutionary Program" (1960), "in *Situationist International Anthology*, 307.
8   A statement that might be read as a reversal of the famous prognostication attributed to Lenin (although almost certainly spurious) that "the capitalists will sell us the rope with which we will hang them." [Ed.]

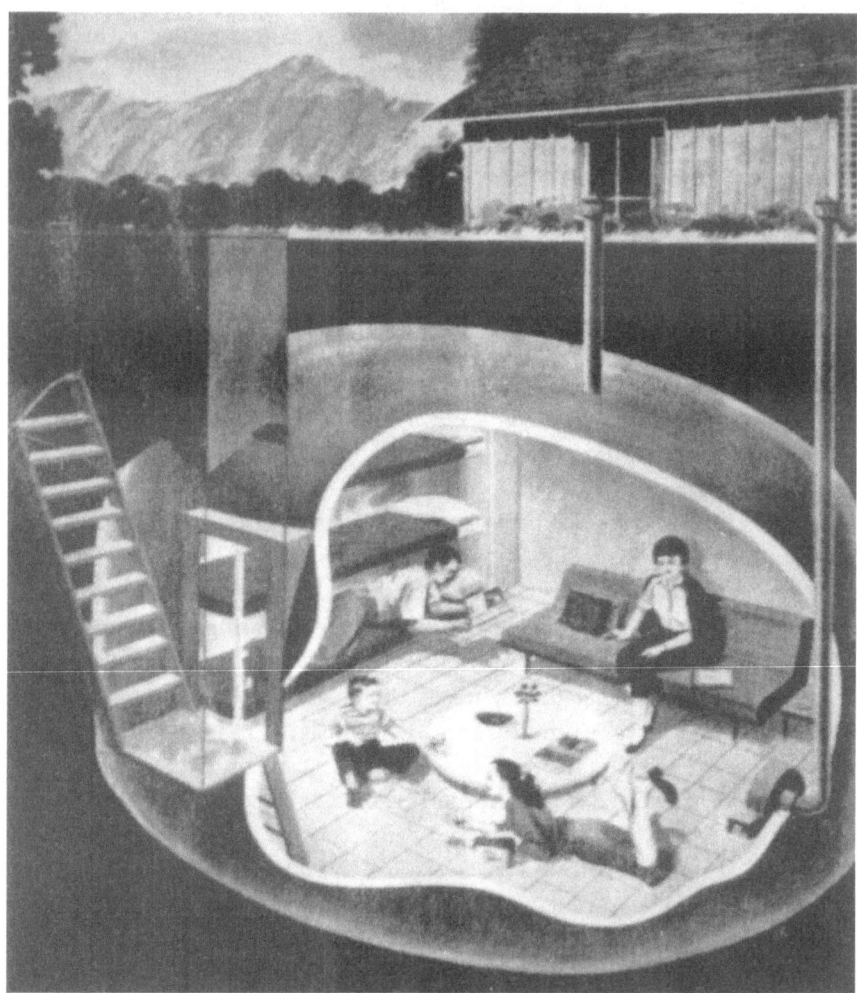

Fig.8.1.1   From *Internationale situationniste* no. 7 (April 1962).

exaggerated and cartoonish, of existence under bureaucratic capitalism brought to its perfection. A neo-Christianity will find a new position there for its ideal of renunciation, a new humility reconcilable with the reviving of industry. The world of shelters recognizes itself as an *air-conditioned vale of tears*. The coalition of all the managers and their priests of various sorts will be able to agree on one unitary keyword: the power of catalepsy, plus super-consumption.

If rarely voted by plebiscite as clearly as by 1961's buyers of shelters, survival as the converse of life is nevertheless found at all levels of the struggle against alienation: in the old conception of art that placed the stress principally on survival through the artwork, as confession of life's renunciation, as excuse and consolation (principally since the bourgeois era of aesthetics, secular substitute for the religious afterworld); and just as much at the most irreducible stage of need, in the necessities of alimentary survival and of habitation, with the "blackmail of utility" that the "Elementary Program of Unitary Urbanism" exposes, eliminating any humane critique of the environment "through the simple argument that people need roofs over their heads."[9]

The new habitation that is taking shape with housing projects is not actually distinguished from the architecture of the shelters. It only represents an inferior rank of it—though their unification is approaching, and the passage from one to the other foreseen without solution of continuity: the first example in France is a slab presently being built in Nice, the basement of which has already been adapted into an anti-atomic shelter for the throng of its inhabitants. The surface's concentration-camp organization is the normal state of a society in formation, the subterranean summary of which represents the pathological excess. That sickness better reveals the plan of this health. The urbanism of despair, on the surface, is in a fair way to becoming rapidly dominant, not only in the population centers of the United States, but also in those much more backward countries of Europe or even for example in the Algeria of the neo-colonialist period proclaimed since the "Constantine Plan."[10] At the end of 1961, the first version of the national plan for French territorial development—whose formulation was later weakened—complained in the chapter on the Parisian region of "the obstinacy of an inactive population to reside within the capital," and this at

---

9   Trans. in this volume, 147.
10 The Constantine Plan (1959–1963) was a plan for economic development in Algeria worked out by the French government in 1958 at the height of the Algerian War following De Gaulle's coming to power. Aimed at valorizing the country's resources, it was also intended to weaken the FLN. Paul Delouvrier, as general delegate of the government in Algeria, was in charge of overseeing its realization. As part of the plan, residential cities for the "indigenous" population were built in Algiers and other large cities on the model of French housing developments. [Ed.]

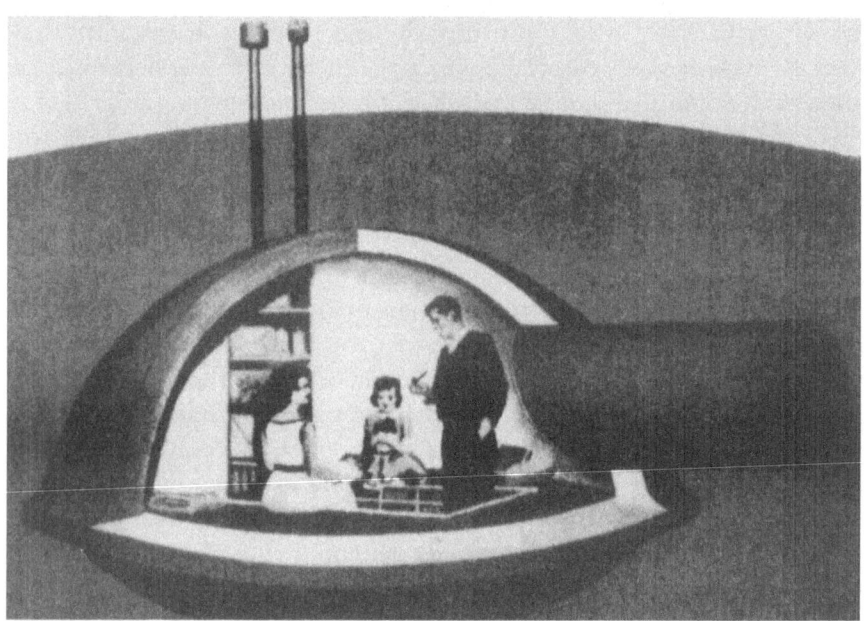

Fig.8.1.2   From *Internationale situationniste* no. 7 (April 1962).

a time when the drafters—certified specialists of happiness and of what is possible—pointed out "that they could be housed more agreeably outside Paris." They therefore ordered the elimination of this painful irrationality by legalizing "the systematic discouragement of dwelling by these inactive persons" in Paris.

Just as the chief activity that counts obviously lies in the systematic discouragement of the managers' calculations that run such a society, up to their concrete elimination, and just as they themselves think much more constantly about it than the doped crowd of executants, the planners erect their defenses in all the modern developments of the land. The planning of shelters for the population, in the normal form of a roof over one's head or in the "affluent" form of family tombs to live in as deterrents, must serve in fact to shelter their own power. The rulers who control the preservation and maximum isolation of their subjects know how on the same occasion to take refuge themselves for strategic purposes. The twentieth-century Haussmanns are no longer reduced to ensuring the deployment of their forces of repression in the grid of the old urban agglomerations. At the same time that they disperse the population, over a vast field, into new cities that are this gridding *in its pure state* (where the inferiority of the masses, disarmed and deprived of means of communication, is sharply increased compared with the ever more technical police forces), they are building *out of reach capitals* where the ruling bureaucracy, for more security, can constitute the whole of the population.

Coinciding with different developmental stages of these government-cities, we can point out: Tirana's "military zone," a quarter cut off from the city and defended by the army, where the residences of Albania's rulers, the Central Committee building, as well as school and hospital institutions, stores, and amusements for this elite living in autarky are concentrated;[11] the administrative city of Rocher Noir, built in one year to serve as capital in Algeria when it appeared that the French authorities had become incapable of continuing normally in a large city—its function corresponds exactly with Tirana's "military zone," except it was made to appear in open country; we finally have the loftiest example with Brasília, parachuted into the center of a vast desert, the inauguration of which rightly coincided with the dismissal of President Quadros by his military, and the prodromes of a civil war in Brazil that only just failed in mopping up the plaster of the bureaucratic capital—which is at the same time, as we know, the exemplary success of functionalist architecture.

Things being what they are, we see many specialists who are starting to denounce a number of disturbing absurdities. This is for want of understanding

---

11 An area to the west of the university, adjacent to Saint Prokopi park, known as Ish-Biloku, reserved for the occupation of important government and party officials. [Ed.]

the central rationality (the rationality of a coherent delirium) that dominates these partial, obvious absurdities, to which their own activities inevitably contribute. Their denunciation of the absurd can thus only be absurd in its forms and its means. What to think of the nine hundred professors of all the universities and research institutes of the areas around New York and Boston who solemnly addressed themselves on December 30, 1961, in the *New York Herald Tribune* to President Kennedy and Governor Rockefeller—a few days before the first flattered himself by having selected, to begin, fifty million shelters—in order to persuade them of the fatal nature of the development of "civil defense?" Or of the teeming horde of sociologists, judges, architects, policemen, psychologists, pedagogues, hygienists, psychiatrists, and journalists who do not cease to find themselves gathered in congresses, commissions, and conferences of all sorts, all in search of an urgent solution for *humanizing* housing projects? The humanization of housing projects is a mystification as ridiculous as the humanization of atomic war, and for the same reasons. The shelters reduce not war but the threat of war, in its "human measure" in the sense of what defines humanity in modern capitalism: its duty as a consumer. This inquiry into humanization simply aims at the joint establishment of the most effective lies for the repressing of people's resistance. Boredom and the total absence of social life characterizing the housing projects of the *banlieues* in a manner as immediate and tangible as the cold temperatures characterize Verkhoyansk,[12] women's magazines come to do reports devoted to the latest fashion in the new *banlieues*—photographing their models in these no-man's-lands—and interview the satisfied people there. Seeing that the stupefying power of the setting is measurable in the intellectual development of the children, the emphasis is placed on their harmful inheritance from classic pauperism's poor housing. The latest reformist theory places its hopes in a sort of culture center—without using that particular word, to keep people from shunning it. In the plans of the Syndicat des architectes de la Seine [Seine Architects Union], the prefabricated "bistro-club" that will everywhere humanize their work is presented as a cubic "plastic cell" (28 x 18 x 4 meters) comprising:

> a stable element: the non-alcoholic *bistro* selling tobacco along with magazines; the remainder could be reserved for different artisanal, do-it-yourself activities. . . . It should become a showcase with all the seductive characteristics that involves. That's why the aesthetic conception and the quality of the materials will be carefully studied to give their full effect night as well as day. Indeed the play of lights should *inform* about the life of the *bistro-club*.[13]

---

12 A town in Siberia near the Arctic Circle in the former Soviet Union, noted for its exceptionally low winter temperatures. [Ed.]
13 Jacques Michel, "Architecture: Le 'bistro-club' pour animer les nouvelles cités," *Le Monde*, December 22, 1961: 9.

Thus we have, presented in profoundly revealing terms, the lucky find that "could facilitate social integration at the level on which the spirit of a small city is forged." The absence of alcohol will be little noticed: we know that in France the youth of the gangs do not currently even need the aid of alcohol to smash everything. The juvenile delinquents seem to have broken with the French tradition of popular alcoholism (whereas the role of alcohol remains so important in the hooliganism of the East) and are not yet, like American youth, using marijuana or stronger drugs. Though wedged in such an empty passage, between the stimulants of two distinct historical stages, they manifest a no less distinct violence in reply precisely to this world we are describing and to the horrible prospect of occupying their hole in it. Leaving separate the factor of revolt, the unionized architects' project makes sense: their glass clubs intend to be as an instrument of supplementary control on the path to that *high surveillance* of production and consumption that constitutes the famous, sought-for integration. The candidly acknowledged recourse to the aesthetics of the store window is illuminated perfectly by the theory of the spectacle: in these de-alcoholized bars the consumers themselves become spectacular, as must the objects of consumption, for want of other attractions. Perfectly reified humanity has its place in the store window, as the desirable image of reification.

The system's internal defect is that it cannot perfectly reify people; it needs to make them act, and to obtain their participation, for want of which the production of reification (and its consumption) would stop right there. The reigning system is thus at grips with history—with its own history, which is at once the history of its reinforcement and the history of its contestation.

Today at a time when, despite certain appearances, *more than ever* (after a century of struggles and the liquidation between the two world wars of the whole classical workers movement, which represented the force of general contestation, by ruling sectors whether traditional or of a new type) the dominant world *passes itself off as definitive*, on the basis of an enrichment and an infinite extension of an irreplaceable model, the comprehension of this world can only be based on contestation. And this contestation has truth or realism only as contestation of the totality.

The alarming lack of ideas that is recognizable in all acts of culture, politics, organization of life, and the rest is explained by this, and the weakness of the modernist constructers of functionalist cities is only a particularly visible example of it. Intelligent specialists only ever have the intelligence to play the game of specialists: hence the fearful conformity and fundamental lack of imagination that make them admit that this or that product is useful, good, necessary. In fact, the root of the reigning *lack of imagination* cannot be understood if one does not have access to the *imagination of lack*—that is to conceiving what is absent, forbidden, and hidden, and yet possible, in modern life.

This is not a theory without links to the way people handle life; it is on the contrary a reality in people's heads, still without links to theory. Those who, taking far enough "the cohabitation with the negative," in the Hegelian sense, recognize explicitly this absence as their principal strength and their program, will make appear the only *positive project* that can tear down the walls of sleep, and the measures of survival, and the bombs of the last judgment, and the megatons of architecture.

URBANISM AS WILL AND REPRESENTATION[14]

What modern capitalism—concentrated and fully established capitalism—inscribes within life's setting is the fusion of what had been opposed as the positive and negative poles of alienation into a sort of *equator of alienation*. An increasingly preventative police supervise the compulsory stay there. New cities are the laboratories of this stifling society, from Vällingby in Sweden to Bessor in Israel, where all forms of leisure are to be united in one single center;[15] similarly, Avilés' housing project immediately expresses the neo-capitalist development now reaching Spain. At the same time, the disappearance of what had been the "jungle of cities"—in its lack of comfort and its luxury, as in its adventures—which corresponded to laissez-faire capitalism, is continuing.[16] The center of Paris is being radically reshaped by the organization of automobile traffic (the quays transformed into highways, and place Dauphine into an underground parking garage), which does not prevent the complementary tendency to restore a few isolated old blocks. As an object of touristic spectacle, as a simple extension of the classical museum, an entire quarter can become a *monument*. All the variants of the civil service construct everywhere their buildings, cut to their measure. Including, at Canisy, the administration of a new activity that, despite its enormity, can be highly appreciated on the market, like all the charlatanisms that respond to real lacks: the specialists of generalization.[17]

---

14 Excerpt from "Le monde dont nous parlons," *Internationale situationniste* no. 9 (August 1964): 12 [Ed.]
15 Vällingby was a Swedish new town (modeled closely on English precedent) planned in the early 1950s as a satellite of Stockholm. [Ed.]
16 A reference to Bertolt Brecht's *Jungle of Cities* (1923); performed in 1962 as "Dans la jungle des villes" at the Théâtre des Champs-Elysées, Paris. [Ed.]
17 Canisy, in northwest France, was the home of the "International Center for Generalization," devoted to the synthesis and generalization of interdisciplinary knowledge. [Ed.]

PERSPECTIVES FOR A GENERATION[18]

THÉO FREY

A mad society intends to arrange its future by generalizing the use of technologically improved individual and collective straitjackets (houses, cities, planned territory), which it imposes on us as a remedy for its ills. We are *invited* to accept and to recognize as our own this prefabricated "non-organic body;" power thinks of enclosing the individual in a different, radically other, self. In addition to flunkies (urbanists, territorial planners), it can count on the *delinquents* who are currently working overtime in the so-called human sciences to help accomplish this task, one that is in effect vital for it. Servants—particularly from an "anthropology" that is no longer speculative but structural and operative—busily occupy themselves in isolating one more "human nature," but this time one directly usable (like the police register) by various conditioning techniques. The ultimate materialization of the process thus begun (supposing that it is given enough *leisure* by the levy of forces of the new contestation that everywhere accompanies it) is exposed from now on as the modernized version of a solution that already has proved itself: the concentration camp, here de-concentrated over the whole of the planet. People in it will be absolutely free, especially to come and go, to *circulate*, while being total prisoners of that futile freedom to come and go along power's paths.

Nowhere mastered (eliminated) by us, the dominant society can only master itself by dominating us. The convergence of present variants of spatial planning little by little materializes this domination. A room, an apartment, a building, a quarter, a city, a whole territory can and must be planned, step by step or simultaneously: with no transition from "how to live happily in a housing project" (*Elle*) to how "to make [this society] agreeable for everyone" (*Le Monde*). Present-day society, in its desire—proclaimed as sickly as it is ingenuously—to *survive*, relies entirely on a *growth* that can nevertheless only develop dully the ridiculous potentialities that are the only ones permitted by its own rationality: *commodity-logic*. That's to say that political economy, as the "logical conclusion [of] the denial of man," pursues its devastative work.[19] Everywhere spectacularly divergent economic theories and policies oppose each other, but nowhere are the absurd imperatives of political economy itself challenged and bourgeois economic categories abolished, in practice, for the benefit of a free (post-economic) construction of situations, and therefore of all of

---

18 *Internationale situationniste* no. 10 (March 1966): 33–35. [Ed.]
19 An appropriation from Marx, "Economic and Philosophic Manuscripts of 1844," in Marx and Engels, *Collected Works*, Vol. 3 ("Marx and Engels: 1843–44") (London: Lawrence & Wishart, 1975), 291. [Ed.]

life, on the basis of the *currently* concentrated and squandered powers in "advanced" societies. This colonization of the future, in the name of a past that has well deserved to be so utterly renounced that the memory of it be lost, implies the systematic reduction of any *radically different vision of what is possible*, despite every *present* in all manifestations of the our current, oppressive society, so that things seem to persist in advancing "by their bad side," *when they are forced to.*[20]

This poor conjuring trick reveals its trademark from the outset: ideology, that is to say an upside-down, mutilated reflection of the real world, of Praxis, but a working ideology the practice of which introduces what appears upside-down and distorted into the real, and no longer just in the mind of philosophers and other ideologues, but in reality: *the world upside-down for good*. This modern process of reducing the gap between life and its representation for the benefit of a *representation* that turns round on its assumptions is merely an artificial, caricatured, spectacular resolution of real problems posed by the widespread revolutionary crisis of the modern world, a "simulacrum" of resolution that will fall at the same time as the great number of illusions that continue to foster it.

Power lives on our incapacity to live; it maintains infinitely multiplied splits and *separations* at the same time that it plans *almost* as it likes allowable encounters. Its masterstroke remains the successful dissociation of everyday life as individual and social space-time from the presently possible reconstruction of ourselves and the world indissolubly—a dissociation whose aim is to separately and jointly control time and space and ultimately to reduce them both, the one and the other, the one by the other. The state of progress of these operations *visibly* expresses the seriousness of an effort in which the sinister vies with the burlesque. The aim: the constitution of a "homogenous," perfectly "integrated" space, formed by the addition of "homologous" functional blocks, structured hierarchically (the famous "hierarchical network of cities, innervating and coordinating a region of a given diameter, and common to industrial societies"),[21] so that in the collection thus achieved the splits, segregations, and multiple conflicts born of the division of labor and separation will be buried in concrete: class conflict, the conflict between city and countryside, the conflict between society and the State, classical ones since Marx, to which must be added the multiple interregional "disparities," of which the current conflict between developed and underdeveloped countries is only the pathological exaggeration. The "ruse of history" is however such that the first apparent successes of this

---

20 See Marx, "The Poverty of Philosophy" (1847), in Marx and Engels, *Collected Works*, Vol. 6 ("Marx and Engels: 1845–48") (London: Lawrence & Wishart, 1976), 174. [Ed.]
21 Typical language of the planner. [Ed.]

planning of law and order—an attenuation of the class struggle (in the old sense) and of the city-countryside antagonism—conceal less and less the radical and hopeless proletarianization of the immense majority of the population, condemned to "live" within the uniform horizon established by the bastardized and spectacular "urban" milieu born of the breakup of the city. This proletarianization—combined with the State-society antagonism that is thereby reinforced, alarming so many sociologists ("We must," writes Chombart de Lauwe, "establish new channels of communication between power and the population")[22]—betrays the literally "unreasonable" nature of the process of "rationalizing" the reification currently underway. At the same time this proletarianization assures it all sorts of worries, completely "irrational" ones from its bureaucratic and alienated point of view, but no less completely justified from the point of view of the dialectical reasoning inherent in all living reality, all Praxis. As Hegel clearly saw, if only to congratulate himself on it, in the system of modern States, the State allows the pseudo-freedom of the individual to develop, while maintaining the coherence of the whole, and it *draws from this antagonism an infinite strength*, which usually happens to be its Achilles heel once a new coherence, radically antagonistic to such an order of things, is established and strengthened. Moreover, any coherent and "successful" planning must be imposed over the whole of the planet in a *generalized urbanism* that involves reducing the phenomenon of underdevelopment, as potentially disturbing to the impossible equilibrium being pursued. But, as though inadvertently, and in a fatal fidelity to itself, capitalism finds itself making war on underdeveloped countries instead of its loudly declared war on underdevelopment, caught as it is in the trap of contradictory, but for it equally vital, demands, and thereby destroying its own claims to survival: all its technocratico-cybernetic "programmings." Such a dialectic guarantees a rude awakening for the leaders of the present prehistoric world who dreamed of putting themselves out of reach by burying us under a coating of cement that *will surely end* by being their own tomb.

In this light, planning should also be understood as the death agonies of *communication* in the old limited but real sense, the residue of which is everywhere tracked down by Power for the benefit of *information*. From now on a "universal communications network" is radically suppressing the distance between things while infinitely increasing the distance between people. Circulation in such a network ends up neutralizing itself, so that the key to the future will consist in making people circulate less and information circulate more. People will stay at home, transformed into mere audiovisual "receivers" of information: this being an attempt to eternalize *in practice* the current—i.e.,

---

22 Paul-Henry Chombart de Lauwe, quoted in Jean Couvreur, "À la semaine sociale de Brest: L'organisation de la cité nouvelle," *Le Monde*, July 13, 1965, 8.

bourgeois—economic categories, in order to create the conditions for a permanent and automatic functioning of the present alienated society, "a more smoothly running machine."[23] The economists' "perfect market" is impossible, especially because of distance: a completely rational economy would have to be concentrated *at a single point* (instantaneous Production and Consumption); if the market is not perfect, it is because the world itself is imperfect, by virtue of which the planners work to make the world perfect. Territorial planning is a metaphysical enterprise in search of a neo-feudal space. The planners' "*Grand Oeuvre*"[24] is the formation of a space without surprises, where the map would be everything and the territory nothing, because it has been completely conjured away and is no longer important, justifying after the event all the "architecture" of those cretinous semanticists who claim to deliver you from Aristotelian tyranny, from "A is not Not-A," as though it had not been established for centuries that "A *becomes* Not-A."

This is so true that today space, which tends to become uniform, is no longer "consumed," time is. The American who tours the world going from one Hilton hotel to another without ever seeing any variation in the setting—except superficially as reconstituted local color, thus integrated and reduced to a gimmick—clearly prefigures the itineraries of the greatest number. The conquest of space, as an "adventure" reserved for an "elite" and reflected spectacularly over the whole of the planet, will be its organized and foreseeable compensation. But, through the expedient of the colonization of space, Power intends to "draw on the future," to "take a long-term view," emptying time of its substance (our realization over the course of a History) in order to cut it up into perfectly inoffensive slices, gutted of any "future" that is not foreseeable, not programmed by its machines. The aim: the formation of a gigantic device intended to "recycle" linear time for the benefit of an expurgated and "shrunken" time, the mechanical, combinatory, and historyless time of machines, which would unite the pseudo-cyclical time of the everyday with a *generalized neo-cyclical time*, the time of passive acceptance and forced resignation to the permanence of the present order of things.

It must be said: "alienation and oppression in society, in any of their variations, cannot be planned, but only rejected as a whole along with that very society."[25] The task of reunifying space and time in a free construction of individual and social space-time belongs to the *coming revolution*: the rout of the "planners" will coincide with a decisive transformation of everyday life, and it will be that transformation.

---

23 Pierre Drouin, "La croissance économique, pour quoi faire? II. – Une machine qui tourne mieux …," *Le Monde*, June 4, 1964, 18.
24 A term with multiple meanings here: both in the sense of "philosopher's stone," the alchemical agent capable of transmuting metal, but also in the sense of "masterpiece." [Ed.]
25 "Manifeste (17 mai 1960)," *Internationale situationniste* no. 4 (June 1960): 36.

EXCERPT FROM *THE SOCIETY OF THE SPECTACLE*[26]
GUY DEBORD

The Society of the Spectacle, *Guy Debord's book of theory, appeared in 1967, systematizing and bolstering the critical themes previously developed in the Situationists' journal. Its 221 theses offered a totalizing critique of the existing world and of every aspect of modern capitalism and its generalized system of illusions. At the same time, it described the forces that had the potential to dispel spectacle: class struggles and revolution, along with the project of an emancipated creativity— nothing less than the domination of all of humanity over its own history. Six years after its first publication, Debord transformed this book into a movie; below is an excerpt derived from the seventh chapter of* The Society of the Spectacle, *critiquing the organization of social space, urbanism, and territorial planning. The left-hand column reproduces the text that appeared on screen; on the right is a description of the accompanying images. Text frames are set into the outside margin of the page.*

Capitalist production has unified space, which is no longer limited by external societies. This unification is at the same time an extensive and intensive process of *banalization*. As the accumulation of commodities mass-produced for the abstract space of the market had to shatter all regional and legal barriers, and all the guild restrictions of the Middle Ages that maintained the *quality* of craft production, it had also to annul the autonomy and quality of places. This homogenizing power is the heavy artillery that has battered down all Chinese walls.[27] [165]

Battleships on the high seas; landing of French, then English, marine-riflemen at Shanghai; an American marine checks Chinese passersby; French soldiers push back a crowd; English soldiers on patrol; barbed wire protecting the Concession's border, guarded by French colonial infantry.

---

26 Guy Debord, "*La Société du spectacle*" (1973), in *Oeuvres*, ed. Jean-Louis Rançon (Paris: Éditions Gallimard, Coll. "Quarto," 2006), 1224–1228. Thesis numbers from the original text are included in brackets. [Ed.]

27 An appropriation of Marx and Engels' famous phrase:

> The bourgeoisie, by the rapid improvement of all instruments of production, by the immensely facilitated means of communication, draws all, even the most barbarian, nations into civilization. The cheap prices of commodities are the heavy artillery with which it batters down all Chinese walls, with which it forces the barbarians' intensely obstinate hatred of foreigners to capitulate. It compels all nations, on pain of extinction, to adopt the bourgeois mode of production; it compels them to introduce what it calls civilization into their midst, i.e., to become bourgeois themselves. In one word, it creates a world after its own image."

See Karl Marx and Frederick Engels, "Manifesto of the Communist Party" (1848), in Karl Marx and Frederick Engels, *Collected Works*, vol. 6 ("Marx and Engels: 1845–48"), London: Lawrence & Wishart, 1976. [Ed.]

In order to become ever more identical to itself, to best approximate motionless monotony, the *free space of the commodity* is henceforth altered and rebuilt at every moment. [166]

British soldiers closing a gate into the Concession.

This society that abolishes geographical distance shelters a new internal distance inside itself, as spectacular separation. [167]

"The society based on the expansion of alienated industrial labor becomes, quite naturally, from one end to another, unhealthy, noisy, ugly, and dirty like a factory."

Byproduct of the circulation of commodities, human circulation considered as a form of consumption, tourism comes down fundamentally to the freedom to go and see what has become banal. The economic planning of the frequenting of different places is already in itself the guarantee of their *equivalence*. The same modernization that has withdrawn the element of time from journeying, has also withdrawn the reality of space. [168]

Tourists visiting Paris in glassed-in buses or "bateaux-mouches"; their guides comment on the sights.

The society that models all its surroundings has developed its special technology for shaping the concrete basis of this ensemble of tasks: its own territory. Urbanism is that taking possession of the natural and human environment by capitalism that, developing logically into absolute domination, now can and must remake the totality of space as *its own setting*. [169]

"Grand ensemble" of new architecture.

"Man returns to a cave dwelling ... which he continues to occupy only precariously, it being for him an alien habitation which can be withdrawn from him any day—a place from which, if he does not pay, he can be thrown out any day. For this mortuary he has to pay.*" (Karl Marx, Economic and Philosophical Manuscripts of 1844)*[28]

---

28 Karl Marx, "Economic and Philosophic Manuscripts of 1844," in Karl Marx and Frederick Engels, *Collected Works*, vol. 3 ("Marx and Engels: 1843–44"), London: Lawrence & Wishart, 1975, 307. [Ed.]

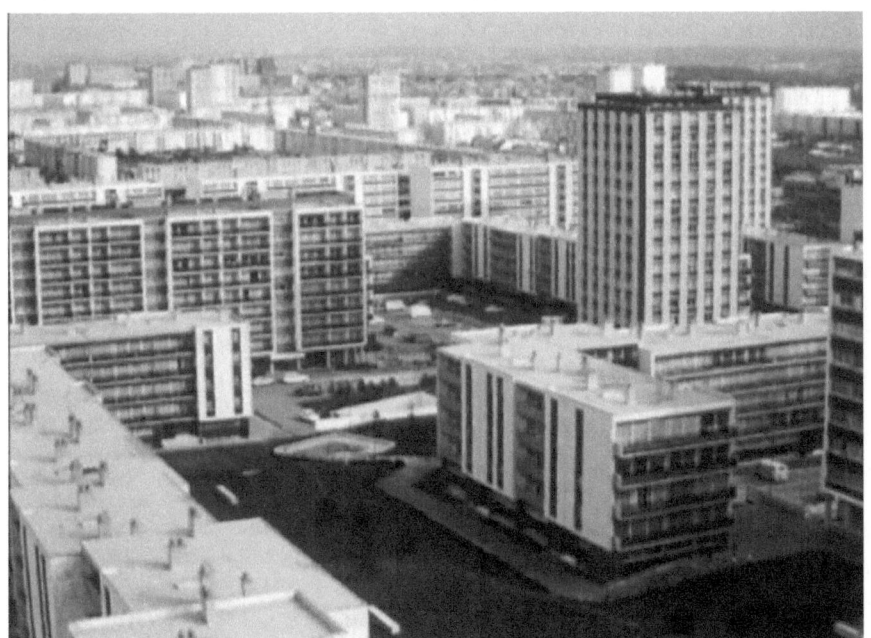

Fig.8.4.1 Still from *The Society of the Spectacle*, dir. Guy Debord, 1973.

If all the technological powers of the capitalist economy must be understood as effecting separations, in the case of urbanism we are dealing with the apparatus of their general basis, with the preparation of the ground suitable for their deployment—with the very technology *of separation*. [171]

CRS[29] *in place on this choice field.*

For the first time a new architecture, which in all previous periods had been reserved for the satisfaction of the ruling classes, is directly intended *for the poor*. The formal poverty and gigantic extent of this new experimental environment arise from its *mass* character, which is entailed at once by those to whom it is addressed and by modern conditions of construction. *Authoritarian decision-making*, which abstractly plans territory as the territory of abstraction, is obviously at the center of these modern conditions of construction, and the *lag* in the conscious domination of these powers is displayed in urbanism. [173, excerpts]

A few models, and productions, of a new architecture—called "marina"—for vacation spots by the sea, but which may also be found in the mountains; the new district of "La Défense," being built in the west of the Parisian region. The cruiser "Aurora" goes up the Neva at the end of the night; it brings to shore its landing party, at daybreak.[30] *The tower of Babel.*[31] *Series of buildings and landscapes in an early Italian painting.*

"The environment, which is rebuilt ever more hastily in the name of repressive control and profit, at the same time becomes more fragile and encourages more and more vandalism. Capitalism in its spectacular stage rebuilds everything as imitation *and generates arsonists*. Thus its setting is becoming everywhere inflammable, like a French high school."

The history that threatens this twilight world is also the force that can subject space to lived time. Proletarian revolution is that *critique of human geography* through which individuals

---

29   Compagnie Républicaine de Sécurité, French riot police. [Ed.]
30   Footage appropriated from Sergei Eisenstein's *October: Ten Days That Shook the World* (1927). [Ed.]
31   Pieter Brueghel the Elder, *Tower of Babel*, c. 1563 (Museum Boymans-van Beuningen, Rotterdam). See fig. 1.11. [Ed.]

and communities construct locations and events corresponding with the appropriation, no longer just of their work, but of their entire history. In this shifting space of play, and of freely chosen variations in the rules of this play, the autonomy of place may be rediscovered, without reintroducing an exclusionary attachment to the soil; and there restore the reality of the journey, and of life understood as a journey containing within itself all its meaning. [178]

EXCERPT FROM *EVERYDAY LIFE IN THE MODERN WORLD*[32]

HENRI LEFEBVRE

TRANSLATED BY SACHA RABINOVITCH

Around 1960 the situation became clearer, everyday life was no longer the no-man's-land, the poor relation of specialized activities. In France and elsewhere neo-capitalist leaders had become aware of the fact that colonies were more trouble than they were worth and there was a change of strategy; new vistas opened out such as investments in national territories and the organization of home trade (which did not exclude the exploitation of "underdeveloped countries" for manpower and raw material and as sites for investments—only they were no longer the main preoccupation). What did the leaders do? All areas outside the centers of political decision and economic concentration of capital were considered as semi-colonies and exploited as such; these included the suburbs of cities, the countryside, zones of agricultural production and all outlying districts inhabited, needless to say, by employees, technicians, and manual laborers; thus the status of the proletarian became generalized, leading to a blurring of class distinctions and of ideological "values." This well-organized exploitation of society involved consumption and was no longer restricted to the productive classes only; capitalism, while requiring that people "adapt" to modern circumstances, had adapted too. Formerly the leaders of industry produced haphazardly for a problematic market; limited family business concerns predominated adding their bourgeois treble to the chorus praising the wonders of trade, of quality, of dearly beloved labor. In Europe after the war a few gifted and intelligent men (who they are is not our concern) saw the possibility of exploiting consumption to organize everyday life. Everyday life was cut up and laid out on the site to be put together again like the pieces of a puzzle, each piece depending on a number of organizations and institutions, each one—working life, private life, leisure—rationally exploited (including the latest commercial and semi-programmed organization of leisure). The *new town* was the typical, significant phenomenon in which and on which this organization could be *read* because it was there that it was *written*. What, apart from such features as the negation of traditional cities, segregation, and intense police supervision, was inscribed in this social text to be deciphered by those who knew the code, what was projected on this screen? Everyday life—organized, neatly subdivided, and programmed to fit a controlled, exact timetable. Whatever the size of their incomes or the class to which

---

32 (1968) (New York: Harper & Row, Coll. "Harper Torchbooks," 1971), 58–59 and 64–67. [Ed.]

they belonged (employee, clerk, minor technician), inhabitants of the new town acquired the generalized status of proletarians; furthermore the new towns (Sarcelles, Mourenx, etc.) were strangely reminiscent of colonial or semi-colonial cities, with their straight roads crisscrossing at right angles and their frequent police patrols;[33] but these were more forbidding and austere, perhaps on account of there being no cafés and pleasure-grounds: the colonizers of the metropolis do not encourage levity …

[…] To subdivide and organize everyday life was not enough; now it had to be *programmed*. The Bureaucratic Society of Controlled Consumption, assured of its ability and proud of its success, is attaining its goal and its half-conscious intentions are coming to light: to cybernetize society by the indirect agency of everyday life.

Everyday life in France is organized according to a concerted program; the so-called superior activities (applied sciences, etc.) are not only increasingly aware of the quotidian, it has become their special province. Daily life is the screen on which our society projects its light and shadow, its hollows and its planes, its power and its weakness; political and social activities converge to consolidate, structure, and *functionalize* it. The other levels of society (with the exception of the state, which operates on a much more exalted plane) only exist in relation to everyday life and the utility and significance of constructs is estimated in direct proportion to their structural effect on it.

If tragedy still exists it is out of sight; the "cool" prevails. Everything is ostensibly de-dramatized; instead of tragedy there are objects, certainties, "values," roles, satisfactions, jobs, situations, and functions. Yet there are powers, colossal and despicable, which swoop down on everyday life and pursue their prey in its evasions and departures, dreams and fantasies to crush it in their relentless grip.

The great event of the last few years is that the effects of industrialization on a superficially modified capitalist society of production and property have produced their results: a programmed *everyday life* in its appropriate *urban setting*. Such a process was favored by the disintegration of the traditional city and the expansion of urbanism. Cybernetization threatens society through the allotment of land, the wide-scale institution of efficient apparatus, and an urban expansion adapted to specific ends (directing offices, the control of circulation and of information).

Thus the dividing process that can still be seen in the new towns is finished and is being replaced by the practical reconstruction of a kind of unity, a

---

33 These were not the only significant features and should not be singled out from the others; thus we should not underestimate the role of semi-programming, National Accounts, and preoccupations with consumer-research in France; mortgages and hire-purchase must also be considered among these features.

tendency officially called "urbanism." The problem of synthesis returns to the fore; the "synthesizer" is very much in demand, and there are many candidates among philosophers, economists, sociologists, architects, urbanists, demographers, and other technicians; nearly all of them bank inconspicuously on a certain "robotization" shaped on their own synthetic model that they would program; the more intelligent among them hope to achieve this by a spontaneous, or democratic, rather than an autocratic, method.[34]

Our theories are more or less in agreement with those of American critical sociology; but though this sociology has elucidated a number of important facts it has neglected the essential concepts of everyday life and modernity, urbanization and urbanism; lacking a general theory of society, of ideologies, and of economics (theory of expansion) it has left the last word to the economists. Unlike Riesman, we do not contrast an "outer-directed" with an "inner-directed" personality; moreover we would prove that though people are directed, even prefabricated, by outer circumstances (compulsions, stereotypes, functions, patterns, ideologies, etc.) they see themselves nonetheless as more than ever self-sufficient and dependent only on their own spontaneous consciences even under robotization. But we would *also* try to prove the failure of such tendencies through "irreducibles," contradictions that resist repression and transposition. Can terrorist pressures and repression reinforce individual self-repression to the point of closing all the issues? Against Marcuse we continue to assert that they cannot.[35]

American critical sociology—notwithstanding the weight of orthodox industry-sponsored "research"—has raised a number of important questions, among which is that of the *social function of business concerns*. Through published works corroborating practical experience, we are now aware that the big "modern" business concern is not content with the status of economic unit (or group of units) or with political influence, but tends to invade social experience and to set itself up as a model of organization and administration for society in general. It usurps the role of the city and takes over functions that are the city's by right and that should, in the future, be those of an urban society: housing, education, promotion, leisure, etc.; furthermore it constricts and alienates privacy by housing its dependants

---

34 It may not be amiss to repeat here that we have no regrets or nostalgias for former times; we do not incriminate the "machine" whether electronic or otherwise; on the contrary. A programmed non-automation of the productive apparatus leads to a programmatizing of the consumer, whereas automation would (perhaps) free creative energies and make them available for works of art. The Bureaucratic Society of Controlled Consumption is heading for fresh contradictions, as only industrial production can be automated and the consumer is elusive and must be tracked down. By displacing basic problems such a society collapses; it is a failure where social life is concerned as the liquidation of humanism proves.

35 Marcuse, *One Dimensional Man* (Boston: Beacon Press, 1964).

in hierarchized dwellings. Its control is sometimes overpowering and, in its own way, the business concern tends to level out society, subordinating social existence to its totalitarian demands and leading to "synthesis."

Cybernetization appeared to operate through the police (Orwell) or through bureaucracy; however conditioning, seeping through the channels of a highly organized everyday life, succeeds mainly on the level of woman or "femininity." Yet femininity also suggests feminism, rebellion, and assertiveness. The robot and the computer are, we repeat, production apparatus; to bypass this appropriation involving a rational world-scale programming, consumption is organized on the pattern of production; only *desires happen to figure among the irreducibles*, and the consumer, especially the female of the species, does not submit to cybernetic processes; while the robot—for the time being—has neither desires nor appetites; its memory alone is unimpeachable. As a result, not the consumer, but consumer-information is treated to conditioning—which may perhaps restrict cybernetic rationality and the programming of everyday life ...

We have just added a ticklish problem to our theory, a poisonous flower to a pretty posy: could the organization of everyday life (with its "brilliance," scintillation, and "modernism") be the French highroad to Americanization? We return to a question formulated earlier on: are we heading for a world-scale homogeneity that would foster or reveal a single absolute system, or, on the contrary, for a state where discrepancies and resistances must inevitably bring about the disruption of the whole structure? Do economically developed nations provide a model, both theoretical and practical, for the relatively underdeveloped, and does expansion feed on development to the point of integration? Will ideology and technology—or the expansion of productivist ideology—prevail in Europe and in France? Is the Americanization of France heading straight for success, under cover of an anti-American policy and using for its ends a social group, the technocrats, at first reactionary but finally submitting in the hope of satisfying a thirst for power? The answers to these questions will have to be deferred.

Acknowledgements

This book would not have come into being if not for Mike Davis, who first suggested a reader that would concentrate on the Situationist International's work on the city, and I would not have been involved in this project if not for the generous support of Rowan Wilson and Tom Penn at Verso, who invited me to edit this volume and who saw it through to publication. Charles Peyton served as an attentive and patient copy-editor of the manuscript, and Mark Martin supervised it through production.

The editor and publisher gratefully acknowledge the permission granted to reproduce the copyright material in this book: AK Press, Éditions Allia, Alice Debord, Éditions Fayard, Éditions Gallimard, the Estate of Asger Jorn, the Estate of Uwe Lausen, the Estate of Marcel Marië, and the Estate of Constant Nieuwenhuys. Every effort has been made to trace copyright holders and to obtain their permission for the use of copyright material. The publisher apologizes for any errors or omissions in the above list and would be grateful if notified of any corrections that should be incorporated in future reprints or editions of this book.

I decided at the outset to undertake new translations of these writings, but I would like to signal here my very great debt to all the previous translators of Situationist writing, whose work I have long relied upon: foremost, of course, Ken Knabb, as well as Donald Nicholson-Smith, John McHale, John Shepley, and Gerardo Denís. Libero Andreotti and John McHale both provided crucial advice at various moments in the editing and production of this volume. And of course, none of this work would have been possible without the presence and love of my daughter, Priya. The work of translation was largely accomplished at two institutions where I had the pleasure of being hosted: the Sterling and Francine Clark Art Institute, where Michael Ann Holly and Mark Ledbury made me feel at home despite my unofficial status there; and the History of Art Department at the University of California, Berkeley, where I have had the great pleasure to teach as a visiting professor.

9.

Bibliography

General

Books

Andreotti, Libero, and Xavier Costa, eds. *Theory of the Dérive and Other Situationist Writings on the City*. Barcelona: Museu d'art contemporani, 1996.

Beneath the Paving Stones: Situationists and the Beach, May 1968. Edinburgh and San Francisco, Calif.: AK Press/Dark Star, 2001.
   Reviews: Gordon, Daniel. *AA Files* no. 44 (Autumn 2001): 85–87.

Harris, Steven, and Deborah Berke, eds. *Architecture of the Everyday*. (New York: Princeton Architectural Press, 1997)
   Reviews: Jones, K. B. *Journal of Architectural Education* 53, no. 2 (November 1999): 124–125.

Fraser, Murray. "Endless Complexity of the Everyday," *Architects' Journal* 208, no. 18 (November 12, 1998): 58.

Home, Stewart. *The Assault on Culture: Utopian Currents from Lettrisme to Class War*. Stirling: AK Press, 1991.
   Reviews: Andreotti, Libero. "Leaving the Twentieth Century: The Situationist International," *Journal of Architectural Education* 49, no. 3 (February 1996): 196–199.

Knabb, Ken, ed. and trans. *Situationist International Anthology*. Berkeley, Calif.: Bureau of Public Secrets, 1981.
   Reviews: Andreotti, Libero. "Leaving the Twentieth Century: The Situationist International," *Journal of Architectural Education* 49, no. 3 (February 1996): 196–199.

Marcus, Greil. *Lipstick Traces: A Secret History of the Twentieth Century*. Cambridge, Mass.: Harvard University Press, 1989.
   Reviews: Andreotti, Libero. "Leaving the Twentieth Century: The Situationist International," *Journal of Architectural Education* 49, no. 3 (February 1996): 196–199.

McDonough, Tom, ed. *Guy Debord and the Situationist International: Texts and Documents*. Cambridge, Mass.: MIT Press, 2002.
   Reviews: Schrijver, Lara. *Archis* no. 2 (2003): 115–116.

Pinder, David. *Visions of the City: Utopianism, Power and Politics in Twentieth-Century Urbanism*. Edinburgh: Edinburgh University Press, 2005.
   Reviews: Rice, Charles. *Journal of Architecture* 11, no. 5 (November 2006): 623–627.
Hardy, Dennis. "The Role of the Situationists," *Built Environment* 32, no. 4 (2006): 449–450.
Plant, Sadie. *The Most Radical Gesture: The Situationist International in a Postmodern Age*. London and New York: Routledge, 1992.
   Reviews: Andreotti, Libero. "Leaving the Twentieth Century: The Situationist International," *Journal of Architectural Education* 49, no. 3 (February 1996): 196–199.
Sadler, Simon. *The Situationist City*. Cambridge, Mass.: MIT Press, 1998.
   Reviews: Deyong, Sarah. *Journal of the Society of Architectural Historians* 60, no. 1 (March 2001): 100–103.
   Linder, Mark, and Joseph Buch. "A Few Things Architects Should/Don't Know about Situationists and Literalists," *Design Book Review: DBR* no. 43 (Fall 2000): 30–35.
   Merrifield, Andy. *Harvard Design Magazine* no. 12 (Fall 2000): 72–75.
   Buch, Joseph. *Architectural Theory Review: Journal of the Department of Architecture, the University of Sydney* 4, no. 2 (November 1999): 110–112.
   Borden, Iain. "Reviewing the Situationists," *Blueprint* no. 150 (May 1998): 47.
   Fraser, Murray. "An Avant-garde in Academic Hands," *Architects' Journal* 207, no. 17 (April 1998): 58.
Schaik, Martin van, and Otaker Mácel, eds. *Exit Utopia: Architectural Provocations, 1956–1976*. Munich and London: Prestel, 2004.
   Reviews: Rattenbury, Kester. "Mystery Guest," *RIBA Journal* 112, no. 11 (November 2005): 14.
   Architecture Today no. 160 (July 2005): 8.
   Basar, Shumon. *AA Files* no. 52 (Summer 2005): 84–87.
Vaneigem, Raoul. *The Revolution of Everyday Life*. Trans. Donald Nicholson-Smith. Welcombe, England: Rebel Press, and Seattle, Wash.: Left Bank Books, 1994.
   Reviews: Andreotti, Libero. "Leaving the Twentieth Century: The Situationist International," *Journal of Architectural Education* 49, no. 3 (February 1996): 196–199.
Viénet, René. *Enragés and Situationists in the Occupation Movement, France, May '68*. New York: Autonomedia, and London: Rebel Press, 1992.
   Reviews: Andreotti, Libero. "Leaving the Twentieth Century: The Situationist International," *Journal of Architectural Education* 49, no. 3 (February 1996): 196–199.

Articles

Andreotti, Libero. "Pratiche ludiche dell'urbanistica situazionista/Ludic Practices of the Situationist Urbanism," *Lotus International* no. 108 (2001): 40–62.
Borden, Iain. "The City of Psychogeography," *Architectural Design* 69, no. 11–12 (November-December 1999): 103–104.
Borden, Iain. "New Babylonians: From the Avant-garde to the Everyday," *Journal of Architecture* 6, no. 2 (Summer 2001): 129–133.
Borden, Iain, and Sandy McCreery, "Critique of Lines," *Architectural Design* 71,

no. 3 ("New Babylonians") (June 2001): 6–7. Monograph reviewed by Jonathan Bell, "The Revolution of Everyday Life," *Blueprint* no. 187 (September 2001): 139.

Chassey, Éric de. "'Place': A Constructed Abstract Situation in the Urban Cultural Continuum of the 1960s," *October* no. 120 (Spring 2007): 24–52.

Costa, Xavier. "Le grand jeu à venir: situationistischer Städtebau/Le grand jeu à venir: Situationist Urbanism," *Daidalos* no. 67 (March 1998): 74–81.

Crawford, Margaret. "The Hacienda Must be Built," *Design Book Review: DBR* no. 24 (Spring 1992): 38–42.

De Cauter, Lieven. "De opkomst van de mobiloteitsmaatschappij: van utopia naar heterotopie/The Rise of the Mobility Society: From Utopia to Heterotopia," *Archis* no. 2 (February 2000): 8–23.

Fournier, Colin. "Webbed Babylon," *Architectural Design* 71, no. 3 (June 2001): 74–77.

General Lighting & Power. "What Is the Difference between a Situationist and an Essex Girl?" *Architectural Design* 71, no. 3 (June 2001): 44–47.

Heuvel, Dirk van den. "Bezetting van verlangen: over de plotselinge actualiteit van het situationisme/Occupation of Desires: Concerning the Sudden Topicality of Situationism," *Archis* no. 2 (February 1999): 72–78.

McLaughlin, Sally, and Aaron Fry. "On Framing: The Situationist Strategies of Détournement and Dérive," *Architectural Theory Review: Journal of the Department of Architecture, the University of Sydney* 6, no. 2 (November 2001): 56–64.

Miller, Ross. "The Situationists: Resurrecting the Avant-garde," *Progressive Architecture* 72, no. 9 (September 1991): 139–140.

Mitchell, William J. "Fools in Cyberspace," *RIBA Journal* 111, no. 4 (April 2004): 16.

Pinder, David. "Subverting Cartography: The Situationists and Maps of the City," *Environment & Planning A* 28, no. 3 (March 1996): 405–427.

Rice, Charles. "Images at the Edge of the Built," *Architectural Design* 71, no. 3 (June 2001): 24–29.

Romito, Lorenzo. "The Surreal Foil," *Architectural Design* 71, no. 3 (June 2001): 20–23.

Röthlisberger, Markus. "Die psychogeographische Enfilade: über die architektonische Inszenierung von Situationen und Ereignissen," *Archithese* 26, no. 2 (March–April 1996): 28–35.

Sadler, Simon. "The Indeterminate Utopia," *Architectural Design* 71, no. 3 (June 2001): 88–92.

Scribner, Charity. "Buildings on Fire: The Situationist International and the Red Army Faction," *Grey Room* no. 26 (Winter 2007): 30–55.

"Situativer Urbanismus: zu einer belläufigen Form des Sozialen," *Arch plus* no. 183 (May 2007): 2–95.

Solís, José. "El entusiasmo situacionista: arquitectura del espectáculo, espectáculo de la arquitectura/The Situationist Enthusiasm: Architecture of Spectacle, the Spectacle of Architecture," *Revista de arquitectura* no. 12 (2005): 54–65.

Stracey, Frances. "The Caves of Gallizio and Hirschhorn: Excavations of the Present," *October* no. 116 (Spring 2006): 86–100.

Toorn, Roemer van. "Architecture against Architecture: Radical Criticism within the Society of the Spectacle," *Berlage cahiers* no. 5 (1995–1998): 82–89.

Violeau, Jean-Louis. "Dérives: Stalker et les espaces autres," *Cahiers de la recherché architecturale et urbaine* no. 9–10 (January 2002): 190–193.

Young, Jason. "Phenomeno-praxis," *Dimensions* 13 (1999): 58–69.

Constant (1920–2005)

Books

Careri, Francesco. *Constant: New Babylon, una città nomade.* Turin: Testo & Imagine, 2001.

Lambert, Jean Clarence, ed. *Constant: New Babylon: art et utopie: textes situationnistes.* Paris: Cercle d'art, 1997.

Reviews: Sadler, Simon. *AA Files* no. 41 (Summer 2000): 84–87.

Fortier, Bruno. "L'Animal situationiste," *Architecture d'aujourd'hui* no. 312 (September 1997): 24.

Wigley, Mark, *Constant's New Babylon: The Hyper-Architecture of Desire.* Rotterdam: Witte de With Center for Contemporary Art and 010 Publishers, 1998.

Reviews: Merrifield, Andy. *Harvard Design Magazine* no. 12 (Fall 2000): 72–75.

Linder, Mark, and Joseph Buch. "A Few Things Architects Should-Don't Know about Situationists and Literalists," *Design Book Review: DBR* no. 43 (Fall 2000): 30–35.

Sadler, Simon. *AA Files* no. 41 (Summer 2000): 84–87.

Heynen, Hilde. *Archis* no. 1 (January 2000): 79–80.

Daidalos no. 69–70 (December 1998–January 1999): 162.

Zegher, Catherine de, and Mark Wigley, eds. *The Activist Drawing: Retracing Situationist Architectures from Constant's New Babylon to Beyond.* New York: Drawing Center, and Cambridge, Mass.: MIT Press, 2001.

Articles

Bresler, Henri. "Construire des situations [obituary]," *Moniteur architecture AMC* no. 155 (October 2005): 34–39.

Careri, Francesco, Armin Linke, and Luca Vitone. "Constant e le radici di New Babylon/ Constant and New Babylon's Roots," *Domus* no. 885 (October 2005): 100–113.

Constant. "New Babylon: An Urbanism of the Future," *Architectural Design* 71, no. 3 (June 2001): 12–14.

Constant, and Jean-Clarence Lambert. "The Amsterdam Studio: A Conversation between Constant and Jean-Clarence Lambert," *AA Files* no. 44 (Autumn 2001): 24–36.

Heynen, Hilde. "New Babylon: The Antinomies of Utopia," *Assemblage* no. 29 (April 1996): 24–43.

"Holanda: Constant," *Arquitectura* (Mexico) no. 93 (March 1966): 25–26.

"Interview met Constant Nieuwenhuys," *Bouwkundig weekblad architectura* 83, no. 17 (August 27, 1965): 315–316.

"Las pérdidas/Disappearances [obituary]," *AV monografias/AV Monographs* no. 117–118 (January–April 2006): 310–313.

Lootsma, Bart. "Now Switch Off the Sound and Reverse the Film ... Koolhaas, Constant, and Dutch Culture in the 1960s," *Hunch: the Berlage Institute report* no. 1 (1999): 152–173.

Lootsma, Bart. "Le film à l'envers: les années 60 de Rem Koolhaas," *Visiteur: ville, territoire, paysage, architecture* no. 7 (Autumn 2001): 90–111.

Novak, Marcos. "Next Babylon, Soft Babylon: (trans)Architecture Is an Algorithm to Play In," *Architectural Design* 68, no. 11-12 (November–December 1998): 11–12.

Pinder, David. "Utopian Transfiguration: The Other Spaces of New Babylon," *Architectural Design* 71, no. 3 (June 2001): 15–19.

Ragon, Michel. "New Babylon: ville utopique du hollandais Constant," *Urbanisme* 41, no. 133 (1972): 54–56.

Rappolt, Mark. "No More Theory; Nothing but Practice: Constant after New Babylon," *AA Files* no. 44 (Autumn 2001): 21–23.

Sosa, José Antonio. "Constructores de ambientes: del mat-building a la lava programática/ Environmental Constructors: From Mat-Building to Programmatic Lava," *Quaderns d'arquitectura i urbanisme* no. 220 (1998): 90–100.

Suzuki, Takanori, et al. "20th Century Architectural Models 2: Discovering Architectural Potential through Practical/Experimental Endeavor," *Kenchiku bunka* 58, no. 667 (October 2003): 19–66.

"The City in Play," *Metropolis* 19, no. 4 (December 1999): 98–104.

Wigley, Mark. "Het grote spel van de stedelijkheid: Constants New Babylon/The Great Urbanism Game: Constant's New Babylon," *Archis* no. 2 (February 1999): 62–71.

Wigley, Mark. "Constant Appeal," *Architecture* 89, no. 8 (August 2000): 55–58.

Wigley, Mark. "The Great Urbanism Game," *Architectural Design* 71, no. 3 (June 2001): 8–11.

Wigley, Mark. "El gran juego del urbanismo: Constant y el paradigma de 'Nueva Babilonia,'" *Arquitectura viva* no. 88 (January–February 2003): 46–49.

Debord, Guy (1931–1994)

Articles

Ibelings, Hans. "Tourism as a Way of Life," *Kritische Berichte* 29, no. 3 (2001): 16–20.

Kaufmann, Vincent. "The Lessons of Guy Debord," *October* no. 115 (Winter 2006): 31–38.

McDonough, Tom. "Oeuvres cinématographiques complètes [and] 2 ou 3 choses que je sais d'elle [and] Playtime" [film review], *Journal of the Society of Architectural Historians* 67, no. 1 (March 2008): 153–155.

McDonough, Tom. "Guy Debord, or the Revolutionary Without a Halo," *October* no. 115 (Winter 2006): 39–45.

Rossi, Aldo Loris. "Guy-Ernest Debord: Venezia e l'urbanismo unitario/Guy-Ernest Debord: Venice and Unitary Urbanism," *Architettura* 47, no. 553 (November 2001): 672–673.

Weber, Samuel. "War, Terrorism, and Spectacle, or: On Towers and Caves," *Grey Room* no. 7 (Spring 2002): 14–23.

Jorn, Asger (1914–1973)

Articles

Birtiwistle, Graham, and Peter Shield. "Asger Jorn's Solutions for Architecture," *AA files* no. 52 (Summer 2005): 34–54.

Dahlmann, Olsen R. "[Relief i Arhus]," *Arkitektur* 4 (1960): 132–138.

Jorn, Asger. "Arkitekturens semantik: Erik Lundberg in memoriam," *Arkitekten* 71, no. 23 (1969): 552–553.

Lefebvre, Henri (1901–1991)

Books

Elden, Stuart. *Understanding Henri Lefebvre: Theory and the Possible*, (London and New York: Continuum, 2004).
  Reviews: Kipfer, Stefan. *Environment & Planning D, Society & Space* 23, no. 6 (December 2005): 928–930.

Lefebvre, Henri. *The Production of Space*, trans. Donald Nicholson-Smith, Oxford and Cambridge, MA: Blackwell, 1991.
  Review: White, Hayden. *Design Book Review: DBR* no. 29–30 (Summer–Fall 1993): 90–93.

Lefebvre, Henri. *Writing On Cities*, ed. and trans. Eleonore Kofman and Elizabeth Lebas, Cambridge, MA: Blackwell, 1996.
  Reviews: Crawford, Margaret. *Harvard Design Magazine* (Winter–Spring 1998): 84–85.

Shields, Rob. *Lefebvre, Love and Struggle: Spatial Dialectics*, London: Routledge, 1999.
  Reviews: Lefebvre, Alexandre. *Environment & Planning A* 32, no. 4 (April 2000): 754–755.

Valença, Márcio. *Environment & Planning D, Society & Space* 18, no. 2 (April 2000): 280–281.

Articles

Barnhill, Robert. "Practicing Another Everyday: Tapping the Virtue of Hyper-repression," *Scroope: Cambridge Architecture Journal* no. 11 (1999–2000): 136–141.

Barth, Lawrence. "Revisited: Henri Lefebvre and the Urban Condition," *Daidalos* no. 75 (May 2000): 22–27.

Borden, Iain. "Mochines van mogelijkheden: het leven in de stad volgens Henri Lefebvre/Machines of Possibilities: City Life with Henri Lefebvre," *Archis* no. 1 (January 2000): 62–68.

Candilis, Georges. "[Town planning]," *Architecture d'aujourd'hui* no. 132 (June–July 1967): 2–17.

Chaslin, François. "Henri Lefebvre et l'utopie," *Architecture d'aujourd'hui* no. 276 (September 1991): 32, 34.

Chevrier, Jean-François. "Mobilité urbaine et théâtre métropolitain," *Cahiers de la recherché architecturale* no. 41 (1997): 121–132, 158, 160.

Clair, René. "Visual Studies: Four Takes on Spatial Turns," *Journal of the Society of Architectural Historians* 65, no. 1 (March 2006): 23–24.

Fyfe, Nicholas R. "Contested Visions of a Modern City: Planning and Poetry in Postwar Glasgow," *Environment & Planning A* 28, no. 3 (March 1996): 387–403.

Gotman, Anne. "Entretien avec Henri Lefebvre," *AMC* no. 14 (December 1986): 6–9.

Hannebert, Jean-Yves. "De l'urbain à la ville: entretien avec Henri Lefebvre," *Techniques et architecture* no. 359 (April–May 1985): 112–113.

Highmore, Ben. "Dwelling on the Daily: On the Term Everyday Life as Used by Henri Lefebvre and Michel de Certeau," *Daidalos* no. 75 (May 2000): 38–43.

Lefebvre, Henri. "El espacio verdadero y la verdad del espacio/True Space and the Truth of Space," *Quaderns d'arquitectura i urbanisme* no. 231 (2001): 58–59.

Lefebvre, Henri. "Les institutions de la société 'post-technologique'," *Espaces et sociétés* no. 5 (April 1972): 3–20.

Lefebvre, Henri. "Le ville et l'urbain," *Espaces et sociétés* no. 2 (March 1971): 3–7.

Lefebvre, Henri. "Réflexions sur la politique de l'espace," *Espace et sociétés* no. 1 (November 1970): 3–12.

"Premios y pérdidas/Distinctions and Disappearances," *AV monografias/AV Monographs* no. 79–80 (September–October 1999): 200–207.

McCannell, Dean. "The Common Landscape after John Brinckerhoff Jackson," *Design Book Review: DBR* no. 40 (Fall 1999): 50–56.

Merrifield, Andy. "Guest Editorial: Seattle, Quebec, Genoa: après la déluge ... Henri Lefebvre?," *Environment & Planning D, Society & Space* 20, no. 2 (April 2002): 127–134.

Soja, Edward W. "Henri Lefebvre 1901–1991," *Environment & Planning D, Society & Space* 9, no. 3 (September 1991): 257–259.

Watson, Victoria. "How Henri Lefebvre Missed the Modernist Sensibility of Mies van der Rohe: Vitalism at the Intersection of a Materialist Conception of Space and a Metaphysical Approach to Architecture," *Journal of Architecture* 12, no. 1 (February 2007): 99–111.

Whitehead, Mark. "Love Thy Neighborhood – Rethinking the Politics of Scale and Walsall's Struggle for Neighbourhood Democracy," *Environment & Planning A* 35, no. 2 (February 2003): 277–300.

Index

Adenauer, Chancellor, 200
Africa, 10, 25, 112, 184
Alabama, 179
Alba Congress *See* Debord, "Statement"
Albania, 205
Alberts, Anton C., 137
Algeria, 179, 203, 205
Algiers, 179
All the King's Horses (Bernstein), 86–87
American blacks, 179–85, 189–90
American Indians, 114
American Survival Products Corporation, 200
Amsterdam, 102, 108–9, 137, 140
 strikes, 196
Aragon, Louis, 79 n.23, 196
Archigram, 2
Architects' Journal, 140
Architectural Review, 140
L'Architecture d'aujourd'hui, 22
Arguments, 165
Armand, Louis, 197
Armstrong-Jones, Antony, 164
Art Nouveau, 113
Asia, 112
Asturias rebellion, 168
Athens Charter (Le Corbusier), 2, 28, 76 n.18, 103, 113
Avilès, 208

Babylon, 30
Ballanche, Pierre-Simon
 "City of Expiations", 45

Essays on Social Palingenesis, 45 n.11
Bandini, Mirella, *L'estetico il politico*, 100 n.7
Bank of France, 170
Barcelona, 185
Bartholdi, Frédéric Auguste, Statue of Liberty, 57
Bastille Day, 45 n.10
Baudelaire, Charles, 11, 38 n.4
Bauhaus, 66
 New, 53, 86
 See also International Movement for an Imaginist Bauhaus
Bavarian Building Regulations, 162
Baylot, Jean, 44–45 n.10
 La circulation à Paris, 45 n.10
Béarn, Henry de, *The New Nomadism*, 41
Beautiful Youth (Debord), 41
Bee Safe Manufacturing Company, 200
Beijing, 143
Belgium, 156
 strikes, 196
Benjamin, Walter, 12
Bentham, Jeremy, 195
Berger, Gaston, 197
Berkeley (student struggle), 182
Berlin, 162
Bernstein, Michèle, 3, 8
 All the King's Horses, 86–87
 on churches, 70
 "Lettrist Intervention", 151 n.15
Bessor, 208
Bible, 45
Bill, Max, 53, 86

Black Power Conference, 192
Blacks (American), 179–85, 189–90
Blanqui, 169
Bloc, André, 136
Boston, 187, 206
Boumedienne, 179
Brasília, 154, 205
Brazil, 205
Brecht, Bertolt, 208 n.16
Breton, André, 6, 8, 10, 63 n.29, 79 n.23
   Communicating Vessels, 6
   Free Rein, 10 n.10, 61 n.25
   Nuit du Tournesol, 86
Brown, Norman O., "The Return of the Repressed", 193–94
Brueghel the Elder, Pieter, *Tower of Babel*, 30, 216 n.31
Brunius, Jacques-Bernard, 6
Brussels, 137, 151
Buffet, Bernard, 66
Bureaucratic Society of Controlled Consumption, 220
Burgess, 79
Burke, Thomas, 50
Busbea, Larry, *Topologies*, 22 n.26
Butler, Judith P., *Subjects of Desire*, 3 n.2

Les Caïds de New-York, 143 n.6
Caillois, Roger, 11
California, 181, 185, 191
Cambodia, 101
Canisy, 208
Carceri (Piranesi), 134
Castro, Fidel, 196
Champaigne, Philippe de, 70
Chasse, Robert, "Hall of Mirrors", 186–89
Cheval, Ferdinand, 3–4, 6, 8, 42, 44
   Palais Idéal, 3–8, 20, 30, 42
Chicago, 144
Chichen Itza, 134
Chinese walls, 213
Choay, Françoise, 28
   L'urbanisme, 29 n.34
Chombart de Lauwe, Paul-Henry, 16–17, 155–56, 158, 211
   La fin des villes, 14 n.16

Paris and the Parisian Region, 14, 19 n.21, 71–78
Chtcheglov, Ivan, 4 n.3, 8, 10, 32, 77–78
   Écrits retrouvés, 32 n.1
   "Formulary for a New Urbanism", 8, 12, 32–42, 62 n.26, 151 n.15
C.I.A.M., 76 n.18, 113
Cinevox, 86
La circulation à Paris et dans le Département de la Seine (Baylot), 45 n.10
City in History (Mumford), 30
Clamart, 153
Cobra, 42, 53
Coca-Cola, 60, 146, 158
Cohen, Margaret, *Profane Illumination*, 11 n.12
Cold War, 200
The Collective Memory (Halbwachs), 77
Columbus, Christopher, 10
Commoner, Barry, 199
Commune (1871), 11, 26, 28–29, 168–76, 196
Communicating Vessels (Breton), 6
communism, 195
Communist Party, 45 n.10
Comte, Auguste, 73
Confessions of an English Opium Eater (De Quincey), 103
Congo, 199
Conord, André-Franck, "Slum Construction", 42, 151 n.15
Constant, 1–2, 17, 22, 141, 151
   "The Amsterdam Declaration", 103–4, 108
   Contribution to *Forum*, 110–11
   "Description of the Yellow Zone", 122–25, 137
   "A Different City for a Different Life", 17
   "The Great Game to Come", 17 n.19
   "Inaugural Report to the Munich Conference", 100 n.8, 106–9
   New Babylon, 2, 17, 19–20, 22, 116, 120–22
   Orange Construction of 1958, 17
   Project for a Gypsy Camp, 20

resignation from S.I., 20, 137–38
"Unitary Urbanism", 112–22
Constantine Plan, 203
Copenhagen, 66, 162
C.R.S. (French riot police), 216
Cuba, 199

Dadaism, 33, 47, 66, 86
David, Jacques Louis, Sacre, 70
David, Michelangelo, 57
Dean, James, 86
Debord, Guy, 1, 3, 6, 8, 10, 12, 14, 17, 19, 32 n.1, 46, 139–40, 166
    "The Amsterdam Declaration", 103–4, 108
    "Architecture and Play", 46–48
    Axis of Exploration, 8
    Beautiful Youth, 41
    and Brueghel, 30
    on churches, 69
    Hurlements en Faveur de Sade, 86, 139
    "Introduction to a Critique of Urban Geography", 8, 10 n.11, 12 n.14, 29 n.37, 59–63, 151 n.15
    "Lettrist Intervention", 151 n.15
    Memoirs, 16
    "On the Commune", 26 n.32, 168–72
    "On the passage of a few people through a rather brief moment in time", 16, 88–90
    Report on the Construction of Situations, 151 n.15
    "Situationist Positions on Traffic", 141–43
    Society of the Spectacle, 29, 213–17
    "Statement by Lettrist International Delegate to the Alba Congress", 90–92, 151 n.15
    "Summary 1954", 6 n.5, 46, 151 n.15
    "Theory of Dérive", 12, 77–85
    "Toward a Situationist International", 94–99, 145 n.10
de Chirico, 38, 62
La découverte aérienne du monde, 16 n.17
De Quincey, Thomas, *Confessions of an English Opium Eater*, 103

dérive, 10–12, 38, 40–41, 46–47, 70, 77–85, 96–97, 101–3, 106, 109
Désert de Retz, 8
De Stijl, 53
détournement, 14, 146
Detroit, riots, 186, 188, 190–91
D.I.N. (German industrial norms), 132
Dio, Johnny, 144
Dionysus, 194
Doomsday System, 199–200
Droulin, Pierre, 212 n.23
Durkheim, Émile, 73

East, 101, 148, 207
Écrits retrouvés (Chtcheglov), 32 n.1
The Edge of Surrealism, 11 n.13
egregore, 41
Eichmann, 156
Eisenhower, Dwight, 195
Eisenstein, Sergei, *October*, 216 n.30
Elle, 66, 209
Engels, Frederick, 169, 172, 177, 194, 213 n.27
England, 52
    Labour Party, 184
    strikes, 196
Espérance-Longdoz, 197
Essays on Social Palingenesis (Ballanche), 45 n.11
L'estetico il politico: Da Cobra all'Internazionale situazionista (Bandini), 100 n.7
Europe, 66, 112, 116, 133, 172, 184, 203, 218, 221
Everyday Life in the Modern World (Lefebvre), 26 n.31, 28 n.33, 218-221
experimental utopia, 19

Faure, Edgar, 70
F.B.I., 144
Feurstein, Günther, 20, 22, 152
    "Function: Provocation", 133–37
    "Unpremeditated Architecture", 125–33, 152 n.17
Fillon, Jacques, 3, 6, 8, 69
    on churches, 70
    "Summary 1954", 6 n.5, 46, 151 n.15

Fin de Copenhague (Jorn), 66, 85
La fin des villes: mythe ou réalité
    (Chombart de Lauwe), 14 n.16
flâneur, 11
Les Fondements de la géographie
    humaine (Sorre), 72–73 n.11
Forum, 141
Fourastié, Jean, 195, 197
Fourmies, strikers of, 195
Fox Hole Shelter, Inc., 200
France, 3, 6, 22, 24–25, 42, 78, 79
    n.23, 160, 172, 176, 203, 207,
    218, 219, 221
    Bank of, 170
    and Watts, 177
Free Rein (Breton), 10 n.10
Frey, Théo, "Perspectives for a
    Generation", 209–12
Friedman, Yona, 28
Friedmann, Georges, *Où va le travail*
    humain?, 73
futurism, 66

Gaudi, Antoni, 4, 133, 136
G.E.A.M. (Study Group for Mobile
    Architecture), 22
General Motors, 187
Germany, 62, 152
    West, 200
G.I.A.P. (International Group for
    Prospective Architecture), 22
Gide, 70, 98
Göteborg Conference, 166
Great Britain, student struggle, 182
Gropius, Walter, 53
Groueff, Stéphane, *Les Caïds de*
    New-York, 143 n.6
Guasco, 137
Guggenheim Museum, 134
Guillemins railroad, 196
Gurvitch, Georges, 72 n.8, 73 n.15

Halbwachs, Maurice
    The Collective Memory, 77
    La Morphologie sociale, 73
Hamburg, 162
Hamburg Theses, 166
Haussmann, Baron Georges, 25–26,
    44, 59, 158, 175, 205
Haussmannization, 25–26

Havel, Jean-Eugène, 160
Hegel, 211
    Phenomenology, 3, 29, 163 n.24
Hegelian urbanism, 3, 29
Herald Tribune, 181, 206
Hilton (hotel), 212
Histoire de l'urbanisme: Époque
    contemporaine
    (Lavedan), 26 n.30
Hofstätter, Peter Robert, 144 n.7, 145
Hollon, Bobbi, 181
Hollywood, 181
Homo Ludens: A Study of the Play-
    Element in Culture (Huizinga),
    46, 114
Howard, Ebenezer, 113–14
Huizinga, Johan, 48
    Homo Ludens, 46, 114
Human Ecology (Quinn), 72
Hundertwasser, "Mold Manifesto
    Against Rationalism in
    Architecture", 20
Hurlements en Faveur de Sade
    (Debord), 86, 139

Image and Form (Jorn), 53, 92
Indians (American), 114
International Movement for an
    Imaginist Bauhaus (I.M.I.B.), 12,
    86, 90, 92
Introduction to Modernity (Lefebvre),
    24 n.28
Israel, 208
Italy, 137
Ivain, Gilles *See* Chtcheglov, Ivan

Jacobinism, 170
Jardin des Plantes, 40
Jorn, Asger, 1, 12, 42, 53, 66, 90
    Fin de Copenhague, 66, 85
    Image and Form, 53–56, 92
Joséphine de Beauharnais, 58
Jugendstil, 113

Kahn, Louis, 134, 136
Keats, John, 194 n.15
Kennedy, 196, 200, 206
Khrushchev, 195–96
Kiesler, Frederick, 158
King, Martin Luther, 179–80

Kotányi, Attila, 137, 151, 166
  "Elementary Program of the Unitary Urbanism Office", 146–49, 155 n.18, 170 n.4, 203
  "Gangland and Philosophy", 143–46, 151 n.15
  "On the Commune", 26 n.32, 168–72

Labour Party (England), 184
Lapierre, Dominique, *Les Caïds de New-York*, 143 n.6
Lasalle, Ferdinand, 161 n.23
Las Vegas, 41
Lausen, Uwe, "The Beautiful and the Good", 161–63
Lavedan, Pierre, *Histoire de l'urbanisme*, 26 n.30
Leary, police Commissioner, 189
Le Corbusier, 2, 6, 8, 34, 42, 45, 66, 77, 91–92, 114, 133, 135–36, 141
  Athens Charter, 2, 28, 103, 113
  "Cité Radieuse", 42, 45
  Modulor, 132
  Unité d'Habitation, 6, 44, 46
  Urbanism is a Key, 47
  Ville Radieuse, 66
Ledoux, 134
Lefebvre, Henri, 2, 19, 24, 26, 152
  Everyday Life in the Modern World, 26 n.31, 28 n.33, 218–22
  "Experimental Utopia", 105–6, 152
  Introduction to Modernity, 24 n.28, 25 n.29
  The Proclamation of the Commune, 172–76
Lenin, V. I., 90 n.2, 169, 201 n.8
Leningrad, 57
Léopoldville, 199
Lettrist International (L.I.), 3–4, 6, 8, 12, 14, 42, 46, 90, 92, 94, 98
  "Skyscrapers by the Roots", 44–46, 53 n.19, 151 n.15
Lettrists, 14, 16, 46, 69, 106
Les Lèvres nues, 92
Lewin, Kurt, 72 n.10
Liebknecht, 174
Liége, strikers, 196–97

Limehouse, London, 48, 50–52
Líster, Enrique, 199
Littré, 156
London, 62
  industrial revolution, 102–3
  Limehouse, 48, 50–52
Lorrain, Claude, 37, 62
  Seaport with the Embarkation of Saint Ursula of 1641, 10
Los Angeles
  Watts riots, 26–29, 177–78, 180–83, 185–86, 196
  Watts Towers, 134
Louvre, 62
Lucky Strike (cigarettes), 195
Ludwig II of Bavaria, 44, 47
Lyon, workers uprising, 195

Maldonado, Tomás, 86
Malevich, 134, 136
Malraux, 60
Mandelbrot, Benoit, 106
Mao, 163
Marcuse, 220
Mariën, Marcel, 63, 92
  "The Commander's Gait", 56–59
Marseille, 6, 43, 46, 99
Marx, Karl, 29, 61, 80, 146, 169, 172, 175–77, 184 n.11, 193, 196, 209 n.19, 210, 213 n.27, 214
Mauriac, François, 61, 70
May '68, 1, 28
Maymont, Paul, 28
McCulley, Johnston, *Zorro*, 32
McDonough, Tom, 17 n.20
McIntyre, LA cardinal, 178
McLuhan, 193
Médium (Vendryes), 79
Melanotte, G., 137
Méliès, Georges, 4
Memoirs (Debord), 16
Mendelsohn, 133
Merlebach, strikers, 196
Merrifield, Andy, *Metromarxism*, 25 n.29
Mesopotamia, 30
Metromarxism (Merrifield), 25 n.29
La Meuse, 196
Mexico, 101
Michelangelo, *David*, 57

Michigan, riots, 190
Mies van der Rohe, 129
Miranti, Gondolfo, 144
Modulor (Le Corbusier), 132
Moles, Abraham, 197
Monaco, 41
Le Monde, 182, 209
Mondrian, Piet, 53, 129
Montgomery, 179
Moore, Wilbert E., 73 n.15
Morise, Max, 79 n.23
La Morphologie sociale (Halbwachs), 73
Morris, William, 114
Moscow, 58
Mourenx, 22–24, 154, 219
Mouvement Républicain Populaire (M.R.P.), 45
Mumford, Lewis, 30, 145
  City in History, 30
Murphy, police Commissioner, 189
Musée de l'Homme, 14

NAACP, 178
Napoléon III, 26
Navarrenx, 24
Nazis, 155–56
Neo-Liberty, 139 n.2
Nervi, 126
Die neue Stadt, eine Studie für das Fürttal, 152
New Arabian Nights (Stevenson), 103
Newark, riots, 186, 188–90, 192
New Babylon (Constant), 2, 17, 19–20, 22, 115, 120–22
New Jersey, riots *See* Newark
The New Nomadism (Béarn), 41
The New York Times, 188, 190
New York, 57, 85, 113, 162, 187–89, 206
  public transit, 113
  Vietnam war protests, 182
Nice, 203
Nivola, Constantino, 134
North America, 112
Notre-Dame, 171
Nuit du Tournesol (Breton), 86
La Nuova Stampa, 99

October: Ten Days that Shook the World (Eisenstein), 218 n.30

Orange Construction of 1958 (Constant), 17
Orwell, 221
Oudejans, Har Th., 137
Où va le travail humain? (Friedmann), 73

Palais Idéal (Cheval), 3–8, 20, 30, 42
Paris, 3, 8, 10–12, 24, 33, 37, 46–47, 59, 62, 79, 84, 86, 113, 140, 163, 203, 205
  consciousness of, 74
  economic centers, 75
  guidebook, 14–17
  housing projects, 153
  improvements, 69
  inconclusive study of, 76–77
  influx of people, 25
  La Défense, 216
  MLK in, 180
  monuments, 77
  public transit, 60, 113
  street names, 68, 85
  technological milieu, 73
  tourists, 214
  traffic circulation, 113, 140, 142 n.8, 208
  See also Commune
Paris Commune *See* Commune
Paris and the Parisian Region (Chombart de Lauwe), 14, 19 n.21, 71–78
Parker, William, 178, 185
Peace o' Mind Shelter Company, 200
Perret, Auguste, 42
Phenomenology (Hegel), 3, 29, 163 n.24
Philips (stereo), 196
Piaget, Jean, 72 n.10
Pinel, Philippe, 33
Pinot-Gallizio, 20, 90, 137
Piranesi, 160
  Carceri, 134
Plato, 145
Poe, Edgar Allen, 37
Pollock, Jackson, 86
Pompeii, 158
Potlatch, 17, 60, 71
P.O.U.M., 185

The Proclamation of the Commune (Lefebvre), 172–76
Profane Illumination (Cohen), 11 n.12
Project for a Gypsy Camp, 20
Proudhon, 61
psychogeography, 4 n.3, 8, 10, 12, 14, 32, 52, 59–60, 62, 69, 77–78, 82, 84–86, 95–96, 106, 109, 119, 121, 139–40
P.T.T. (French General Post Office), 68
Pyramid of Cheops, 134

Quadros, President of Brazil, 205
Quick, 200
Quinn, James Alfred, *Human Ecology*, 72
Quoist, 75 n.17

Reims, Cathedral, 134
Renault, 153, 195
Revue française de sociologie, 152
Ridgway, Matthew Bunken, 63
Riesman, 220
Rietveld, 134
Rimbaud, Arthur, 1
Rocher Noir, 205
Rockefeller, Governor, 206
Rodia, Simon, 134
Rumney, Ralph, 140
Ruskin, John, 113–14
Russia, 59, 184

Saarinen, 136
Sacre (David), 70
Sadler, Simon, *The Situationist City*, 16 n.18
Saint Augustine, 159
Saint-Just, 171
Sarcelles, 24, 154, 163–64, 166, 219
Scharoun, 134, 136
Schöffer, Nicolas, 28
Schweitzer, Doctor, 196
Schwitters, Kurt, 47
Seaport with the Embarkation of Saint Ursula of 1641 (Lorrain), 10
Second World War, 6
Seine Architects Union, 206
Selma march, 179
Situationist archive, 4 n.3

Situationists
  writings, 20 n.24, 151 n.15
  "The Bad Days Will End", 168 n.1, 196 n.20
  "Construct yourself a little situation without a future", 4 n.3
  "Critique of Urbanism", 22, 24, 28, 149–55
  "The Decline and Fall of the Spectacle-Commodity Economy", 177–85
  "A Different City for a Different Life", 17
  "Emergency State Ended in Detroit", 190–93
  "Geopolitics of Hibernation", 198–208
  "The Great Game to Come", 17 n.19
  "Lettrist Intervention", 151 n.15
  "Limehouse Nights", 48–52
  "New Theater of Operations within Culture", 12, 14
  "Next Planet", 6, 42, 44, 151 n.15
  "On the Commune", 26 n.32
  "On the Poverty of Student Life", 197 n.23
  "On the Role of the S.I.", 163–67
  "Plan for Rational Improvements to the City of Paris", 69–71
  "Situationist News", 137–38
  "The Sound and the Fury", 196 n.20
  "Unitary Urbanism at the End of the 1950s", 99–103, 150 n.13, 151 n.15
  "Urbanism as Will and Representation", 208
  "While Awaiting the Boarding Up of Churches", 68
  See also Bernstein, Michèle; Brown, Norman O.; Chasse, Robert; Chtcheglov, Ivan; Conord, André-Franck; Constant; Debord, Guy; Feurstein, Günther; Frey, Théo; Jorn, Asger; Kotányi, Attila; Lausen, Uwe; Lettrist International; Mariën, Marcel; Vaneigem, Raoul; Wolman, Gil J.

The Situationist City (Sadler), 16 n.18
Smith, Adam, 195
Society of the Spectacle (Debord), 29, 213–17
Sociocultural Causality, Space, Time (Sorokin), 71
Sorokin, Pitrim A., *Sociocultural Causality, Space, Time*, 71
Sorre, Maximilien, *Les Fondements de la géographie humaine*, 72–73 n.11
South America, 112
Spain, 22, 25, 208
  anti-Franco war, 185, 199
Spengler, 193
Stael, Nicolas de, 86
Statue of Liberty (Bartholdi), 57
Stendhal, 70 n.5
Stevenson, Robert Louis, *New Arabian Nights*, 103
Stockholm, 162
  riots, 196
Subjects of Desire (Butler), 3 n.2
Sudreau, Pierre, 24
Surrealism, 6, 8, 10, 14, 28, 33, 69 n.4, 79, 152 n.17
Sweden, 200, 208
Switzerland, 200

Tamerlane, 63
Taut, 134
Team 10, 1, 28
Terror of 1848, 11
Thomas, Dylan, 86
Time magazine, 28
The Times, 52
Tirana, 205
Topologies (Busbea), 22 n.26
Touraine, Yves, 158
Tower of Babel (Brueghel), 30, 216 n.31
Trocchi, 166
Twentieth Century Sociology, 73 n.15

unitary urbanism, 12, 14, 16–17, 20, 90–92, 94–95, 97, 99–104, 106, 108–11, 115–16, 119–20, 137–42, 146, 148–52, 154–55
  research bureau, 109, 137

Unité d'Habitation (Le Corbusier), 6, 44, 46
United Nations, 199
University of Edinburgh, student struggle, 182
L'urbanisme: utopies et réalités, une anthologie (Choay), 29 n.34
Urbanism is a Key (Le Corbusier), 47
US, 45, 141–42, 183, 188, 192, 198–201, 203
Utrecht, 134

Vällingby, 208
Vaneigem, Raoul, 166
  "Basic Banalities", 200 n.6
  "Comments Against Urbanism", 155–61
  "Elementary Program of the Unitary Urbanism Office", 146–49, 155 n.18, 170 n.4, 203
  "On the Commune", 26 n.32, 168–72
  The Revolution of Everyday Life, 158 n.20, 194–97
Vantongerloo, 134, 136
Vendryes, Pierre, *Médium*, 79
Venice, 139 n.2, 140
Venus de Milo, 57
Verkhoyansk, 206
Versailles, 170, 176
Versnel, Jan, 17
Vesnin, 136
Vichney, Nicolas, 199
Victory of Samothrace, 57
Vienna, 162
Vietnam war, 182, 188, 190–91
Vitrac, Roger, 79 n.23
Volkswagen, 195, 197

Wagner, 47
Wallace, governor of Alabama, 179
Wallon, Henri, 72 n.10
Warsaw, 77
Watts (riots in LA), 26–29, 177–78, 180–83, 185–86, 188, 196
Watts Towers (LA), 134
Weiner, Norbert, 118
Welfare State, 161–62, 195–97

West, 101, 148
Wilkins, Roy, 178
Wolman, Gil J., 69–70, 90
   on churches, 69
   "Lettrist Intervention", 151 n.15

Wols, 86
Wright, Frank Lloyd, 101, 134

Xpuhie's palace, 134

Zorro (McCulley), 32

www.ingramcontent.com/pod-product-compliance
Lightning Source LLC
Chambersburg PA
CBHW031614210526
45464CB00004B/1573